Green Shift

A

Green Shift

Towards a green sensibility in architecture

John Farmer

Edited by Kenneth Richardson

With supplementary text by:

Judith Farren Bradley
Stuart Durant
Trevor Garnham
Kenneth Richardson

Published in association with WWF-UK

Butterworth Architecture
An imprint of Butterworth-Heinemann

Butterworth-Heinemann
Linacre House, Jordan Hill, Oxford OX2 8DP
A division of Reed Educational & Professional Publishing Ltd

  A member of the Reed Elsevier plc group

OXFORD   LONDON   BOSTON
NEW DELHI   SINGAPORE   SYDNEY
TOKYO   TORONTO   WELLINGTON

First published 1996

WWF-UK is a Registered Charity number 201707
WWF-UK will be paid 10% publishers net receipts on the first
1500 copies sold then 12½% net receipts thereafter

British Library Cataloguing in Publication Data
Farmer, John
    Green Shift: Towards a Green Sensibility in Architecture
    I. Title II. Richardson, Kenneth
    720.47

ISBN 0 7506 1530 3

Library of Congress Cataloguing in Publication Data
Farmer, John, d. 1994.
    Green shift: towards a green sensibility in architecture/John
    Farmer; edited by Kenneth Richardson.
    p. cm.
    Includes bibliographical references and index.
    ISBN 0 7506 1530 3
    1. Architecture – Environmental aspects. I. Richardson, Kenneth,
    M.Sc. II. Title.
    NA2542.35.F37   95–40532
    720'.47–dc20   CIP

Typeset by Scribe Design, Gillingham, Kent
Printed and bound in Great Britain

Contents

WWF and Green Shift

WWF-UK commissioned John Farmer to trace the development of green thinking in architecture. The resulting book more than meets that original brief. John Farmer has here presented an interdisciplinary and holistic overview, pulling together a wide range of unsuspected and disparate elements that contribute to a continuing tradition of green architecture.

Architects know that their profession involves them across a broad spectrum – from the practical to the visionary. They deal in materials and construction but also in symbols and the psyche; in shelter but also in meaning. The profession therefore attracts the multi-talented and the polymath such as John Farmer.

Going beyond architectural considerations, the book weaves the professional weft into the wider social warp. The resulting fabric contains vivid strands of history, politics, art, literature, science and religion, all in turn shadowed by the impact of war, of nuclear threat and of environmental unknowns. As here described, each one of this multiplicity of strands has its particular contribution to make to the evolution of a green architecture.

Author's preface

Although concern for green issues is now widespread in architecture as well as elsewhere, there is little the architect, or the general reader, can turn to in order to help put into context the various attempts now being made to design in green ways. For some designers this means retreating from mass production and high technology in favour of a sophisticated knowing primitivism, while for others the mass industrial and scientific techniques that, used rampantly, have contributed to our various ecological crises are seen as crucial to solving them. Some of this ecologically concerned effort is contructional, some is aesthetic – symbolic of green values, paralleling such expressions in the other arts. With only a few exceptions all are unconnected to the mass of current design, and without connection either to the history of modern architecture as presently perceived – except to one aspect or other of the organic tradition. Even this is too confined in the way it has been perceived, to show fully the continuity of thought and action, of which green design is the latest manifestation. How the changing view of nature affected modern architecture beyond the arts and crafts movements and the organic tradition, in often scientifically inspired ways, has been obscured by emphasis in the classic accounts of modern architectural history on the developing enthusiasm for technology and the equating of this unreservedly with progress.

For the architecture of the industrial period reflects fundamental changes in the way that we have come to see nature, as much as it reflects the stages in our technologically driven social and material progress. Affecting more than the buildings seen as part of organic tradition, these changing mutating reflections are the past to which present green endeavour can look for continuity and perhaps inspiration.

The book is in six parts, comprising twenty chapters grouped chronologically and thematically. In many of these the house is used as a focus for discussion. The book as a whole is a history of modern architecture as seen from a green standpoint. The last chapters look at the variety of green directions at present being pursued and discuss the advantages and disadvantages of the options available technically, as well as what green architecture looks like compared to the modern and other buildings of the present and past.

John Farmer

Editor's preface

John Farmer (1934–94) studied architecture at the Regent Street Polytechnic in the late 1950s, and began practising as an architect in the 1960s – a period of cold war politics and 'you've never had it so good' consumerism that did much to form his own green sensibility. One of the last of his many sensitive and imaginative designs was for a possible redevelopment of the town centre of Littlehampton, to which he and his wife Vicki moved in 1988; and a recent scheme produced by the local council shows clear evidence of his thinking.

At the end of the 1960s he began teaching architecture at Kingston, where he became a Senior Lecturer in 1971, and Principal Lecturer in charge of the undergraduate course in 1982. Generations of students remember his inspirational teaching with affection and gratitude, and it is fitting that two of the colleagues who have helped bring this book to completion were originally his students.

Research and writing played an increasingly important role in his life in the later years. In the early 1970s he studied history and theory of architecture at the University of Essex, where he began his work on Ruskin. In 1987 he was awarded a PhD by the Royal College of Art for his thesis on 1940s Romanticism; and prior to his sudden death in 1994 he was coordinating the research of the Kingston School of Architecture's Green Audit.

At the time of his death, the text of *Green Shift* – a WWF commission – was incomplete. Fortunately a condensed version of 20 000 words had been supplied to the publisher and some chapters had been fully written up. Comparing these with their equivalents in the condensed version, and with the aid of copious notes located by his widow Vicki Farmer, it was not difficult to see how he intended to develop the remaining chapters. A number of these have been completed largely using material found among his papers.

Other chapters have been completed with contributions from John Farmer's friends and colleagues in the School of Architecture and the School of Art and Design History at Kingston University. The last chapter incorporates a substantial collaborative contribution from the School of Architecture's Green Audit group of which he had been leader. The chapter incorporates his own introduction to the Green Audit prospectus and ends with the material he had already written for the closing pages of the book.

The illustrations are from various sources. Original photographs have been taken by the Green Audit in association with John's son, Augustus J. Farmer, with photographic equipment provided by WWF and support from the Faculty of Design. Others have been chosen from John Farmer's personal slide collection. A third group has kindly been made available by the Kingston University Knights Park Library from its own collection.

During the editing of the book, the Green Audit group (now co-ordinated by Sue-Ann Lee) has functioned as an invaluable editorial advisory team, and has provided the glosssary. I am also particularly indebted to Trevor Garnham, who has painstakingly read through the text and helped to clarify it. With the exception of the final chapter, where we took the decision to incorporate research planned under John Farmer's leadership, our aim has been to complete the text as he had envisaged it; and to make it contribute to that perceptual shift that his title (with its play on the red shift of the astronomers) is calling for.

Kenneth Richardson
March 1995

List of illustrations and acknowledgements

Every effort has been made to trace owners of copyright material but the editor would be glad to hear from any copyright owners of material produced in this book whose copyright has unwittingly been infringed.

2.1 Architecture without architects: Chinese underground village – dwellings below, fields upstairs. From Bernard Rudofsky, *Architecture without Architects* (1974) © Academy Group Ltd.

2.2 Mandan earth lodge, a traditional North American dwelling. Drawing: Laurie Bradley.

2.3 Prefabricated parts for yurta, a traditional dwelling of central Asia. From Enrico Guidoni, *Primitive Architecture* (1979) © Academy Group Ltd.

2.4 Completed yurta covered with felt and cane matting.

2.5 Charcoal burner's hut. Photo: John Farmer.

2.6 Skara Brae excavations, Orkney. Photo: Trevor Garnham.

2.7 Henry Moore, 'Crowd looking at a Tied-up Object' (1942). Courtesy of The Henry Moore Foundation. © The Henry Moore Foundation.

3.1 Bramante, Tempietto, Rome. Courtesy of Kingston University Slide Collection.

3.2 Primitive hut: drawing by Sir William Chambers.

3.3 Grotto at Stourhead, Wiltshire. Photo: Green Audit.

3.4 Boullée, Cenotaph for Newton. From Helen Rosenau, *Boullée and Visionary Architecture* (1976) © Academy Group Ltd.

3.5a–b Ledoux, Saltworks at Chaux, near Besançon. Photos: Trevor Garnham.

3.6 Ledoux, House of the Director of the River.

3.7 Ledoux, House of the Rural Guards.

4.1 Cottage at Stourhead, Wiltshire. Photo: Green Audit.

4.2 Cottage in Marie Antoinette's *hameau* at Versailles. Courtesy of Kingston University Slide Collection.

4.3 Cottage ornée, Lyme Regis. Photo: John Farmer.

4.4 Cottages at Nuneham Courtney, Oxfordshire. Photo: Green Audit.

4.5 Cottages at Milton Abbas, Dorset. Photo: Green Audit.

4.6a–c Nash, cottages at Blaise Hamlet. Photo: Green Audit.

4.7 Repton's woodman's cottage, Blaise Castle estate near Bristol. Photo: Green Audit.

4.8 Nash's dairy, Blaise Castle estate. Photo: John Farmer.

4.9 Lord Ongley's housing at Old Warden, Bedfordshire. Photo: Green Audit.

Part One
Introduction

1 Architecture: a green history for our times

This book is an account of how buildings from the eighteenth century to the present time have reflected the momentous changes that have occurred in our perceptions of the natural world and of our place in it. It also gives an alternative focus to the history of modern architecture as it is usually described.

As the view of nature changes from the rational explanations of Newton and others in the eighteenth century to the chaos theorists of today, so the excitement and understanding of architects, riven like society by moods alternating from euphoria to fear, gives rise to buildings whose forms, colours and textures are subject to the shifting world views about the nature of nature. Out of these views, of sympathy, of awe, of the usefulness of nature, comes slowly the attitude that we now call green or ecologically aware. Present in thoughts and deeds a hundred and more years ago, it has only in the last few years assumed centre stage. Many have contributed to it, some of whom in architecture at least have long been seen as irrelevant and backward looking.

This study as well as being a history of the emergence of green thought in architecture will rehabilitate such people and the buildings that they affected or designed. Undervalued currents of thought and feeling will be given prominence, so that they are no longer seen as interesting dead-ends in the flow of modern progress, but rather as pointers to what has to happen in the future if humankind and the rest of the planet's occupants are to prosper together. In addition, a number of familiar trends in twentieth-century architecture will be reinterpreted in terms of the fears, anxieties and instinct for survival that are an integral part of a green sensibility.

The architecture of modern times has been discussed in many ways: from the social and political, through the tracing of architectural movements, and sometimes their connections to the other arts, to the effect of technological advances. Often descriptions of architectural development have been restricted to a scholarly recording of facts. When more opinionated, probably the most important model in the writing of modern architectural history – and therefore of the way that it has come to be perceived – has linked the evaluation of buildings to the expression of technological progress and its benefit to society. In the early histories of modern architecture like those of Nikolaus Pevsner, Emil Kaufmann and Sigfried Giedion, a line is traced of architects and their building in the recent architectural past that leads to what we know as the modern movement, or Modernism. It is a line that excludes as well as includes, that is often puritanical and uninterested in popular culture, that aims to convert and change. It often assumes too that to use a new material, as well as an image redolent of the machine, is intrinsically superior. These polemicists for the modern movement were concerned to legitimate it by tracing its ancestry in the previous centuries. Kaufmann's 1933 book *From Ledoux to Le Corbusier* saw, rightly, the continuity of ideas between French Neo-classical architects and Purism, while Pevsner's 1937 *Pioneers of Modern Design* took the nineteenth-century engineers and the British Arts and Crafts movement as the founders of Modernism. Giedion in 1941 published *Space Time and Architecture: The Growth of a New Tradition*; more rambling and encyclopaedic, less polemical than Pevsner, it too tended to downgrade the effects of Neo-classicism but included much more on the work of what became known as the organic architecture of Wright and Aalto. These works, and others that followed in their wake, collectively gave a credible ancestry to modern architecture. After the changes brought about by the Second World War, the history of modern architecture was most effectively rounded out by Reyner Banham. Banham's thoroughly researched *Theory and Design in the First Machine Age* (1960) also rehabilitated the Expressionist strand in twentieth-century architecture – a strand that had been sidelined because it did not fit into the lineages traced by the polemicists for Modernism. In 1966 he added an account of the greatest of the post-war changes, that of the coming of Brutalism.

By the late 1960s, though, both the Modernist version of architectural history and the problem of how to proceed when designing for the present, had become urgent issues. The two were inseparable. Brutalism had brought to a climax the alienation of many ordinary people from modern ways of building. There was also a growing dominance of a culture by consumer needs, which artists had been exploring through pop art (a movement with which, in the 1950s, Brutalism itself had been briefly linked). When architects began tentatively to follow, led by Robert Venturi, it was to become the final break-up of the consensus that had tended to gather around Modernist developments as they had occurred, from the International Style to Brutalism. The spare puritanical buildings of late Modernism were attacked by Venturi in his books *Complexity and Contradiction in Architecture* (1966) and *Learning from Las Vegas* (1972). These attacks concentrated on the late phase of the International Style that had become the house style of big business and executive living, as well as of much public housing.

An acceptance of popular consumer culture on the one hand, and of learning from past buildings on the other (particularly those from transitional fraught epochs like our own), Venturi argued, was necessary to bring modern architecture into serious contention with the concerns and attitudes of our age. To do this consumer culture was to be both enjoyed and confronted architecturally with the memories of a selectively tough and complex past. Venturi's was an approach that sought to continue the traditional verities of the past while realistically accepting their present place in a culture of rapid change. Above all, it created the climate in which Banham's pupil Charles Jencks could pronounce in 1977 the death of Modernism and proclaim the advent of Postmodernism.

Whether or not one accepts Jencks's verdict (and there are many who would not) the important point is that the cause of Modernism had been well served over the previous half-century by architectural historians; in its early utopian phase it had been validated not just in terms of the *Zeitgeist* (the spirit of the age), of technological determinism and social responsibility, but also in terms of its historical antecedents.

In the new pluralistic architectural culture of the postmodern era, many architects have felt that an important part of designing buildings was about flair in choosing and juxtaposing their forms, spaces, colours and textures in more varied ways, less constrained by black and white ideas about the right and wrong way of doing so – and that in the later twentieth century with its intermingling of cultural ideas there was room no more for ideologies like the Modernism of the past to gain a stranglehold. As part of the new attitude to what was important in the past, traditional architects like Lutyens were appreciated by modern designers and rehabilitated by historians.

Since then, the architectural debate has embraced, in addition to Postmodernism, a bewildering proliferation of movements: high-tech, deconstructive building, classical revivals, vernacular revivals and more. All have had their adherents, and in some cases the benefit of a further re-writing of architectural history to validate them – for example, the enormously increased emphasis on the continuing tradition of Classicism in David Watkin's *A History of Western Architecture* (1986).

There is one trend in contemporary architecture that could only recently be included in this list. Given the widespread knowledge by the 1960s of the harm as well as the benefits that machine-age society, in peace as well as in war, had brought to humans, as well as to the planet, it is puzzling as to why the new architectural debate at that time did not really engage with green issues. Vital aspects in music and literature of the popular culture, that Venturi recommended paying attention to, were concerned with them. There is no equivalent to, say, Joan Baez, in the buildings or words of Venturi, although there is in much of the pop culture he recommends. Nor is there any account in his approval of the billboards of Las Vegas of the views of those like Tom Wolfe who equated the freeform signs and pools of Vegas with Mafia corruption. Generally the architects and theorists stood apart from these aspects of 1960s culture. Only the wigwams and 'woodbutchers art' sheds of Woodstock culture responded. The clamour over green issues, that had started with a prophetic few a hundred years or more earlier, had now reached a wider audience, but mainstream architecture was not yet paying attention. It would be a decade before it began to.

This book attempts to put that past into focus. On a broader canvas it aims to show that urgent attempts by architects now to produce a green architecture in both blueprint and in reality have in their ancestry a sequence of ideas and buildings, just as the Neo-classical works of Ledoux, and those of the great engineers, lay behind the modern movement in architecture. By setting out the past from this green point of view, and then by discussing the present, a start may be made in shaping a critical history of green architecture. In such a view the achievements that promise much to the future will not always be those that a Pevsner, or even a Venturi would hold to. A partisan, though accurate, re-reading of this kind seems sorely needed now, both because we doubt the benefits of unchecked material progress, and in narrower architectural terms because we need to confront the pretentious obfuscation with which the competing factions deluge the architectural press. Before starting this task I was surprised that so few attempts have been made to do this. The word organic, misused often in hopelessly fuzzy ways, has come to stand for that strand in architecture which has empathy in one way or another with natural forms. The narrower definition of the idea of the organic which Giedion, and then Bruno Zevi set down formed an honoured but marginal adjunct to the mainstream of modern architecture; it was always a loose one and has become more confused since. In contrast to this conception of the organic we have the idea of a green architecture, of buildings which use lightly the earth's resources, and which are expressive also of a way of living which thinks in terms of partnership with nature. It may be organic in those senses, but equally may be 'inorganic', relating to physical rather than biological aspects of nature. The past that leads to the green present is wider and more inclusive that the organic, as that has been understood in architecture.

I remarked a little earlier that it seemed odd that so little appraisal of the green past of building had been undertaken. Writing this book has enabled me to understand this situation a little better and to see what needs to be done. It involves pushing against the drift, the weight of an orthodoxy about how major buildings of our industrial times have come to be interpreted. That is difficult, whether as in my case the orthodoxies of the modern architectural past were inculcated at an impressionable age; or, I would guess, even more so if one finds oneself at a similarly impressionable age now, surrounded by a frantic image-a-second, thought-a-minute culture that can confuse the trivial with the serious for mere novelty or mere material gain.

The book is more about British buildings than others because I know these best, although as we near the present the ratio of European and American buildings increases. This is usually where these have, at best, tepid equivalents in Britain, or where they are important to what happens in Britain. I am concerned primarily with modern Western industrial society starting from the beginnings of industrialization in the eighteenth century and ending in the present. Earlier, or other, cultures come into view only as they affect Western culture. Where possible domestic buildings are chosen as examples: comparing that basic shelter which is the house across time and culture gives an obvious thread to discussion of social and constructional variations, although I have not made this an absolute rule – there are other buildings too important to leave out when tracing the relationship between nature and architectural expression. Mostly the buildings chosen are examples of high design: the buildings of designers who through the intensity of their work express in heightened form a society's aspirations and difficulties in sometimes inspiring, sometimes consoling, sometimes fearful forms. In architecture the need to reconcile that expression with the functional and social duties of a building emphasizes the peculiar difficulties of architectural expression as an art form, as well as explaining its overwhelming impact when successful. It is the art we can inhabit; because it also caters for our brute needs, it can show more comprehensively than any other how fast or how fragile are the connections of mind to body, or the relationship of human society to the natural world.

Part Two
The first return of the primitive hut

The primitive hut is a concept, an ideal, a point of reference for architectural theorists. Folk building can illustrate the principles – of functional simplicity, of oneness with nature – underlying the concept and the ideal. The search for the origins of architecture has been a recurring concern; but the return of the primitive hut as a focus of that concern in the eighteenth century showed just how far architecture had moved away from its roots in the natural world.

The return to nature as a source of inspiration for thinkers of the Enlightenment was inseparable from the rise of science; and its was nature as understood by Newton that was to find expression in the work of the great Neo-classical visionaries. But the return to nature could be a more direct, more Romantic urge, such as we find in the cult of the cottage. Ruinlust (the term is Rose Macaulay's) expressed both the rational and Romantic elements in the culture of the eighteenth century. Perhaps more importantly, ruins show very clearly the symbiotic relation between buildings and nature.

The chapter on folk building is placed at the beginning of this part of the book for two reasons. It is a topic that has been of particular relevance and concern to architects from the eighteenth century to the present day; and it has an obvious thematic relation to the concern with the primitive hut. The remaining chapters give a selective reading of the history of the architecture of the second half of the eighteenth century, concentrating on buildings that express or symbolize nature – the nature of the physicists as much as the nature of the poets. One should not overstate the difference; Pope could write 'God said Let Newton be! and all was light', and Wordsworth could write of being 'Rolled round in earth's diurnal course, With rocks, and stones, and trees'. For Blake, on the other hand, there was a sharp antithesis between his Romantic visions of nature and the blind rationalism of the Enlightenment – 'may God us keep', he wrote, 'from single vision and Newton's sleep'.

The historians' coverage of Neo-classicism reflects their ideologies as Chapter 1 has shown; what they tell us about the cottage is likewise determined by their own agenda, and if this is to promote Modernism (Pevsner) or Classicism (David Watkin), it will not be very much. The cult of the cottage in the late eighteenth and early nineteenth century is part of Romanticism; it parallels much of the poetry and painting of the time and subsumes the earlier fashion for the picturesque. A green perspective will shift our perceptions of its importance. The quest for classical ruins interests historians primarily as a factor in the various classical revivals of the period. Here too a green perspective enables us to see its wider cultural significance.

2 Folk building

We must be clear that there is no fixed generic label for folk building, for what Bernard Rudofsky awkwardly but accurately called 'Non-pedigreed Architecture'. Words like vernacular, anonymous, spontaneous, indigenous or rural could be used – as the word traditional often is. The term 'vernacular' – meaning originally the everyday architectural language of a particular region – has been adopted by most architects and historians. I prefer 'folk' for its resonances with folk music, folk tales, etc. For me the term 'folk building' shades over into buildings which are already more consciously designed in a Western sense, but in which traditional methods and materials are used in a still largely pre-industrial culture. In folk traditions we find slowly evolving ways of putting buildings together, based upon the available resources gathered by hand, or at best with the use of rudimentary tools: buildings with their size, forms and surfaces directed by a combination of necessity and ritual. Controlled by these slowly developing functional traditions and the way of life of the particular culture, the earliest buildings would have particular forms, from the circular kraals made from plant forms of southern Africa, or the rectangular clay cubes of northern Africa, to the steep-roofed timber, clay or stone buildings of northern Europe. The range of buildings embraced by my term folk building extends from anonymous shelters built out of rudimentary need, of which the cave is the earliest form, to those buildings where functional requirements and symbolic importance combine with constructional ingenuity to make buildings whose sophistication parallels those of our industrialized culture.

The folk element in Western ways of putting buildings together shades off as buildings become consciously 'designed'. Increasingly quickly rational amendments were made in the ways of building compared to what had come before. In the houses put up by builders in the eighteenth and nineteenth centuries from pattern books, for example, the traditional methods and materials still largely prevail. They do however rely upon the invention of architects who, producing the pedigreed 'architectural' houses and pattern books derived from them, guide the modifications that take place and hasten them through fashionable change.

It was a similar process that earlier in England had led the architectural and building decisions of the master masons and priests in the great cathedrals to be replicated in humbler ways in smaller churches and in secular buildings too. In Elizabethan England printed books illustrated with woodblocks became available, and the process of assimilating overseas ideas through pattern books from the Low Countries (with Renaissance detail changed by misunderstanding but also by northern

Gothic tradition) first appeared in the work of architects like Robert Smythson. Combined with folk ways of crafting buildings this produced the unique houses and civic buildings of the Elizabethans. This was exceptional then as a fusion of (architectural) poet and peasant but a century or two later in Georgian England it became the norm, except in the more inaccessible areas of the country.

The interaction between architectural ideas developed by the educated architect and the presence of living craft traditions changed in the eighteenth century. The imposition of at first alien classical designs onto traditional methods of construction gave way to a reinterpretation of the expressive tradition of the vernacular by the educated architect. Then as the industrialization by mass production methods and by the development of new materials began to affect ways of building it was the folk ways of building that began in their turn to be affected. The ideas of the past that stimulated the Gothic revivals of the nineteenth century and particularly the Arts and Crafts movement that followed owed at least as much to examples of humble folk building as to the great cathedrals and palaces. As the century progressed the need for smaller secular buildings, particularly houses, made the examples of church and civic pomp in building less central a concern. The idea of the simple house takes over from the palace and cathedral as a central architectural problem, embodying the turn of the century aspirations for an educated well-housed population.

The role of ideas derived from folk building in this century is mixed. From its clear inspiration in the English Arts and Crafts movement and the associated garden city ideas to the formation of the new towns, but also in the use of brooding fantastic forms in Expressionist explorations of the dark places of the mind, folk sources have been both idealized and seen as images of a brutish existence. They have also served as a source to be well and truly assimilated in a new modern machine-age architecture.

In 1963 an exhibition was held at the Museum of Modern Art in New York called Architecture without Architects. Its organizer was Bernard Rudofsky who wrote at the time:

Architectural history, as written and taught in the Western world has never been concerned with more than a few select cultures. In terms of space it comprises but a small part of the globe – Europe, stretches of Egypt, Anatolia – or little more than was known in the second century AD. Moreover the evolution of architecture is usually dealt with only in its late phases. Skipping the first fifty centuries, chroniclers present us with a full dress pageant of formal architecture, as arbitrary in its way as ... dating the birth of music with the advent of the symphony orchestra ... Architectural history is equally biased on the social plane. It amounts to little more than a Who's Who of architects who commemorated power and wealth; an anthology of buildings by and for the privileged – houses of true and false gods, of merchant princes and of princes of the blood – with never a word about lesser people ... such self-imposed limitations appear absurd.

This exhibition of Rudofsky's photographs from his travels around the world's remaining archaic architecture struck a chord at the time. The backpacking hippie trails like that across the Middle East to India, Afghanistan and Nepal were opening up and as more and more ordinary people began to travel widely and informally the twentieth century's intermittent interest in ideas of the primitive was reawakened.

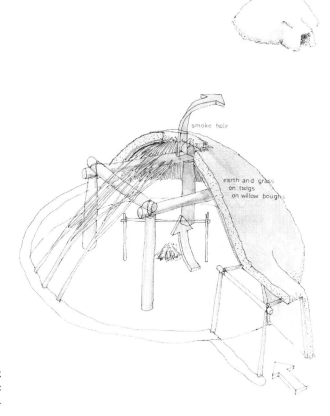

Figure 2.1
Architecture without architects: Chinese underground village – dwellings below, fields upstairs. From Bernard Rudofsky, *Architecture without Architects* (1974) © Academy Group Ltd.

Figure 2.2
Mandan earth lodge, a traditional North American dwelling. Drawing: Laurie Bradley.

Figure 2.3
Prefabricated parts for yurta, a traditional dwelling of central Asia. From Enrico Guidoni, *Primitive Architecture* (1979) © Academy Group Ltd.

Figure 2.4
Completed yurta covered with felt and cane matting. From Enrico Guidoni, *Primitive Architecture* (1979) © Academy Group Ltd.

Earlier interests like that of the Cubists in African art and Le Corbusier in north African houses, of sculptors like Moore and architects like Wright in central American sculpture and architecture, were joined by an intense awareness of the deep past. This interest in the ways of behaving and building of archaic peoples, in the monuments of the deep past back beyond that of the classical period of ancient Greece, and in the folk traditions that still survived had many and complex causes. Among them were clearly the unsettling effects of rapid change, and the loss of confidence in the values of the West after a second technologically driven war which had ended with the invention of the ultimately destructive atomic bombs. From simple nostalgia for the way things had been (or were imagined to have been), to a constructive desire to learn from the past when moving into the future, the need to connect to the past became widespread.

Earlier a bestselling book by Jacquetta Hawkes called *A Land* (1951) had explained the psychology of the approach that the interest in the deep past called up, and the wish to make thick walled primitive looking buildings in the present. She did this by recalling the steps of the geological formation of the British Isles, the laying down of the remnants of fossilized life forms in the strata as time passed and species came and went, on the surface of which the fragile present, its peoples, their buildings and the flora and fauna of the earth lived and died. Hawkes's book connected the fragile surface of the land with its human timescales to the aeons of geological time compressed underfoot by discussion of the work of her friend Henry Moore the sculptor:

Even when already isolated by a developed consciousness, men lived in clefts in the stone, or raised great blocks of it to greet gods created to express human unity with the rest of creation. With sharpening consciousness they began to quarry it, cut and shape it to express their various ideals. Anyone who enters a Gothic Cathedral must be aware that he is walking back into the primeval forest of existence, with birds, beasts, monsters and angels looking through the foliage. But with classical building man was giving expression to that upper part of his consciousness which would cut itself more from its background to live in the Ionic temple of the intellect. Yet in spite of the Ionic temple, in spite of the even greater perils of the concrete office block, the most sensitive and civilized men have never forgotten their origins, their relationship with the land. Now Henry Moore can be used to symbolize a reaction towards it. His curves follow life back into the stone, grope round the contours of the woman he finds there, pull her out with accumulating layers of time, the impressions of detailed life, marking the flesh of her universal existence.

Hawkes's book calls for a rebalancing of the forces of mind and nature. Written, as so much was at the time, under the threat of precipitate nuclear war, it is an ecological tract.

Whether aligned with the renewal of interest in folk architecture as campaigned for by Rudofsky or with either positive or negative musings about the deep past, many late twentieth-century architects gave their buildings similar resonances. Like Moore in his sculptures, some found links with the deep and archetypally imagined past, sometimes with uplift and optimism, sometimes as metaphorical pits of despair. Others began to re-integrate traditional forms into the language of modern architecture. Others again 'dropped out' and joined the instinctive do-it-yourself trend in making handmade houses – some inspired by pure Rudofsky-like folk sources, others by the urban junk culture of Western cities or Third World shanty towns. In the expediency of their material, the Third World shanties come close to the primitive huts of their ancestors in the putting together of what is available – jerry cans and cheap or waste industrial products instead of the leaves and wood of the forest and the clays and stones of the earth.

Now again the urge to re-examine the fundamentals of human need, to strip away the superfluous in the cause of saving the earth is strong. For some this will be a return to folk ways combined with the use of our scientific know-how, for others a purer return to the primitive. With the concern for the earth that was emerging in the 1960s now becoming widespread, folk ways are again being looked to for guidance. In architecture the fitness, utility and material spareness of much folk building is stimulating as we explore how to regain in our buildings a balance between ourselves and our resources, between humankind and nature.

*

As late twentieth-century people, though, the limitations of folk cultures in helping us to know what to do are evident, unless we opt for a return to living in mudhuts and swinging from the trees. It is important to be hard headed about this for the directness and freshness of folk buildings, like those we make in play during childhood, and the slower sense of time they evoke, can bring out the rose coloured spectacles.

Life in those folk buildings was often hard and rudimentary, even when a benign climate, fertile soil and a peaceful society avoided anything worse. As Aldous Huxley pointed out, it was only in a countryside like England's that the feeling for nature and for those who worked the land developed as sympathetically as in our Romantic poetry. Put Wordsworth in the tropics, Huxley argued, and the snakes, insects, carnivorous beasts, the fevers and the fetid heat would put an end to discussion of tropical equivalents to the daffodils dancing in the wind – at least in anything like the same unthreatened paradisiacal way. Awe and wonder could thrive in the jungle – or the desert – but the cosiness of the relationship would disappear. Even in the reasonable English climate it did not follow that those living by subsistence in the countryside would necessarily agree over idyllic pastoral values. Today's farmworker is likely to prefer a standard bungalow with all mod cons – a blot on the landscape to the planners – to an old cottage. Jane Austen knew about this. In *Mansfield Park* there is a conversation between a tenant farmer and a group of educated people from the big house who are out walking the countryside and admiring its picturesque qualities. Where they see unalloyed beauty, the farmer sees only more toil and trouble ahead in the infertile scrub and clumps of resistant trees that pepper the view.

When we look to the past or across into the remaining folk cultures of our time, it should perhaps be with a similar collision in mind – a collision between a hankering for the apparent stability of a life lived in balance with natural forces which folk building seems to express, and a doubt about how the effect of living in such a way would foul up what we enjoy about the way we live now. In folk building there is a slow pace of change in choice of materials, constructional methods, and ways of painting and carving developed by the needs of a particular climate and the constraints of limited technology. These combine with long established traditions of belief and ways of life to make for a seemingly effortless inevitability of form and decoration – at least to our eyes. It is easy though to underestimate the confinement, boredom and ignorance, the sense of cramped lives.

The buildings of our own folk past, when we come across them now, are usually changed from what they were in themselves or in their setting. This is increasingly the case in less developed parts of the world. Modern plumbing, ways of cooking and storing food, the lighting, heating and other aspects of modern life bring older buildings into our time with their less appetizing bits pruned (though new and visually unseemly things may be added too).

Only in early photographs and in reading accounts of life in the past can a fuller realization of what remains in built form be understood. Visiting those museums where folk buildings are re-erected free of modern revisions can to an extent de-romanticize. On the one hand there is the satisfying utility of the buildings, the unity of buildings with their surroundings in material form and texture (often even when crowded into mock-up landscapes and pretend streets). On the other hand, even on the brightest summer day, and manifest in winter, there is the evidence of bare subsistence: of lives lived in the cold and damp without so many of the things we would regard as necessities. There was until Victorian times only candlelight to extend the day's activities.

The inconveniences, and terrors, compared to our experience vary of course according to the age and importance of the buildings concerned. The nearer our time, the more comfortable is a general rule, as in the late renaissance of the Rococo style in Europe (and its Georgian equivalent in England) when the cossetting of one's bottom on a chair increased as unqualified visions of a comforting divinity slipped progressively over the horizon. These material improvements inevitably affected the humbler non-pedigree buildings in their turn. The burghers of central Europe in the eighteenth century would for instance have had intimations of coming twentieth-century concepts of convenience (helped by the number of servants available). Well insulated buildings were lit by large glassed windows with enclosed wood-burning stoves circulating hot air through the house by ducts built into the walls, and the candlelight magnified by reflecting mirrors and given sparkle by the crystal glass chandeliers. Such buildings are on the cusp of an industrial way of thinking in which ever quickening logical method is applied to inventing and refining more and more ways of doing things. Even a more backward English house of the period with its thermally less efficient sash windows and open fire grates might have been tolerable for the owners – although not for the slaving servants. For all those who were not part of the ruling classes life would have been much harder, with only marginal improvements upon the peasant cottage in the fields or the charcoal burner's hut in the woods. (In this century such ways were still hard as an account like Flora Thomson's of her Lark Rise hamlet can testify.) In such dwellings an earth floor, straw bedding, a roof-hole instead of a chimney, wind-hole instead of a window, at best glazed with the caul from a new-born calf, would be shared with the precious animals that provided food and clothing. Houses of this kind from the Medieval or later ages are basic enough, but to visit earlier settlements like those of the Bronze or Iron Ages is to move back into a brute existence. To compare the way of life in these with the crafted beauty of objects recovered from sites by archaeology is to marvel at the human need and determination to make sense of the world through making things.

When a settlement is recreated from the archaeological evidence like the Iron Age village at Uberlingen on the Bodensee lake in southern

Figure 2.5
Charcoal burner's hut.

Figure 2.6
Skara Brae excavations, Orkney.

Germany the starkness is blunted, however accurate the reconstruction. Its neatly thatched huts built out over the lake manage somehow to suggest Club Mediterranée fun as much as a subsistence way of life where if no fish were caught, or if the crops failed, the people would go hungry. At Chysauster on an austere hill in Cornwall overlooking the Atlantic, or more sombrely at Skara Brae on the Orkney Islands coastline, the chill aspects of life in such buildings cannot be avoided, even allowing for the cooling of climate that has occurred since those times. Both places have much of their stone walling but are now roofless. Iron-age Chysauster has eight courtyard houses with walled garden plots, the earliest found in Britain. Skara Brae has free-form covered alleyways. Chysauster is made of random-shaped granite block walls laid dry. There would have been wooden roofs covered either with mud or, as in the recent reconstruction, with thatch. At Skara Brae the local red sandstone was used. As it splits easily into regular blocks (unlike granite) it is used in smaller pieces in the dry stone walling and in larger pieces to span over doors, for covering the entrance passage and for paving. Uniquely Skara Brae has the most ancient furniture to have been found in Britain, in the dressers and beds made of flagstones, the wooden equivalents used at Chysauster and other places having rotted away. Skara Brae excavations show its Neolithic people died young. Their short lives were lived in cold fraught circumstances racked with disease and an ignorance of cause and effect beyond that gained by painful trial and error, which rendered these people helpless before so many more events in the world around them or in themselves than we are today. There were gods to propitiate and without the Christian hope, or that of other developed religions, of better times later. To stand among these buildings, or others like them, even more than among the standing stones or the tumuli from the Stone Age to the Iron Age, to stand there and imaginatively re-inhabit their present (and our past), even on a warm day with the sea and sky blue, birds singing, wild flowers abounding, is surely to become alone and helpless in body and mind, aware only of the most rudimentary and risky forms of human living.

In a drawing made by Henry Moore in 1942 the state of mind of people living in this way was made absolutely clear. A crowd of expectant people clad in simple drapes are looking up at a huge object wrapped about with materials, probably skins, tied together with ropes. It appears to be a large standing stone – a menhir – but one cannot be sure. Other smaller stones lie around. The time is obviously the distant past. The people are engrossed in the contemplation of a fetishistic, perhaps consoling, perhaps menacing object. By hiding the object from view while showing that it resonantly exists, that it is there, Moore paradoxically intensifies its real identity and preserves its ritual power. For it removes us from being present day voyeurs of a past scene. Instead for a moment when looking at the drawing, we can become active participants in a primal ritual act before the most solid awesome object these people can summon; we can share these people's view of the cosmos where even the stars could be moving wallpaper for all they knew. The rapt accord between object and watching people is made tighter for us by the obscuring wrappings. We know it to be stone, a significant stone, as well as if we had seen it naked. Moreover, we see it as they see it. *We see as much as they know.*

Figure 2.7
Henry Moore, 'Crowd looking at a Tied-up Object' (1942). Courtesy of The Henry Moore Foundation.

*

We have now to handle the problems caused by our industrial civilization's destructive aspects with its threat to the ecological balance of the earth. The coming of these problems to crisis point is not news. For over a century there have been those who have seen the dilemmas raised by technology as well as the advances made. From the time of John Ruskin, whose writings first posed the issues to architects, a look backwards into folk ways has been seen as an unavoidable part of renewal. It is a looking back to see what went wrong. It is clearly not enough now to repeat the way that the past two hundred years have mythologized the idea of the noble savage as an image of renewal. Rampant technology can obviously only be controlled by other technology. Nevertheless there has undoubtedly been, and will continue to be, an inspirational quest for simplicity: how to do much with little, how to achieve beauty through utility, how not to be too greedy. From the Arts and Crafts movements to Le Corbusier's late buildings and onwards that myth of simplicity has profoundly inspired architectural expression. That quest for renewal moves back in time into the deeper past (and into the deeper structure of nature as our understanding of that grows) as we move nearer to the present.

Rousseau saw 'primitive' peoples as uncontaminated by 'civilized' values, making a bridge between educated man and nature, a reminder of basic truths about the human condition, a corrective. We know now that 'primitive' cultures just like advanced ones can fail, and not only by being overrun by cannier or more warlike peoples, or by natural cataclysms like earthquakes or tidal waves. Problems induced by destruction of their habitat have caused extinction too, whether by overpopulation of the available fertile land as happened to the New Mexican Pueblo Indians, or by self-destructive beliefs such as the craze for statues of the Easter Islanders which is now thought to have caused the destruction of their forests. Now a sense of a shared common human threat, whether from outside destruction or by human miscalculation, has joined the idealization of the noble savage and, for architects, his primitive hut. An elegiac strand has been added to the idea of renewal, often displacing it in the years since 1945.

So the idea of renewal from the buildings of folk or primitive culture becomes more a matter of shared sympathy and of lessons in how to endure. Our awareness of the instability of the past and our uncertainty about the use or validity of its beliefs increases, although provoking nostalgia for what look like less complicated slower times. The intrinsic conviction of the forms from the past confront doubt and continue to tantalize and reawaken atavistic needs. (These can of course express themselves in varying ways: it is salutary to remember that folk ways inspired the SS training huts in the dark woods as well as those of the rambler and boy scout.)

In both constructive and destructive ways folk traditions have left their mark on the buildings of the modern age. Alongside changes in our perspective on nature given us by science, they mark a point from which our relationship with the natural world and our place in it has been pursued in architecture. In their expression in architecture folk traditions have been a bridge as well as sometimes showing a chasm, as our views of the cosmos change.

I began this chapter by referring to the concept of 'non-pedigreed' architecture coined by Rudofsky for his 1963 exhibition. It is time now to turn the clock back, to move from a twentieth-century concern with the primitive huts of actual folk building to the primitive hut conceptualized by eighteenth-century theorists in their search for the origins of architecture – a search which this book takes as the starting point for its history of modern architecture. In relation to this chronological history, folk building may stand as a timeless backcloth, a universal frame of reference, something to be discussed before moving on to an architecture of names and dates. But it also has its place at the start of this alternative history for the enormous significance it has held for architects and architectural thinkers from the eighteenth century to the present day.

3 The search for the origins of architecture

The Renaissance belief in building according to classical rules derived from the example of Rome came by degrees more open to variation. At first though came the struggle to adapt the written descriptions of Roman building in Vitruvius's *Ten Books on Architecture*, which had been rediscovered at St Gall in the fifteenth century, to the buildings required by Quattrocento Italy. The most complicated problem was in adapting the forms of the Greek and Roman temple, which were without public inside space, to the needs of the Christian church with its different ritual and spaces for worship.

Figure 3.1
Bramante, Tempietto, Rome.

This process was slowed by the continuance of Gothic habits, particularly when classical ideas spread to northern Europe, the heartland of Gothic. By the fifteenth century the imperial classical past had been emulated. A building like Bramante's little Tempietto in the courtyard of St Peter's in Montorio marked a calm poised climax in the development of classical architecture. With the ability to understand and manipulate the classical rules, though, came increasing invention, and eventually showy virtuoso display. Mannerism, the sixteenth century's freer use of classical language in architecture, has been explained as culturally linked to the turmoil caused by the advent of Protestantism, and to the other social and political factors including war involved in that momentous change. There must also, more simply, have been the impulse to change, inherent in Renaissance ideas of progress and eased by the properties of classical architectural language, with its separable elements, and possibility of making up new rules for combining them. The Vitruvian rules had anyway to be modified to suit new building demands. Architectural virtuosity continued as architects invented the flowing spaces and forms of the classical Baroque and then that movement's aftermath in the decorative theatrical extravagances of the Rococo. By then doubt was growing whether this was the right way to use the classical tradition or whether Classicism was even the right architectural language to use.

Gothic had begun to be revived in northern Europe early on. It had never really gone away. A classical architect like Hawksmoor could readily when required build in a Gothic mode alongside the older Gothic buildings at All Souls in Oxford, just as earlier in Jacobean times a castle like Bolsover had been deliberately rebuilt by Robert Smythson to house consciously chivalric goings-on that harked nostalgically backwards. By the eighteenth century the traditions of how to build in a Gothic style could not have faded, there were too many buildings around for that to be so, but a civilized, Georgianized version of Gothic came to be fashionable, a counterpoint to the omnipotence of classically derived Georgian.

Certainties over the exact nature of the classical language faltered. People had found that Vitruvian mathematical proportions, central to ideas of perfect classical form, did not always coincide with those found in the remains of some Roman temples. Ideas of the harmony of the universe being expressible in architecture, by whole number ratios, as proposed by neo-Platonic classical theory were not discredited, although they might look a little gauche compared with the sophisticated calculations behind Newton's explanation of the workings of the solar system. Vitruvius's examples were in any case of Roman buildings, he having been a (rather unsuccessful) Roman architect. Greece, occupied by Islamic Turkey, was only now being explored by those interested in architecture. Two architects, Stuart and Revett, went and measured Greek classical remains in the early 1750s. They found them to be in both detail and proportion substantially different from Roman remains, as well as from Vitruvius. There was no longer a certain agreed base. Choice abounded, compounded by knowledge of how other cultures built, brought home by European explorers, traders and colonizers. Questions arose about whether classical buildings should be Greek or Roman, Gothick, or more exotically even Chinese or Indian, connecting either to the past or to the far-flung present. Architecture in practice centred for the most part upon the European classical ideas, the exotic being largely confined to fun buildings for the garden or pleasure palace.

For many architects, using ideas from various sources was fine. Moving from using sources imperfectly understood, but vividly imagined, to being increasingly correct archaeologically, the freer use of styles became more systematic as knowledge grew. Stuart and Revett's pioneering work in measuring the antiquities of Athens was followed by others. John Wood recorded the Roman ruins of Baalbec and Palmyra, Napoleon commissioned an exhaustive study of Egyptian monuments, Hitorff measured the reconstructed Greek temples including conjecturally their vivid coloured decoration. Egyptian, Hindu or Chinese building styles also become more historically accurate. It is a process that French rationality brings to finality. Durand's early nineteenth-century book of plans, sections and elevations of buildings of all kinds from around the world, arranged according to type and drawn to the same scale, indicates a new kind of rationalizing certainty. It overtook Fischer Von Ehrlach's free conjectural reconstructions of the Wonders of the Ancient World, a hundred years earlier, where ignorance of what something had looked like was enlivened by a mixture of imagination and mythologizing.

Others were not so content to enjoy the aesthetic choices laid out before them in the hedonistic imaginative way of a Von Ehrlach, Hawksmoor or later a John Nash. Neither could they be satisfied with a rational systematizing of choice based upon styles such as Durand produced. For them the uprooting changes, the fall away from certainty meant striking at the first causes. In this they were part of the eighteenth-century impulse, stirred by Rousseau, to examine the past; to go back to beginnings in order to re-invigorate the present. Behind the intellectual curiosity is the desire to get some order, something more certain in deciding what buildings should be like. In a sense it is a futile mission, the first of many in the modern age, in that it involves trying to pin down an impossible certainty – the very need to have such a certainty implying a situation where it cannot be attained. The ways of thinking that produced the possibility of unity had gone, except in a problem-solving material sense.

Rousseau thought that in the development of civilization fundamental human qualities and needs had become overlooked, swamped, even corrupted by superficial distraction and artifice, as the French aristocracy of his time undoubtedly displayed. To those of a reforming ascetic nature, the noble savage, standing at the beginnings of human endeavour, was seen to have a simple dignity. For architects the interesting question concerned what buildings the savage would have lived in. What would his hut and his settlement have been like? Well, the dwellings of less developed peoples and Europe's own folk buildings have evidence to show here. More interestingly in terms of renewal of the present, how would primitive shelter have developed to metamorphose into the style of the classical golden ages, or into the stone forest of the Gothic cathedral? Intellectuals took the question seriously while some saw it as an opportunity for fun and games.

The serious discussion tended to divide between the extremely logical approaches of French theorists like the Abbé Laugier and the less systematic approach of more poetic architects and theorists like Ledoux, in which the sense of time passing is acute, of a primitive past being also the future to which in time their own culture will revert. Laugier followed Vitruvius in speculating that the earliest buildings would have been spare arrangements of tree trunks arranged vertically to support roofs sloped enough to discharge rainwater. Laugier connected suppositions of this kind, with their metaphorical connections of forest, to the columnar structure of the Gothic cathedral and the classical temple. From this he advocated a rational geometrical architecture based upon simple architectural elements, principal among which was to be the column in its role of holding (simple) roof above (simple) floor. The space between earth and sky within which we live is spoken of in terms of the primacy of the column. In practice the placing of the column ahead of the continuous wall as a structural support caused practical difficulties when buildings were still largely built with loadbearing walls. (Later Laugier would be seen as an early advocate of framed structure.) Architects, among them Sir William Chambers, drew versions of this primitive hut that by stages led to the perfect forms of the stone-built classical temple, its triglyphs and dentils having supposedly derived from its timber antecedents. Vitruvius himself had written:

... it was the discovery of fire that originally gave rise to the coming together of men ... finding themselves naturally gifted beyond the other animals in not being obliged to walk with faces to the ground, but upright and gazing upon the splendour of the grassy firmament, and also being able to do with ease whatever they chose to do with their hands and fingers, they began in that first assembly to construct shelters. Some made them of green boughs, others dug caves on mountain sides, and some, in imitation of the nests of swallows and the way they were built, made places of refuge out of mud and twigs. Next by observing the shelters of others and adding new detail to their own inceptions, they constructed better and better kinds of huts as time went on.

... with their natural gift sharpened by emulation, their standards improved daily. At first they set up forked stakes connected by twigs and covered these walls with mud. Others made lumps of dried mud, covering them with reeds and leaves to keep out the rain and heat. Finding that such roofs could not stand the rain during the storms of winter, they built them with peaks daubed with mud, the roofs sloping and projecting so as to carry off the rainwater.

Vitruvius goes on to reinforce his argument by detailing some of the primitive buildings that are 'to this day constructed of like materials by foreign tribes: for instance in Gaul, Spain, Portugal and Aquitaine...' The effect more generally of eighteenth-century speculation about the primitive was to make the revival of earlier styles more popular. Roman Classicism was joined by Greek and, of the Greek orders, Doric was seen as the strongest, the most elemental. The Parthenon became seen as the most perfect building of classical antiquity. Egyptian architecture, and fabled buildings that came from other pre-Hellenic cultures like the Mausoleum of Halicarnassos, also inspired new ways of building. Doric Greek became widespread, and more occasionally Egyptian and other now distant imagery made an architectural appearance in palaces, houses, hotels, factories and other buildings of the eighteenth and early nineteenth centuries. More directly speculation about the primitive produced a spate of primitive huts which were built as eyecatchers in the gardens of the rich. These were consciously styled versions of the way the poorest peasants like the forest charcoal burners still lived and reflected the fashionable novelty of the idea of public nakedness in body or in buildings to the bewigged, powdered and heavily dressed people of the time. Sometimes they were used as hunting lodges when of a more opulent kind, sometimes as hermitages where a man would be paid to assume the role of a hermit (as happened at Badminton in Gloucestershire where the building still exists, although no longer containing its paid mystic). In the landscape gardens of the age there

Figure 3.2
Primitive hut: drawing by Sir William Chambers.

Figure 3.3
Grotto at Stourhead, Wiltshire.

usually was a construction of an even more elemental kind – the grotto. Derived from the Renaissance revival of a feature of ancient Roman gardens, the grotto was decorative in the feldspar and tufa lining its walls, and had water nearby or running through; built deeply into the earth, containing a classical statue or two, it was an entertaining and pleasurably shivery experience, that socially could lead to the kind of relaxing between the sexes that a horror film served to do in the back row of the cinema. It was also a reincarnation of the rudest shelter of all, of the one that nature provided without the need for human intervention. The earliest habitations of humankind, their rocky surfaces and arbitrary geometry satisfyingly primitive, even when consolingly and brightly decorated by statues and glitzy rocks and shells in their consciously civilized recreation as a grotto, provided fun for the nobleman as well as a reminder of where his forebears had once lived.

This use of the untrimmed rocky surface, of the natural appearance of stones piled up as in nature, came to signify a reminder of the elemental, the raw state of things against which, or in harmony with which, the rationalizing processes of human invention were juxtaposed. The highly finished sculpted and painted cave-like forms of a Rococo church like that of the Asam brothers, St John Nepomuk in Munich, had its facade mounted upon seemingly arbitrary rock forms that erupt from the pavement to merge with the geometrical shapes above. In other late Baroque or Rococo buildings the grotto rises above ground to take the form of a chiselled primitive chamber. The reforming puritanical phase of Classicism (known as the Neo-classical) that followed took the grotto, the primitive hut, and Classicism stripped of its later Baroque accretions, and found a revolutionary expressive power in using these to reflect new scientific ideas about the nature of the cosmos.

Newton proposed a view of the universe in which the heavenly bodies circled harmoniously, held by gravity, in mathematically predictable orbits. The image presented to the non-scientist was of a smooth well-oiled celestial mechanism, like that of a watch, its behaviour predictable, that ran its automatic course. God was still in the picture, though a little less central, his role now that of the watchmaker rather than omnipresent and arbitrary manipulator. The geometry of the system, reflected in the way that earthly things functioned too, was connected by architects to the geometric and number ratios of Renaissance theory which under-pinned the aesthetics of this architecture. The abstracting distancing quality inherent in having in mind the shape and movement of heavenly bodies in space when designing buildings must have helped to cut through the decorative clutter of late Renaissance building. This Newtonian immensity of space, parallelling that other distancing of the primitive in time, set the stage for radical innovation.

The twin influences upon architectural form of Newtonian physics and the noble savage is shown graphically in two drawings by Ledoux. In one he explicitly connects the underground circular chamber of his proposed cemetery at Chaux to a view of the earth circled by other planets, as the inscription makes plain. In the other, a naked man sits on rocks under a tree on an island surrounded by ocean. Above in two clouds the gods are gambolling. The inscription says 'The shelter of the wretched': the inescapable rootedness of man on earth and the perfec-tion of the heavens above, whose glory the architect longs to reflect in his buildings. By stripping back classical architecture to its geometric essentials, inspired by the spherical purity of the planets, and by taking the Enlightenment equation of light with life, with knowledge progress-ing among the shadows of the enclosing darkness on earth as in plane-tary space, the new architecture came into being. Ledoux's contemporary Boullée talked of the way that personal contact with nature could lead to philosophical and architectural thoughts:

Figure 3.4
Boullée, Cenotaph for Newton. From Helen Rosenau, *Boullée and Visionary Architecture* (1976) © Academy Group Ltd.

Happening to be in the country where I was skirting a wood one moonlit night, my attention was excited by an effigy of myself, produced by the action of the light ... Owing to my peculiar frame of mind, the effect of this phantom self was one of deep sadness. The shadows of the trees drawn on the ground affected me profoundly. My imagination working on the theme, I began to ... note every-thing that was sombre in nature. What did I see? A mass of objects, black against the palest light. Nature seemed to mourn beneath my eyes. Struck by the effect upon my feelings I endeavoured from that moment, to apply the same principles to architecture: I sought to create a general effect through the use of shadows. To this end I thought that light (as I had observed it in nature) could complete everything engendered by my imagination. That was how my mind went to work whilst I was creating this new style of architecture ... I can imagine nothing more melancholy than a monument fashioned out of a surface that is level, bare and denuded, a material that absorbs all light, that is void of all detail, and whose decoration is formed by a play of shadows thrown by still deeper shadows.

Boullée is here talking of funerary architecture but the idea of bare surfaces enlivened by the play of light on their forms was an important part of the new approach. Ledoux, in his buildings for the Royal Saltworks at Chaux before the Revolution and in his unbuilt schemes for Chaux, made mostly when he lost his royal patrons and failed to find republican ones, designed a wide variety of buildings, of which only a few were constructionally beyond the available technology. (The same could not be said of some of Boullée's projects.) The idea of an *architec-ture parlante* – 'parlante' in the sense of a building's forms speaking of its function symbolically, which true to Enlightenment ideals was

Figure 3.5a–b
Ledoux, Saltworks at Chaux, near Besançon.

Figure 3.6
Ledoux, House of the Director of the River.

Figure 3.7
Ledoux, House of the Rural Guards.

morally instructive where necessary – came to fruition in these build-ings, and those of his contemporary Lequeu. Ledoux, unlike Lequeu, tended to move this expressive way of designing from representational to more abstract forms in his later work, although strict geometry is there earlier, sometimes radically as in the House of the Rural Guards. As Ledoux explained in his Pacifière (Justice) building, 'parlante' ideas in architecture became for him identified with geometry:

If artists were willing to use the symbolic system – the form of the cube is the symbol of justice, seated on a square stone – they would reap as much glory as poets. They would exalt the minds of all observers and not a stone in all their works would fail to speak to the eyes of the passer-by ... Thus as Chastel says ... the 'Pacifier', a structure designed to incite, by its very appearance, the desire for universal peace, should be a cubic block surmounted by a cylinder, on a (squared) base. It is the abstract dignity and intractable rigour of forms that should influence the citizens' souls...

The main buildings of Chaux are firmly geometric but with the function of the place expressed in their detail. The rough grotto-like entranceway is a reminder of the underground rocks from which the salt is mined, and the recurring sculpted motif of the salt pouring from vessels tells of the journey the salt has in solution through pipes to the saltworks. In the unbuilt projects the geometric forms and sturdy unadorned columns of a stripped Classicism were marshalled to evoke the building's purpose often using nature metaphorically in the process. A gunpowder factory has formalized volcanoes for its chimneys. The House of Pleasure, designed to accommodate a programme of sexual instruction, has its plan interlock forms that geometrically interpret and juxtapose vagina and penis. In the houses for the country workers around Chaux, the primitive hut becomes the vehicle upon which Enlightenment ideas are expressed in architectural form. A House for the Woodcutters takes Laugier's preference for columns as elemental elements. Logs (the woodcutter's source material) form walls made of columns with a roof based upon Vitruvian precedent. A House for Coopers is formed of two spare interlocking barrel forms. A House for the Director of the River takes an oval form set upon a podium through which a stream rushes from a waterfall situated behind and above the house; as an image of control over nature, by a channelling domination of the natural, it has great expressive power. Of the House of the Rural Guards, Sedlmayr wrote:

Round about 1770, twenty years before the outbreak of the French Revolution, we encounter for the first time in the whole history of architecture a building projected in the shape of a complete sphere. It has the appearance of a spaceship that has touched down upon the earth, which it touches at one point, and a gangway has been laid beside it ... This fantastic design for a building is (by) C N Ledoux, the leader of the architectural revolution. The design is in no way related to the purpose of the building, ... by a sudden lightning flash ... we are confronted here by the greatest upheaval architecture has ever known; indeed for such an idea even to be conceivable ... even as a ... fantastic exercise of the imagination, it was first necessary for architecture to be equated with geome-try. The sphere is an unarchitectural, or even an anti-architectural form. Cubes, pyramids, cylinders, and cones may be considered as the 'basic' forms of the building. The hemisphere may be added but not the sphere. The pyramid has in certain epochs been used as the basic form of entire buildings, and so has the hemisphere – but never the sphere itself. Even in the case of the other forms named certain limits have to be set if we are to transform them from geometrical to basic architectural forms. The cylinder, for instance, is an architectural form only when it stands upright, not when it lies upon its side, the cone only when it rests upon its circular base, not when it is balanced upon its point. That alone is truly tectonic which recognises the earth as its basis. Even certain types of architecture, such as the Gothic and the Baroque, recognise the earth as their potential resting place, to which they are related and to which they come soaring down. The sphere denies this earth basis. Where the sphere is made the basic form of the building, we must assume a dogma which rests upon two axioms: First the geometrical – or rather the stereometric – basic forms are also the basic architectural forms. Second, every basic geometrical form is capable of becoming by itself the basic form of an entire building.

This passage is quoted at length, as it sets down the basis on which a late questioning of some aspects of Modernism could be valid from what might be called a traditionalist point of view. The House of the Rural Guards has the purest of forms for the age of Newton, a sphere like that of the planet seen excitedly through a telescope, a miniature – an aedicule – of the earth itself. It can be thought of too as that other Enlightenment symbol, this time much magnified rather than reduced, that of the eyeball. (The image of the eye had been already used by Ledoux in two-dimensional ways in his Besançon Theatre.)

This house, an intermediary in its scale between these two symbolically important images, speaks of rational knowledge and ideas and progress overtaking – swamping – the memory of the primitive hut. It speaks too, in its vestigial contact with the ground, of how tenuous was its link with the earth, how thin the thread connecting the developing ability to theorize abstractly about the cosmos was to nature as seen by the noble savage. At this time, however modern the thought processes were, the technology made for only slow progress in the human control of nature. In these circumstances the house is, as Sedlmayr says, a kind of spaceship, its alien nature emphasized ('parlante' style) by its use for Rural Guards whose function is to control. It is now two centuries since this exposition of the future collision between modern ways and older ways was given substance by Ledoux in this little house, which starting from the premise of a primitive hut changed in his hands into intimations of the modern space invader.

*

Never envisaged for serious re-use by civilized humans, however entranced they were by Rousseau's ideas, the primitive hut was thought of as a mythical root from which to trace the route to present truth. Most had agreed that the complexities of the late Baroque, and the court life it represented, had to go. The primitive hut in the eighteenth century was a concept reminding civilized architecture not to move too far from its roots in nature and in utility. In the related interest in the cottage and cottage living, architects would find more literal ways of connecting earlier folk ways of living to buildings of the time, artificially at first, with more verisimilitude later.

4 The cult of the cottage

Enthusiasm for the cottage had begun with the urge by landowners to adorn their estates. At first it would be just architectural scenery, a variation on the temple, grotto or tower empty of inhabitants, like the cottage strategically placed to frame a view at Stourhead. Later estate workers would live in these homes, sited as they principally were to improve the views from the windows of the great house or the prospect as the gentry drove or walked their grounds. These cottages, often sited as gatehouses, were appropriately picturesque, exaggerating the architectural silhouette and detail of ordinary folk building.

Picturesque meant quite literally the kind of beauty that made a good picture. It was applied to landscape, and to buildings in the landscape. It referred in particular to the classical landscapes of the seventeenth-century French artists Claude Lorrain and Gaspard Poussin as well as to the rather wilder scenery of the Italian Salvator Rosa. Cottages that appeared in these paintings would be copied by English cottage designers.

The cottages might often incorporate a reminder of the folk architecture seen by the gentry, or by their architects, on the Grand Tour. A thriving trade in architectural pattern books of cottage design grew which could include Swiss, Italian, Chinese and other styles, as well as

Figure 4.1
Cottage at Stourhead, Wiltshire.

the variations on British tradition. The desire for picturesqueness could coincide with more comfortable homes for the lower classes, but often the concern for outside appearance led to awkward inside spaces. It was in the philanthropic and sensible interest in housing workers on the country estates or in model housing near the new factories that the cottage was improved to allow workers some advance in their home comforts. In estates like that at Milton Abbas in Dorset, Old Warden in Bedfordshire and later the Lovelace housing around East Horsley in Surrey, as well as in the more rudely functional housing laid out by industrialists at Saltaire in Yorkshire and New Lanark in Scotland, there emerged serious attempts to improve the welfare of the lower classes.

Behind the concern for the country buildings of the lower classes, as in the more fundamental but related search for the origins of architecture in the primitive hut, were those Rousseau-esque notions of the purity, harmony and freshness of life that lay with those untouched by civilization, whether they be savage, child or country peasant. So in the eighteenth century in different ways, in the name of reform, for the pleasure of a prettier view or for the enjoyment of bucolic games, the cottage became a cult object. The improvement of the cottage in model schemes paralleled the developments in agriculture which were improving the quality and variety of livestock and plants, while the aesthetic interest in the cottage, however selfishly concerned with a better view, or a dressing up of the estate to show its fashionable status, nevertheless widened what might be designed, and who it might be designed for. No longer would the admired buildings of the past be only those of the highest status. The palace, the cathedral and the city hall had been now joined by the cottage.

The cult of the cottage moves into a new phase with the *hameau* of Marie Antoinette built in 1782 by the court architect Richard Mique. Marie Antoinette and her court would play in her *hameau*, with its duck pond, or she might for a while be a milkmaid in a Rambouillet dairy using her milk pails and yoke of Sèvres porcelain. The cottage had now

Figure 4.2
Cottage in Marie Antoinette's *hameau* at Versailles.

Figure 4.3
Cottage ornée, Lyme Regis.

become entangled with aristocratic games, a relaxation from the artifice of court life by playing at being peasants using peasant-like implements in peasant-like houses.

However much we want to smile at Marie Antoinette playing the milkmaid, one cannot avoid the feeling that this group of stylized farm buildings are symptomatic of the onset of Romanticism. Architecturally speaking they are part of a trend known as Romantic Naturalism. Very probably neither the queen nor Mique had actually read Rousseau's *La Nouvelle Heloise* published two decades earlier, with its return to primitive nature as a source of ideas for modern life; but the idea of trying to experience the life of the peasant surely goes beyond the detached pleasures of the picturesque. And though the use of thatch and exposed timbers certainly is picturesque, our total experience of this group of buildings is not reducible to how they look.

In England the immense gap between the actual experience of living in a cottage close to nature and its vicarious enjoyment was to narrow. The cottage ornée, for all its contradictions, was to give the aristocracy a genuine taste of that closeness to nature that was affecting the design of substantial country houses also, and in 1798, with the debate on the picturesque generated by Payne Knight and Uvedale Price dominating the architectural thinking of the time, the architect James Malton published his enormously influential *British Cottage Architecture*. This was addressed:

to those Noblemen and Gentlemen of Taste, who build retreats for themselves, with desire to have them appear as cottages, or erect habitations for their peasantry or other tenants: And to the Farmer, as a guide in the construction of his dwelling, that it may agree and correspond with the surrounding scenery.

Malton's intended readership points to an interest significantly wider than the trend that was already developing, of picturesque cottages to be lived in by the poor and enjoyed by the rich. In England in the 1790s the cottage is as central to the culture of Romanticism as the poetry of the period, but with this difference: both in the context of patronage and of the picturesque tradition, it is characteristically situated in a relatively domesticated environment. A half-century earlier, James Thomson in *The Castle of Indolence* (1748) had written:

Now the black Tempest strikes the astonished Eyes;
Now down the Steep the flashing Torrent flies;
The trembling Sun now plays o'er Ocean blue,
And now rude Mountains frown amid the Skies;
What'er Lorrain light-touched with softening Hue,
Or savage Rosa dashed, or learned Poussin drew.

But this was not to be the kind of landscape in which Malton and his many successors were to develop their cottage designs. J. M. Gandy (*Designs for Cottages* and *The Rural Architect*, both 1805) is the exception here, setting a number of houses in relatively wild surroundings (notably his shepherd's cottage). However, their handling of the vernacular might indeed be compared to the use made of the folk ballad by Wordsworth and Coleridge. Sir John Summerson (*Heavenly Mansions*, 1949) has suggested that Gandy 'was consciously attempting to do in architecture what Wordsworth had, some years previously, done in poetry', that one might see Gandy 'as a frustrated Wordsworth of architecture'. He goes on to cite Gandy's avoidance of conventional detail; his 'uncouth disposition of doors and windows and the grotesque acceptance of the "lean-to" ... the coarsely projecting eaves and the squat chimneys'. This may indeed be an architectural equivalent of Wordsworth's 'plainer and more emphatic language', and a protest against the 'false taste, false feeling' that disgusted Wordsworth in the genteel school of picturesque landscape; but Malton likewise embraces a wide range of approaches and clientele, and some of his designs relate more closely than Gandy's to their vernacular origins, in a way that parallels Wordsworth's construction of his poetic diction. Actual rather than mythic primitive huts have inspired them both.

While Malton's championship of the picturesque in architecture seems, for most of his essay, to go no further than his initial description of cottages as 'the most pleasing, the most suitable ornaments of art that can be introduced to embellish rural nature', he can be scathing about 'those tasty little dwellings in noblemen's and gentlemen's pleasure grounds'; and at times he can rise to a full-blooded Romanticism which takes him very close to Wordsworth:

The matured eye, palled with gaudy magnificence, turns disgusted from the gorgeous structure, fair sloping lawn, well turned canal, regular fence, and formal rows of trees; and regards, with unspeakable delight, the simple cottage, the rugged common, rude pond, wild hedge-rows, and irregular plantations. Happy he! who early sees that true happiness is distinct from noise, from bustle, and from ceremony; ...

Here it is more than just the eye that is 'palled' or 'disgusted'; and the 'unspeakable delight' is more than a genteel aesthetic pleasure.

It is not difficult to find instances where the integration of the cottage with nature very clearly transcends the requirements of the picturesque. Humphrey Repton's unbuilt water porter's cottage for Holkham (1789) had already gone way beyond any recognizable vernacular sources in

Figure 4.4
Cottages at Nuneham Courtney, Oxfordshire.

Figure 4.5
Cottages at Milton Abbas, Dorset.

its extreme asymmetry and curvilinearity. And what became known as the Rustic cottage – a genre exemplified by John Plaw, and to which Soane had contributed in his designs for a dairy at Hamels (1788) – made a Romantic use of the Neo-classical primitive hut which would have shocked Laugier as much as it offended Uvedale Price and Payne Knight. Plaw is notable not only for his primitivist designs, but also for the introduction of the terms 'cottage ornée' and 'ferme ornée' in his books of the 1790s. Within the broad category of the picturesque, these are important concepts, denoting a degree of conscious artificiality that is at odds with Romantic Naturalism.

It is in the 1790s too that the picturesque and now unmistakably Romantic cult of the cottage interacts (and to some extent merges) with another developing tradition – the building of cottages outside the newly established parks of great landowners to house agricultural workers, typically ones who had been displaced by the enclosures. In some cases (Nuneham Courtney, Oxfordshire, 1761; Milton Abbas, Dorset, 1773–86) the accommodation provided had been relatively generous; but they had attracted criticism on aesthetic grounds. The Milton Abbas cottages, often attributed to Sir William Chambers, have a Georgian regularity and symmetry which is only partly mitigated by their attractive thatching, and the undoubtedly picturesque way in which they descend the hill. Nuneham Courtney – which replaced a whole village (very possibly Goldsmith's 'Sweet Auburn') – was much praised for its comfort but lambasted by the picturesque writer William Gilpin and later by the encyclopaedist of cottage architecture John Loudon, for its regularity and symmetry. Very different in approach was Nash's Blaise Hamlet (1811), the first architecturally significant integration of the 'model village' tradition with the picturesque.

Nash was of course already established as a designer of picturesque residences; in 1800 at Luscombe, in Devon – a castle in name and imagery but in fact a relatively small country house – he had incorporated some of the characteristics that Malton had enumerated. It does 'agree and correspond' with the (admittedly 'improved') landscape; it is asymmetrical for consciously aesthetic as well as practical reasons. The interrelation between the house and its natural surroundings achieved by Nash in collaboration with Repton embodies Romantic attitudes that go beyond the picturesque, and find expression in the French windows of the drawing-room, dining-room and conservatories – windows that do not just 'frame the view' (Girouard) but provide physical access to nature. The Nash–Repton collaboration here is also important in the context of their very different contributions to the Blaise estate. Repton's 'nature' is not Wordsworth's; but a tree is still a tree, and 'the living air and the blue sky' are there to be experienced. Closer to Romantic Naturalism is another country house of the period, the exquisite Knowle (thatch, dormers, etc.), which like Luscombe was built to be lived in. Such houses are part of the broader cultural context in which we must situate Nash's cottages at Blaise.

It was in 1789 that the Quaker financier John Hartford acquired the Blaise Castle estate at Henbury near Bristol. He had a local architect build him a new house, but entrusted the improvement of the estate to Humphrey Repton who in 1795–6 produced a series of picturesque landscape designs that incorporated a woodman's cottage:

This cottage will give an air of cheerfulness and inhabitancy to the scene which would without it be too sombre, because the castle tho' perfectly in character with the solemn dignity of the surrounding woods, increases rather than relieves the apparent solitude.

Repton later elaborates on the role of this cottage in the landscape, in a way that brings sharply into focus its simultaneously functional and aesthetic character:

The effect of this building from the house can be very little conceived from the drawing, because it is one of those objects which derives its chief beauty from the ideas of animation and movement. A temple or a pavilion in such a situa-

Figure 4.6a–c
Nash, cottages at Blaise Hamlet.

Figure 4.7
Repton's woodman's cottage, Blaise Castle estate near Bristol.

tion would receive the light and produce an object to contrast with the sameness of wood and lawn, but it would not appear to be inhabited; while this, by its form will mark its intention, and the occasional smoke from the chimney will not only produce that cheerful and varying motion which painting cannot express, but it will frequently happen in a summer's evening that the smoke from this cottage will spread a thin vale along the glen, and produce that kind of vapoury repose over the opposite wood which painters often attempt to describe, and which in appearance so separates the two sides of the valley that the imagination will conceive it to be much wider and more extensive than it really is. The form of this cottage must partake of the wildness of scenery without meanness; it must look like what it is, the habitation of a labourer who has the care of the adjoining woods; but its simplicity should be the effect of Art and not of accident, it must seem to belong to the proprietor of the mansion and the castle, without effecting to imitate the character of either. I think a covered seat at the gable end of a neat thatched cottage will be the best mode of producing the object here required, and the idea to be excited is 'la Simplicité soignée'.

In short it is to be simultaneously a real-life primitive hut and a picturesque adornment of the landowner's estate.

Following the death of his Bristol architect, Hartford brought in Nash to add further buildings to Repton's landscape, and these included a dairy (circa 1804). This was to be a genuine working dairy just as Repton's cottage was for a genuine working woodman; but stylistically it is more intricate and is instantly recognizable as a cottage ornée in contrast to Repton's 'vernacular'. It also anticipates Nash's designs for the hamlet, to be built on the other side of the Kings Weston Road on land acquired by Hartford in 1807.

In designing the hamlet (nine cottages disposed informally around a green, with a pump off-centre in the middle), Nash worked with Repton's son George. It has been commented by Pevsner that 'with their

Figure 4.8
Nash's dairy, Blaise Castle estate.

fancy dress parade of styles and irregular planning and silhouettes these buildings epitomized the picturesque in architecture'; this is undoubtedly true, but does not go far enough. As homes for elderly retainers, they are on a human scale and nicely balance the needs for community and privacy. Approaching them through a gate in a wall and a narrow passage is curiously reminiscent of entering the Begijnhof in Amsterdam. Each house opens directly on to the green, with its asymmetrically placed pump, and has sheltered outward-facing seating (recently renewed); but each has also a substantial garden to the back and side. Though satisfying their patron's taste for the picturesque with their endlessly varied ornate chimneys and their variety of roofing materials (stone, tile, thatch), they are separated from his estate and exist primarily for the comfort and enjoyment of their inhabitants.

This small group of cottages in exaggerated folk style show in their neat cottage gardens and architectural intricacy the spell cast by the cottage ornée as desire for such buildings moved out from the landed estates, to be adapted as fashionable country and seaside residences by the middle class. Nash's cottages are in striking contrast to the imagined vernacular of Repton's earlier woodman's cottage on the Blaise estate. Both individually and in their total ensemble they are a rural predecessor and analogue of his Park Villages in Regent's Park. (Park Village West with its winding street makes a good comparison.) The Romantic overall effect of Blaise contrasts strongly with Milton Abbas, where we are still looking at nature as it was understood by the poets of the Enlightenment.

In the sophistication of its architecture, the cottage ornée, incorporating as it did cottage elements within the framework of the successive stylistic changes from Georgian to Victorian, was always to a degree removed from the original cottage built within rural folk tradition. The decades that followed saw a spate of publications on cottage design, culminating in John Loudon's great encyclopaedia of 1842. Loudon himself may have been responsible for the revamping of Great Tew in Oxfordshire. *Rural Residences* (1818) by J. B. Papworth, best known for his work in Cheltenham, was one of the most influential works in the 1820s and 1830s and he himself had a hand in many rural buildings up and down the country. In 1837, some forty years after Repton had written about the cottage's role in contributing 'animation and movement' to a landscape, Ruskin wrote an article for Loudon's *Architecture Magazine* entitled 'Introduction to the Poetry of Architecture' in which he too spoke of the need for 'the presence of animated existence in a scene of natural beauty'. It is inappropriate to embellish a 'peaceful and unpretending scene' with 'a building fit for the abode of wealth or pride'; whereas 'the cottage is one of the embellishments of natural scenery which deserve attentive consideration':

It is beautiful always, and everywhere. Whether looking out of the woody dingle with its eye-like window, and sending up the motion of azure smoke between the silver trunks of aged trees; or grouped among the bright cornfields of the fruitlike plain; or forming grey clusters along the slope of the mountain side, the cottage always gives the idea of a thing to be beloved: a quiet life-giving voice, that is as peaceful as silence itself.

Landowners continued to build model estates for their workers and in most cases simultaneously 'improve' their estate by providing picturesque views, well into the Victorian period. Lord Ongley's picturesque terraces of cottages at Old Warden in Bedfordshire (circa 1850) are a good example. The Earl of Lovelace, who was related to Byron by marriage, extended his extraordinary stylistic additions to East Horsley Towers to embrace a proliferation of freestanding cottages from 1856 onwards, spreading out along roads to the north and south. Stylistically there is too much going on here in the endlessly inventive and colourful decoration of their flint walls; but they are handsome and substantial buildings, providing very much more accommodation than the more consciously cottagey designs of the picturesque period.

Figure 4.9
Lord Ongley's housing at Old Warden, Bedfordshire.

Figure 4.10
House on the Lovelace estate, East Horsley, Surrey.

Figure 4.11
Holly Village, Highgate, north London.

In many ways the most remarkable of these mid-Victorian examples is Baroness Burdett Coutts's Holly Village (1865) in Highgate, north London: a group of eight cottages designed by the architect H. Darbyshire for a select group of family servants which will bear comparison with Blaise Hamlet (and makes a most striking contrast with the philanthropic housing by the same architect for the same patron in Bethnal Green). Architecturally the cottages of Holly Village come closer to the Gothic revival secular vernacular of the period with their gabled dormers and entrances and their gingerbread bargeboards. Stylistically they are all of a piece. But there is also a romantic Hansel and Gretel feel about them, a fairy tale quality that is reinforced by the impregnable holly hedge that protects them from intrusion and prying eyes. What links them very strikingly with Blaise Hamlet is the way they are grouped around and look on to a green: though it is not a fashionably picturesque, consciously irregular piece of landscaping but a garden with paths, flowerbeds and cypress trees. There is the same self-consciousness as at Blaise, but in the half-century that separates them the proliferation of back-to-back terraces of degraded cottages in the industrial towns has given new force to the cult of the rural cottage and the idyll it enshrines. It is an idyll, one might add, that flies in the face of the actual rural cottages from which most of the migrants to the city had come.

Lightly at first, architecture had followed, as always, the shift in society's concerns and needs. The rise of a mobile middle class and then the great demonstration of the power of the mob in the French Revolution had turned urgent attention to the mores of the underclasses. The dallying with the cult of the cottage in the eighteenth century took on more urgent overtones in the nineteenth century when the agricultural cottage was being built in massed rows in the new industrial towns without regard for the hygienic and social problems that this would cause. Then the vision of country cottages set in pastoral landscape came to be idealized as a better way of housing: not just as a game or for a prettier view, but as an example to set before the tough new problems of the industrial city, of which the early model workers' dwellings in country and city would be seen as precursors.

As the nineteenth century progressed, exploration of the origins of folk building was stimulated by the Lake poets, then Ruskin and eventually the arts and crafts ideas of Morris and his followers. When the cottage became the model for new building to emulate at the end of the century it was to the language of the rude original rather than to the artifice of the cottage ornée that designers turned. Awash with sentiment as the vanishing old ways of cottage living then were, it was in the uncovering of the actual simplicities of the old crafts traditions that the Arts and Crafts movements found their most potent sources for change.

*

In what ways, we must now ask, does the cult of the cottage from the 1790s to the mid-Victorian period represent a return of the primitive hut? To answer this we must first decide what are the essential and common features of a range of overlapping cottage types. Scale is the first thing that comes to mind for the cottage is by definition small, on the human scale (Le Corbusier was to call it disparagingly our shell). Secondly it always relates (however perversely) to a real or imagined vernacular – in its essentially functional design (whatever the ornamental artiness of the cottage ornée) and its use of folk building techniques and materials. Thirdly (and this overlaps with the previous point), it is related clearly to the world of nature – in its asymmetries and curvilinearity, in its use of natural materials and its siting in the landscape. In all three of these factors it matches the common denominators of the primitive hut as illustrated by Laugier, Chambers and others. When one considers the social context and stylistic excesses of the cottage ornée, or the nature of the agrarian revolution which led to the building of picturesque model villages, such a convergence is remarkable. Only rarely (for example with the Swiss Cottage, or with some of John Plaw's more consciously

Figure 4.12
Cottage ornée at Ockley, Surrey.

primitivist designs) was such an identification with the primitive hut the result of conscious intent.

The cottage was certainly a cult: it was sentimentalized – as the site of virtue and simple pure joys – by Goldsmith in the mid-eighteenth century in his rhyming-couplet lament 'The Deserted Village' and it was romanticized half a century later for its closeness to a nature that was God's language, by Coleridge in 'Frost at Midnight'. But the reality that lay behind Goldsmith's poem is not at issue, and anyone who has sat up by a wood fire in a thatched cottage on an English winter night will have shared Coleridge's experience. His cottage is close to nature; and at night nature comes specially close to the cottage as the owl cries and the icicle forms on the thatch:

The frost performs its secret ministry,
Unhelped by any wind. The owlet's cry
Came loud – and hark, again! Loud as before.

The very existence of such a cult is testimony to man's desire to escape from artificiality, to renounce a world 'where wealth accumulates and men decay' (Goldsmith), and the possibility to embrace 'that solitude which suits abstruser musings' (Coleridge). Goldsmith's villagers will encounter a very different nature in the tropics, he well knows; and Coleridge has had to wait until the inmates of his cottage are all at rest before he can enjoy that solitude. They are realists both. Despite everything, the cult of the cottage remains an affirmation of green values.

5 Ruinlust

*Perhaps the most striking of the eighteenth century conventions was that of ruin...
The classical enthusiasts ... had returned from Italy and Greece, with so keen an
appreciation of the survivals of antiquity that they had adorned their parks with
miniature parthenons and set up shattered porticoes on the banks of most unsuit-
able lakes. But these classical ruin-builders regarded their efforts rather as the
modern sightseer regards his diary or sketchbook; they wanted a memento of the
Grand Tour ... consequently their ruins were only ruins because the buildings
which inspired them were also in decay; they were not dilapidated for dilapidation's
sake. To the Gothistic eye, however, a ruin was in itself a thing of loveliness – and
for interesting reasons. A mouldering building is a parable of the victory of nature
over man's handiwork. The grass growing rankly in a once stately courtyard, the
ivy creeping over the broken tracery on a once sumptuous window, the glimpse of
sky through the fallen roof of a once proud banqueting hall – sights such as these
move to a melancholy pleasure minds which dwelt gladly on the impermanence of
life and human effort, which sought on every hand symbols of pantheist philosophy.*

Michael Sadleir, 'Jane Austen and Gothic Romance' from
Things Past: Collected Essays (1944)

Ruins also connect the present to the past. Sadleir's contemporary John
Piper thought too about how the blitzed ruins he had painted related to
the cult of ruin in Romantic painting. Writing in the *Architectural Review*
he quoted approvingly a passage by John Ruskin:

*A building of the eighth or tenth century stands ruinous in the open street;
children play around it, the peasants heap their corn in it, the buildings of
yesterday nestle about it and fit new stones into its rents ... No-one wonders
at it, or thinks of it as separate and of another time; we feel the ancient works
to be a real thing and one with the new ... antiquity is no dream; it is rather
the children playing about the old stones that are a dream. But all is continuous; and the words from generation to generation are understandable ...*

The Gothic revivalists tried to make connection with Christian values
through Gothic architecture, just as the classical revivalists had dreamed
of a new golden age that would take strength from the ruinous remains
of Greece and Rome.

Ruskin, in reviewing picturesque theory early in the nineteenth
century, had the effect of firming up the connections made in the
eighteenth century between picturesque qualities and traditional vernacular ways of building; and this aspect of picturesqueness is inseparable

Figure 5.1
Piranesi, ruined entrance to villa known as Sette Bassi.

from the significance carried by the ruins that were so often to be found in the same landscape paintings. An obsession with ruins was to be taken up by the cult of the picturesque in the second half of the century where it merges with the cult of the sublime in landscape; but its appearance in the 1750s is significant.

If we return to the conjunction of Doric gateway and grotto in Ledoux's Saltworks, mentioned in Chapter 3, we may find here an apt image of the different directions that the concern with the primitive hut could take, and of its simultaneous classical (rational) and Romantic (primitivist) potential. Something of this classical/Romantic duality is also to be found in Piranesi's treatment of the ruins of ancient Rome and in the sensibilities of all the eighteenth-century architects and archaeologists who were caught up in the passion for ruins that his drawings fuelled.

Ostensibly the archaeological energies of Piranesi and of the succession of Englishmen who likewise came to Rome to see the ruins was directed at a better knowledge and understanding of the construction of Roman buildings. This was the basis of the Neo-classical movement of the second half of the century. Publications such as Robert Wood's *The Ruins of Palmyra* (1753), the first volume of Stuart and Revett's *Antiquities of Athens* (1762) and Robert Adam's *Ruins of the Palace of the Emperor Diocletian at Spoleto* (1764) continued to provide a mass of information for practising architects while simultaneously generating a Romantic enthusiasm for ruins. They also gave the Neo-classical age a clearer sense of past time, and of the relation of buildings to nature and time, than any previous period had enjoyed.

Figure 5.2
Engraving from Robert Wood, *The Ruins of Palmyra* (1753). Reproduced from Robin Fedden, *Illustrations from Syria* (1946).

While on the one hand the urge to construct buildings that followed Roman proportions and constructional principles blended with the urge to embody contemporary ideas of the primitive hut, there also emerged a Romantic attachment to ruins for their own sake. Neo-classical architects in England and elsewhere would not only produce designs inspired by an archaeologically correct understanding of classical buildings, they

Figure 5.3
Sir William Chambers, ruined arch in Kew Gardens.

would also create artificial ruins derived, as Sadleir points out, from the ruined buildings they had seen. Sir William Chambers who would later produce his own version of the primitive hut with his 'rustic cabins' included a ruined Roman arch in his buildings for Kew Gardens, and the frequency with which we find miniature temples, ruins and grottoes all together in the gardens of classical English country houses is clear evidence of the different ways in which the sensibility of the period showed itself.

This is less surprising than it might seem when one realizes that a whole range of seemingly rational Enlightenment attitudes are centred on highly romantic idealizations of a real or imagined past golden age, of the noble savage, of childhood. The primitive hut itself was such an idealization. Here it was a real and not entirely lost past that could be idealized as a golden age. (The Gothic revival of the nineteenth century would include exactly the same attitudes to the Middle Ages.) When it later became assimilated to the picturesque movement, the cult of the classical ruin did not lose this potential for idealizing the past.

The instinctive mid-eighteenth-century feeling for the relation between ruined buildings and nature is made explicit by Uvedale Price and again appears in Ruskin. Price is specifically concerned with the pictorial, though the aesthetic pleasures include the association of ideas. 'The ivy, shrubs and vegetation which usually accompany old ruins', in addition to enhancing their picturesque qualities, announce something of 'age, decay and abandonment'. But in the nineteenth-century Gothic revival we find Ruskin himself concerned that buildings should show 'the golden stain of time'. He was all too familiar with and dismissive of 'the theory that the essence of the picturesque consists in the expressing of 'Universal Decay', and contemptuous of 'The artist who looks to the stem of the ivy rather that the shaft of the pillar'. It is a matter of emphasis, of concentrating more on the ageing of the building:

But so far as it can be rendered consistent with the inherent character, the picturesque or extraneous sublimity of architecture has just this of nobler function in it than that of any other object whatsoever, that it is an exponent of age, of that in which, as has been said, the greatest glory of the building consists; and, therefore, the external signs of this glory, having power and purpose greater than any belonging to their mere sensible beauty, may be considered as taking rank among pure and essential characters; so essential to my mind, that I think a building cannot be considered as in its prime until 4 or 5 centuries have passed over it; and the entire choice and arrangement of its details should have reference to their appearance after that period, so that none should be admitted which would suffer material injury either by the weather-staining or the mechanical degradation which the lapse of such period would necessitate.

The 'golden stain of time' shows the ancient building – whether ruined or still intact – to be obedient to nature's laws. For Ruskin it is assimilated to nature in a deeper sense than that of picturesque theory, retaining in its symbiotic relationship, its separate architectural identity and integrity.

The ruinlust of the architects who wandered around remains of Rome and Greece in the middle of the eighteenth century was part of that wider wanderlust that sought out buildings and civilizations remote in both place and time. The cult of the primitive hut was part of that sensibility too but as Uvedale Price in the late eighteenth century and Ruskin in the nineteenth both saw, it was also part of a wider appreciation of the interaction of buildings and nature over time. Buildings mature then decay in time. In an old building the processes of change are going on in slow discreet ways within the fabric, the natural tendency of materials to disintegrate through time and weather held in check by the constructional knowledge put together over centuries of trial and error. Such a building is in balance, an object given balance by the organic processes it engenders and supports. Where overt ruination occurs these processes are speeding up, and can be more spectacularly seen. To quote Geoffrey Grigson, writing in the mid-twentieth century (*An English Farmhouse and its Neighbourhood*, 1948):

A ruinous building does work its healthy function in human feelings and thought, not only because it shows death, but because its death does nourish these lichens and these green algae, does nourish this moss on this thatch, this rose-bay willow herb on the beams, does give birds places they can build in cracking walls, does give crannies to insects from bee to woodlouse. For us in order, in our muddle of disintegration, a ruin should give special delight, because beyond symbolizing disorder and death, beyond nourishing wilderness it yet imposes some order on that wilderness. Some order of the rectangularity of walls, triangularity of eaves, the parallel of the roof timbers half-shown, half-concealed.

Like earlier appreciators of the picturesque, Grigson makes lichen stand as the delightful symbol of this balance between decay and renewal in the processes of ruination, just as Uvedale Price had seen lichen as a necessary part of picturesque beauty. Lichens are the symbiosis between the living countryside and the now dead materials that humans have taken from that countryside to make into buildings. On unruined country buildings lichens are the tiny symbol of that process that can be seen in the full swing of a building's ruination through natural decay:

Lichens ... cannot stand the smoke of large towns ... not a patch of silver, gold or grey will you meet ... in London, Sheffield or Glasgow; lichens are pre-eminently something of the countryside, rejoicing in such buildings as an extension of their natural home on rock or tree – just as swallows and house-martins have found artificial caves and cliffs in cow sheds and under the eaves of houses ... we owe much to lichens ... lichen on brick, on tile, on wood ... and then the green weatherstains of algae – growth all of it, which unites the buildings to the earth out of which they emerge

This use of natural ruin to provide moral lessons as well as aesthetic delight through a mixture of analytic method and poetic insight is thoroughly, I think consciously, Ruskinian. Grigson like Ruskin in his time, whose prose style he seems on occasion to pastiche, would seem to have been largely ignored in the lessons he felt the country had to offer the city. In writing the way he did – *An English Farmhouse* might well have been called 'The Stones of Wiltshire' – he too was going against the progressive grain of the time.

Part Three
Natural selection and industrialization

This group of chapters carries the story forward into the nineteenth century, and focuses for the most part on Victorian England – though at times it is necessary to trace the earlier origins of a particular line of development. In particular, for thematic reasons I discuss Bavarian Rococo here rather than in Part Two.

Science and industrialization are seen as the dominant factors: science extending and reshaping our understanding of nature, industry bringing both challenges and threats to traditional relations with the natural world. Changing attitudes to plants, animals and children, all central to the culture of the period, are reflected in the Victorian home.

At the centre of the conflicting currents of thought and feeling, and of their impact on the theory and practice of architecture, is the figure of John Ruskin; and in Ruskin we first meet ways of thinking that are recognizably ecological. When discussing the coming of modern architecture in his book *Theory and Design in The First Machine Age* in 1960, Reyner Banham argues that what distinguished 'the men from the boys' in the first years of this century was their attitude to the writings of John Ruskin. To rubbish Ruskin then was to be on the side of constructive progress in architecture. This book will show that now, as then, Ruskin and those who thought like him have been ignored at great cost: that the fundamental criticisms of the machine made by Ruskin, closely followed by Morris, have still to be addressed before we can be convinced that technological progress will improve rather than regress the human condition.

The Oxford Museum – a museum of natural history – was intended, in the way it was to be built, and as a finished building, to be an example to Victorian society of not just how to build but also how to behave. It was to act as a bridge, an expression of the unity of scientific enquiry and Christian belief. In its construction it was to represent a model for connecting past traditions with the new materials and new needs of the time. In its way of building it was to show the fast industrializing society around it how a building could only be beautiful if all who took part in constructing it were working creatively. For all these reasons the Oxford Museum was to be a key building in the development of Victorian Architecture – in Ruskin's hopeful words, 'the more honoured the more it becomes excelled'. The museum was to be, for a time at least, the exemplary building of its period as the Doge's Palace in Venice had been at the height of Venetian culture.

Ruskin's critique of industry and its effects, and his concern with truthfulness in architecture – truth to function, truth to materials – did much to create the climate in which Arts and Crafts architecture developed. The Arts and Crafts house, in its return to a closer relation with nature as well as to the building traditions of the English countryside, provided a model that was to be followed in Europe and America.

The final chapter of this section takes a wider look at the influence of nature on architectural form. In the organic forms of Art Nouveau and Jugendstil architecture we find the new cosmos seen through the microscope and discovered in the oceans. The ideas of vitalism, of life force, of nature in continual movement, bring the awesome idea of natural selection into fascinating detail that mirrors the new industrial culture's restless change and movement.

These forms could be replicated by industrial production, though the ideas behind their use were individualist and craft-based. Gestures of symbiosis between the human habitat and the forms found in nature were bound to give way to a more rational and metaphoric use of natural forms in our own century; but at the close of the nineteenth century the interaction between industrial production and the most recent understanding of natural selection was flowering in the architecture of Horta, Guimard and Gaudi.

6 Rocks, apes and Victorian homes

It may seem at first sight far fetched to claim that much Victorian building reflects the momentous discoveries of natural science such as Lyell's accurate estimates of geological time and Darwin's establishment of the descent of humankind from the ape. Yet alongside the technological advances in iron and steel construction, sanitation, and ways of manufacturing building components and putting them together, and connected to the historical and technical search for an architectural style appropriate for the age, was a response to the changing perspective of the human place in the natural order. Buildings reflected the psychological groundswell in society caused by the new knowledge.

The physical changes were apparent in town and country as the industrial revolution proceeded. The pits, slagheaps, factories with their tall chimneys, the industrial processes, the growth of urban housing for rich and poor were matched by the changes in ways of life, as mechanization led to railway travel and the crowded life became the norm for so many more than before in cities and towns. As people moved to work in towns, the countryside became relatively depopulated in places. The contrast between the tumultuous hell of manufacturing cities and towns and the still tended but underpopulated countryside was poignant.

Against this background of turbulent change in the appearance of things and in ways of life, the new discoveries of science made for an equivalent destabilizing of the psyche. The firm belief in a Christian God whose word was to be found in holy scripture was confronted, with all that this involved for a Protestant society which placed religious reliance upon the Bible as the written word of God. Geological time as expounded by Lyell broke with the idea that the book of Genesis could be taken literally, or be anything other than a metaphor for the creation. It also had unnerving implications for existing assumptions about space as well as time. Lyell in his *Principles of Geology* published in 1833 had shown that the earth's present state was the result of slow changes through aeons of time, combined with periods of quicker change, in which an originally molten planet cooled, its geological formations clashing and crushing, its seas being formed though rains of unimaginable density and duration, with successive forms of vegetation and of animal life adding to the laying down of sediment into soil and rock layers. This explicit provable account of earthly creation, of a planet among other planets spinning through space forming itself into its present state, without the consoling anthropomorphic imagery of a benevolent Godhead setting earthly things in motion, remains an unsettling thought a century and a half later in our own time. To the Victorians it was deeply unsettling as well as riveting news. It carried too the implication of continuing earthly change through each moment of human time, however small and unnoticeable that change might be, and eventually certain catastrophe with the decay and death of the planet as the energy of the sun finally dissipated.

The gradual connecting of humankind with his animal ancestors, that coalesced in 1858 with Darwin's account of *The Origin of Species*, was the other radical change presented to the Victorian perception of themselves and their place in the world. Before 1858 the evidence had piled up, in for instance Darwin's own work on orchids and the means by which they propagated, of the disinterested waste, the surplus organisms that proliferated in the struggle to continue life from one generation to another, whatever the order of organism involved – a struggle the Victorians could identify with as their large families were thinned out in childhood by disease and accident. Darwin's theories of an often cruel struggle in nature in which successful species had to evolve and adapt, and in which the fittest only survived, was found by some as reason for allowing the uncontrolled industrialization, and all its attendant stresses for the population, to continue without limitation; thus the race maintained its strength, the weakest being allowed to go to the wall for the sake of the future. In this sense the worst of the factories and housing ghettoes of the time could be said to be reflecting a view of human life as necessarily analogous to the workings of the rest of the natural world, with nothing being done to interfere with such inevitable processes. Then there was the shocking news that humankind and the animals were close relations, with the hairy apes the closest of all.

*

As anyone will know who has moved to a Victorian or Edwardian house from a Regency or Georgian one, or vice versa, there is a solidity, an opulence, as well as a loss of elegance, in such houses compared to earlier ones of similar status. Typically the Victorian house has a middle-class sense of the values of home and hearth, of the house as a fortress against the world. The availability of cheap and varied raw materials, the mass production of building materials and improving technology marked a physical change in building practice and appearance. Most pre-Victorian houses have had bathrooms and drainage systems added, a process that started in the nineteenth century. This makes it difficult to appreciate what a technical shift had taken place. Houses of the Regency and earlier were complicated versions of the primitive hut: rudimentary drainage if any at all, candle lighting, little inside decoration beyond wood panelling, floors usually bare with few coverings. The refinements of proportion and workmanship may obscure the physical nature of such houses, which in their technology are crude, while the demands of classical styling, like the need for parapets to hide roofs and rainwater pipes, could make for a drop in constructional quality compared with earlier folk building. The later Victorian house by contrast is modern in its heating, sanitation and lighting. The open fire and sash window were thermally inefficient – in mainland Europe the stove and double casement were in common use; the Victorian heating boilers used coal, and the lighting was by gas; but in principle the systems of the modern Western house were established by the later part of the nineteenth century, considerably helped by American inventions. Gluttonous in its demands on resources, and obsessive in its architectural detailing, it would usually have been much more comfortable than

Figure 6.1
Solid Victorian house, north Oxford.

earlier houses, with its solidity and the thickness of its furnishings, as well as the new technologies of water closet, artificial lighting and the emergence of central heating which made for a totally different experience of home life: its technical breaks with the past paralleling the momentous changes in the way we understand the world that occurred in its time.

We have seen that the concept of geological time, as opposed to the seven days of Genesis time, the raw savagery of natural selection and the revelation of our family relationship to the ape were all part of the cultural background as such houses were being built. We must now see how this finds expression in their architectural style. Like all Victorian culture, the architecture is ebullient, and richly, densely literal in its historical and natural detail. Hugh Casson has spoken of a typical Victorian interior as being like a slice through Victorian plum pudding, and the exteriors are often as encrusted. It is possible to see some rapport between the overarching concepts of Victorian science and such architecture, as in the striking coinciding of the new diagrams of geological strata with the polychromatic striation of buildings, although the precedent of Gothic building is clearly another factor in this. The attention to sculpted and patterned forms derived from nature as well as from historical ornament, which in furnishings as well as architecture are such a feature of Victorian design, is connectable again to historical enthusiasms, although the singular reliance on plant forms may well have to do with the scientific disturbing of an easy kinship with the animal kingdom. A building – that 'exhalation from the earth' as Victorians quite often put it – might be strengthened in its connection to the earth by a continuation of the bandings of the earth's strata marked upon its walls and roofs (particularly if they obeyed Ruskin's assertion that such bandings must go right through the thickness of the materials). This strengthening might incorporate, as well as the consoling connection to past architecture, the still friendly natural world of plants, of 'the lilies of the field … that toil not neither do they spin'.

In ordinary houses from mid-century there is that ebullience, that richness, that heaviness. Is it an image of confidence, or of fear? Are the rich literal surfaces loaded with belief in the satisfactions of material progress or are they literally full in order to reassure, to have something to hold on to? To intensify reality as seen on a clear day, rather than as imagined with the new information supplied by science? Nature, even up to the outbreak of the Great War, looked ever bountiful, and non-destructible, except to a few who had noticed the disappearance of creatures like the auk, the moa, the dodo, and now the bison. The richness of natural and historical forms could calm, could reassure, could call one back to the here and now. Perceptive artists would have to find another way of expressing, of showing there was a problem, rather than just erecting a physical barrier, solidity, to keep out thoughts of the dark.

*

Whether knowledge that humans had apes (and by inference all the other living creatures) as relatives had anything to do with it or not, the later nineteenth century saw great scientific and popular interest in the way that animals and other creatures lived and made their homes. For those who believed that God had designed nature the rational thing to do was to examine nature for lessons in how to do things and learn thereby from divine inspiration, while for others the fascination of the natural world was enough impetus to look and be inspired perhaps by what they saw. As well as the collecting of natural objects and arranging them in collections, many people kept artificially maintained habitats in the home such as aquaria and ferneries. Conservatories proliferated in which plants not hardy enough for the climate could flourish. Zoological collections were widely established. The establishment of the South Kensington museums included plans for ones devoted to natural history, geology and science. In short it was a heyday for natural history.

Figure 6.2
Stuffed otter (Kingston Museum)

In the books that disseminated knowledge of this natural world this sense of excitement is often evident. The forms, patterns, colours and textures of nature – of the rocks, clouds, plant forms and creatures – have of course a continuous commentary of a hedonistic as well as moralistic kind in the writings and drawings of Ruskin. Elsewhere the tone and aim may be less wide, but the idea of nature as a teacher, whether by divine or other right, remains. A look through popular books on nature of the time makes clear their role in kindling the imagination, a fascination mixed with unease where creepy-crawlies and the like are concerned. In general ways books like Rhind's *The Vegetable Kingdom* (1840?), Wolf's *Zoological Sketches* (1861), or the great German encyclopaedia of natural history *Brehms Thierleben* (1876) convey in their illustrations the magical impact of the things that they describe. The potential patterns and, with more delayed effect, the forms to be extracted from nature were traced initially by Christopher Dresser in *Unity in Variety* (1859) and in the articles he wrote for the *Technical Educator*, then later by others. Much of this writing and illustrating of natural forms is coolly rational and seeks to apply the forms, or more usually patterns, to mainstream Victorian design in the ornamental tiles, carpets, curtains and china of the Victorian homes. Its effect has been to make the characteristic clutter of Victorian possessions have patterns derived more from nature than before, but it seems not to intend more substantial aesthetic change than that.

Another side of this purveying of nature's forms, this application to design of the images of nature and the thoughts that they provoke, is more conducive to change. It happens when an alternative world is revealed, or when a piece of the world we inhabit is shown in such a way that it appears new. The Victorian home had to an extent already allowed people to experience alternative worlds within its walls in the aquaria, fern cases and conservatories that, in their fashionable sequence, were as ubiquitous as the TV and the video are in our homes. The fish, the ferns, the conservatory plants and, more discreetly, the view through the microscope – much more than the domestic pets habituated to human ways – showed to those who saw and thought about them other ways in which these very distant relatives went about their natural business. Through imaginative rumination these gave rise to images that would extend and alter human ways of seeing and expressing. They were the more potent, as were the images in books, for being apprehended within human walls rather than outside, whether that outside were to be the garden or the jungle.

A couple of books by the amateur scientist and popular author the Rev. J. G. Wood can act as indicators for part of the progression from scientific knowledge to a wider cultural sympathy for the ways and images of non-human life, that affects the forms that some houses assumed at the turn of the nineteenth century. Wood's *Homes Without Hands – Being a Description of the Habitations of Animals, Classed According to their Principle of Construction* (1865), is well described by its title. His *Nature's Teaching – Human Invention Anticipated by Nature* (1876) is a companion volume to show that there is 'scarcely an invention of man that has not its anticipation in Nature'. Wood's belief in the divine inspiration of nature adds an imperative confidence to his descriptions and assertions, but the text and especially the engraved plates in *Homes Without Hands* carry an imaginative charge that must for many have made the divine imperative unnecessary. Empathy was worked up by such images (of which there were many), born of close contemplation of the goings-on in the aquaria, or the beehive, or from observations of animals, birds, fish or insects nesting in the wild; or indeed of that sense of affinity with plants that the novelist John Cowper Powys writing half a century later would describe as 'being absorbed in the chemistry, faint, flowing and dim of that strange vegetable flesh which is so far older than the flesh of man or beast!'

The result could be merely sentimental, mawkish even. The anthropomorphic turning of animals into banal versions of humans, as in the Victorian vogue for stuffed animals arranged in human dress assuming human behaviour, anticipated those aspects of Disney that would do the same. A more promising aspect of this collision between the facts of animal life and late nineteenth century culture came through the activities of writers, in some cases naturalists too like Beatrix Potter, who placed human characters into plausible animal furs and animal habitats, there to act out essentially human dramas in disguise. The animals being stripped-down, elemental versions of humanity became characterizations of the child who had not yet become the human adult. In so doing they avoided the impurities, if not the sheer nastiness of adult behaviour, the more so for not being human but only a distant relative of the now-suspect species – suspect, that is, for those to whom humankind was separating dangerously from its necessary equilibrium with nature. Seen this way and grounded as they were in the homely comfort of the earth itself, the squabbles of Beatrix Potter's creatures represent a kind of

Figure 6.3
Nineteenth-century conservatory, Blaise Castle.

Figure 6.4
Victorian bee-house, from Shirley Hibberd, *Rustic Adornments for Homes of Taste* (1856).

Figure 6.5
Mrs Tittlemouse's house

Figure 6.6
The house under the ground, from J. M. Barrie's *Peter Pan* (1921): illustration by Mabel Lucie Attwell.

earthly paradise, more convincing because so much less esoteric than any of William Morris's historically coloured dreams. Mrs Tittlemouse's little home with its snug living room, draughtproof bed, ample store cupboards and delightful situation is a mythical, unrealizable version of the Arts and Crafts house (the subject of a later chapter), which could not help be spoiled by the basic fact that it had to be designed for adult human living. Its nostalgic images of childhood expressed in idealized animal living were consoling, a reminder of what the adult has left behind, and which however intense the memory can only be re-imagined fleetingly through art. It is a mood that at its near-pathological is summarized in J. M. Barrie's dictum that 'the best is over when you are ten', a view of life given an aching passion in A. A. Milne's Christopher Robin stories, most particularly in their ending when the boy and the bear part company leaving their ghosts among the trees, the air heavy with the feeling that nothing is ever going to be as good again – as indeed it wasn't to be either for the real life Christopher Robin or for his generation.

The most fully realized of these animal homes are those of Ratty, Moley and Badger in Kenneth Grahame's *The Wind in the Willows* (1908). Moley and Ratty's homes are everything that, in its deepest psychological impetus, the Arts and Crafts home was intended to be. Badger's home has the added edge of having been converted from the ruins of past human habitation, a fundamental home gouged out from the basements of a civilization that did not last, that had lost contact with

Figure 6.7
Eeyore's house from A. A. Milne's *Winnie-the-Pooh* (1926): illustration by E. H. Shepard, ©
under the Berne Convention, reproduced by
kind permission of Curtis Brown, London.

Figure 6.8
Badger's house, from Kenneth Grahame's *Wind in the Willows* (1908): illustration by E. H.
Shepard, © under the Berne Convention,
reproduced by kind permission of Curtis
Brown, London.

its natural roots, whereas Toad's house, 'a fine upstanding house, the
best on the riverbank', which does not snuggle down and integrate with
the contours and colours of the landscape, is like its owner a portrait of
the destructiveness, as well as the vitality, of modern ways.

The potency of images of animal homes such as those imagined by
Potter and Grahame is clear in the way that, within the constraints of
the needs of human living, Arts and Crafts architects made spaces that
resonated with similar feelings. In the novel, human homes take on this
imperative connection between a human (rather than animal) character
and his or her kind of home and its setting. Earlier Dickens had used
images of houses to reflect, caricature even, his characters. There is
Peggotty the fisherman with his boathouse, as much part of him as a
hermit crab's shell; Wemmick and his aged P. with their tiny mock fortified house, a haven of kindness away from the city and dishonest city
ways. Later H. G. Wells in *The History of Mr Polly* (1910) introduces a
home, The Potwell Inn, at the end of the book in which Mr Polly after
a lifetime of commercial failure, nagging wife and uncomfortable house
becomes the general factotum of the inn; giving up all struggle to understand life he sinks into comfortable routine in the old building beside
the river. Mr Polly, Moley, Ratty and Mrs Tittlemouse are in their essentials one, as are their homes. All are connected, too, with an imaginative

empathy, strong at the time, with how animals manage their homes; and this spirit, alongside the spirit of childhood and a respect for traditional ways of building, infuses the Arts and Crafts house.

There are of course many influences at work in this particular mode of the late Victorian home, and we shall meet these in a later chapter. But to the extent that we see the Arts and Crafts house nestling in the landscape as akin to an animal burrow, it joins these other images as part of the cultural legacy of Victorian natural history.

7 The cult of childhood

I have already spoken about childhood in the previous chapter. It is time now to look a little more deeply into this aspect of Victorian culture.

For Rousseau the child, and the savage as representative of the childhood of the race, were purer forms of humanity, their behaviour and culture unsullied by civilized artifice. The maltreatment of children in the early industrial revolution, and the exploitation and repression of many of the native peoples as Europeans colonized the globe, are both shameful aspects of our history; in attempting to right such behaviour reformers helped spread an understanding of how both the child and the savage felt about the world and how they expressed themselves. The growing understanding and concern for children merged with the earlier phase of idealization.

The idea of the Fall is important in understanding our modern attitudes towards childhood. For Jean-Jacques Rousseau, whose *Emile, ou de l'Education* was published in 1762, it was also a way of understanding man's behaviour towards nature. Here Rousseau formulated, in his account of the ideal education of the boy Emile, a very modern account of the Fall of Man:

Everything is good coming from the hands of the Author of all things; everything degenerates in the hands of man. He forces one soil to nourish the productions of another, one tree to carry the fruits of another; he merges and confounds the climates, the elements, the seasons; he harms his dog, his horse, his slave; he throws everything into disorder, he distorts everything; he loves deformity, monsters; he wants nothing as Nature made it, not even man himself. To please him, man must be broken in like a horse; man must be adapted to man's own fashion, like a tree in his garden.

Among the precursors of Rousseau, among those who counselled us to return to a more natural or more primitive state, was the Jesuit Marc-Antoine Laugier. As the Abbé Laugier we have already met him in Chapter 3; he was the author of the seminal text of Neo-classical architectural theory, the *Essai sur l'Architecture* (1752), and he sought to encourage architects to embrace reason and to turn to nature as their mentor. Significantly it is to a child that a muse points out a rough shelter made of tree trunks and leaves – the legendary primitive hut – in Laugier's frontispiece.

Architects, and by implication all humanity, were thus exhorted to cast off the corruptions of the centuries. This enthusiasm for untutored innocence – an innocence which had been lost in the Garden of Eden – was an important current of thought and feeling during the

Figure 7.1
Hermes inscribing the elements of the sciences on columns, from Rousseau's *Émile, ou de L'Education* (1762).

Enlightenment. We are still attached to the idea of innocence and it is embedded in green thinking.

Rousseau even thought that Emile should be taught geometry through play:

I do not even pretend to teach Emile geometry; he shall teach it to me. In drawing a circle, I will not use a compass, but a point at the end of a cord which turns on a pivot ... when I want to compare the radii of a semi-circle, Emile will laugh at me and tell me that the same cord, held with the same tension, cannot describe unequal distances ...

Figure 7.2
A muse points out the origins of trabeated architecture to a child – the fledgling architect – from Laugier's *Essai sur L'Architecture* (2nd edn, 1755)

Rousseau's influence in initiating a cult of the child is immeasurable. Without him we might have had to wait a long time for the full recognition of the need for nurturing the sensibilities of the child. This acknowledgement of the child as a fully sentient being was to become widely manifest in the literature of the nineteenth century.

A process of extolling the states of infancy and childhood had begun, in England, with William Blake. His *Songs of Innocence* – innocence associated with childhood – were written in 1789. By then Rousseau's ideas had become common intellectual property. Blake's sentiments are sometimes quite close to Rousseau's although they are metamorphosed. For Blake transmuted all the things of which his mind took possession. 'Infant Sorrow', a little poem from *Songs of Experience*, of 1794, has something of Rousseau about it:

My mother groan'd! my father wept.
Into the dangerous world I leapt:
Helpless, naked, piping loud:
Like a fiend hid in a cloud.

Struggling in my father's hands,
Striving against my swaddling bands.

Figure 7.3
Little Nell from Dickens's *The Old Curiosity Shop*
(1841)

Bound and weary I thought best
To sulk upon my mother's breast

Here is another aspect of childhood that was to be cultivated by the Victorians. Unbounded creative energy – represented by the child – is fated to be constrained by the adult world in which the spirit and the imagination are forever fettered.

Early in the nineteenth century poems by Wordsworth and Coleridge imagine the world as seen by the child, to create a sense of wonder. The child's eye view is used to open out that of the adult. This re-civilizing of the adult by 'uncivilized' example is there in Dickens's novels where the child, whether Little Dorrit or Nell of *The Old Curiosity Shop*, give through their innocence, moral rectitude and stoicism, an example to the corrupt world of adulthood; or like Oliver Twist or Little Joe the crossing sweeper in *Bleak House* give, through their helpless state, the opportunity for good people to behave well. Charlotte Brontë wrote about the sensibility of the child in *Jane Eyre* (1847), a romantic tour de force in its portrayal of the anxieties of a childhood in which adults are frequently malevolent and cruel.

We still impute an innocence to childhood and, very significantly, we still invest children with a creative sense which we believe is to be destroyed by us later. This is one of our prevailing myths. It is we adults who have created the culture of childhood. The quaint mid-Victorian cottage houses of the nursery, those box-like constructions with windows at each corner and curtains pulled back in an old-fashioned way, are adult creations which generations of children have dutifully copied in their drawings.

Figure 7.4
Little Dorrit as 'Little Mother' from Dickens's
Little Dorrit (1857)

*

The importance attached to childhood in the nineteenth century made the education of children specially important. How were their innocence and creativity to be safeguarded and nurtured? Nature was to be the crucial touchstone. The period which was to witness the first growth of industrialization was still as yet bathed in the sunlight of the Enlightenment, and it was this generation which was to try to make realities of Rousseau's unrealizable education project. Heinrich Pestalozzi, who knew Rousseau's ideas well, was the first modern educator. In 1805, his school in the village of Yverdon in Switzerland was to be a place of pilgrimage for the founder of modern educational theory, Friedrich Froebel. Froebel drew inspiration from what he saw at Yverdon and always acknowledged his indebtedness to Pestalozzi. Froebel's thinking inevitably possesses the characteristics of the era from which it sprang and it is easily possible to detect in his ideas much that savours of Neo-classical idealism. This is particularly the case with his attachment to universal order.

Froebel's well-known 'gifts' were intended to introduce children to ideas of order and beauty. The 'first gift' was a soft ball attached to a piece of string which would teach the child to discriminate between self and object, between having and not having. The 'second gift' consisted of a wooden ball and a cube: the cube with its six faces would introduce the concept of repetition; the wooden ball would also behave very differently from the soft ball and would roll on a flat surface. Goethe had a monument to Good Fortune in his garden at Weimar which consisted of a cube supporting a sphere; the sphere, which symbolized unity, was also a representation of the sublime. During the Neo-classical era taxonomical systems – 'natural systems' – were sometimes represented as spheres. All the diverse elements in the natural world, it was believed, could be related to one another within a diagram in the form of a sphere.

Froebel's 'third gift', which was intended for children between the ages of three and five, was a wooden cube which was itself further subdivided into eight cubes. With these the child could build the simplest familiar everyday objects – the 'forms of life'. Among these might be the chair upon which Grandmother sat when she was telling her stories, or an arch in a garden. The child could also arrange the blocks into 'forms of beauty' – crystal-like radiating configurations. These would teach children about the interdependence of beauty and order.

The 'fourth gift', intended for five-year-olds, was a cube divided into eight rectangular blocks. It recapitulated what had gone before and prepared the way for the gift which was to follow. The 'fifth gift' was a block which was divided into twenty-seven smaller cubes, some of which were again subdivided by being cut diagonally. With the 'fifth gift' the child could learn the rudiments of geometry – as far as Pythagoras's theorem – and construct more complex 'forms of beauty' as well as build little houses, a church, a school and a factory. Even a Gothic lancet window was possible. All the 'gifts' had a precise didactic role.

Although Froebel's teaching methods were introduced into Britain in the 1850s it was not until the late 1880s that children in board schools – as state or national schools were then called – began to adopt Froebel's methods. Frank Lloyd Wright played with the 'gifts' as a child. The tale has become part of the Wrightian hagiography, and Wright's preoccupation with geometry is often traced back to this childhood experience.

One of the most significant parts of Froebel's teaching, in the present context, was his concern that children should be taught to love nature. God was manifest in His own creation and nature was 'spirit visible'.

All manifestations of nature could be used to teach moral lessons. Thinkers in the nineteenth century continued to be preoccupied, as they had been earlier, with what the philosopher R. G. Collingwood described as 'the problem of discovering some intrinsic connection between matter and mind – some connection which would preserve the special character of each, and yet make them genuinely and intelligibly parts of the same world'. This can explain why so many vain attempts were made during the nineteenth century to bring a spiritual dimension into science – to spiritualize science.

In the 1840s at Froebel's first kindergarten in Blankenburg each child cultivated his or her own minute plot of land, while the whole school tended and harvested a collective vegetable garden. Echoes of Froebel's particular mode of prostration before the altar of Nature – as well as Rousseau's and Pestalozzi's – are to be found in William Morris's writings. Matthew Arnold recognized the importance of teaching the children of the masses about nature – he sometimes uses the German term Naturkunde – though he believed that the study of nature would not in itself transform the character of the child (the child needed to be moralized before he or she could appreciate the lessons of nature).

Walter Pater was perhaps the earliest writer to have ascribed a responsiveness to aesthetic stimuli, as opposed to geometrical understanding, on the part of children. In his essay 'The Child in the House', published in *Macmillan's Magazine* in 1878, Pater discusses the aesthetic sensations of children. This is based upon his own recollections.

... the child finds for itself, and with unstinted delight ... in those whites and reds through the smoke on very homely buildings, and in the gold of the dandelions at the road-side ... in the lack of better ministries to its desire of beauty.

*

The enthusiasm for untutored innocence resurfaced at the end of the nineteenth century with the seductive primitivism of Gauguin. In general the savage had remained just that to nineteenth-century culture: to be exploited, governed, and where possible converted to Christianity. Only late in the century does the culture of the savage or the primitive affect the culture of Europe. Gauguin after painting the peasants of Brittany goes to Tahiti in search of the ways of his Peruvian childhood and introduces the power of the primitive to Europe.

With the idea of the tabula rasa – the clean slate – constantly in mind the West would seek to begin anew. Roger Fry wrote enthusiastically about the art of the Bushmen of the Kalahari in *The Burlington Magazine* as early as 1910 and saw in it, misguidedly though understandably, some of the qualities of the art of children. Fry organized an exhibition of children's art (to be precise the drawings of the children of artist friends) at the premises of the Omega workshops in 1917. Earlier, in Secessionist Vienna, Franz Cizek had begun to explore the creative efforts of children and his work was praised by the Futurist Marinetti. The child-like qualities of Paul Klee's paintings during his Bauhaus teaching period are there for all to see. The primitive – as well as the child-like – became essential ingredients in the Modernist agenda.

Thus primitivism becomes the engine of Modernism. Both child and savage can give licence to outrageous behaviour and uninhibited artefacts. Futurism, the found objects of Duchamp and the use by Paul Klee of the conceptual view of the child to express adult themes, are ways in which the child is used to inform and progress adult expression.

At the turn of the century however the idea of childhood was being used in a different way as a retreat away from adult themes, from expressing the world the way it is, or how it might be, back to how it was – or more likely how it should have been. The nostalgia for one's own pre-adult past is what marks out Arts and Crafts architects like Voysey, Baillie Scott and Olbrich from what architecturally follows. We shall return to these later.

8 John Ruskin and the idea of ecology

John Ruskin's name has already featured in a number of places. If there is one man who can be credited with the founding of a green sensibility in the wake of Lyell and Darwin it is Ruskin. Heavier industrialization with the consequent social upheavals, the growth of industrial and commercial cities and revolutionary pressures and fears had accompanied the scientific discoveries of Lyell in geology and Darwin and others in natural history. The reforming propositions Ruskin put forward for the arts and then for society were besides much else the first systematic reaction of a kind we would now call green. Ruskin's advocacy of Gothic architecture as a model for his time, his analysis of industrial ills and the eventual advocacy of social change, his later practical experiments in cleaning-up pollution, getting involved in selling unadulterated food and organizing a community, were all grounded in his crucial experiences in the 1850s, after Lyell and alongside Darwin's revelations, when he invoked the example of Venice as an example of what had happened and could yet happen to the British empire. It was then too that he was involved in the design and the construction of the Oxford Museum, a building that he openly intended to be a moral and aesthetic exemplar to set against what he saw as the rampant destruction unleashed by uncontrolled capitalism. Ruskin's part in that building, the subject of Chapter 9, tells of the adjustments it forced upon his attempt to re-build humans' relationship with their own past and the forging of what we might now call a green sensibility.

In the 1850s Ruskin published *The Stones of Venice*. It told of the establishment of Venice as a city, built up gradually on wooden piles sunk into the bed of its protective lagoon, of its subsequent rise to power as a Christian trading empire and its later slow decline through the later Renaissance to the Austrian occupation in Ruskin's time. The book was more though than an architectural and social history. Ruskin saw a coinciding of the Gothic and early Renaissance stages of Venetian building with the time of the Republic's highest achievement in terms of secular power and Christian influence. A characteristic Venetian architecture developed which, though it changed as Byzantine and Romanesque styles gave way to Gothic, always remained Venetian, the aesthetic of a sea-city, responsive to its functional needs, using its available materials, and fusing the multiplicity of exciting architectural ideas that more than anywhere else in Europe came together in Venice, which was geographically and commercially the major trade route between East and West. Venetian architecture had arisen in the most unpromising of circumstances from a society that had made a city and then an empire from beginnings on the mud flats of the lagoon.

Figure 8.1a–b
Venice: palaces on the Grand Canal.

Venice became for Ruskin a series of object lessons – its past an inspiration, its present a warning, to his own Victorian society; a city of beautiful buildings going to slow ruin, under foreign occupation, its citizens no longer in control of what had been a powerful empire. Its days of power coincided with a Christian Gothic architecture and its days of decline with the advent of the classical styles he hated (represented most powerfully by the buildings and influence of Palladio). Venetian building had given priority to the colours, forms and textures of the surfaces of a building which was to Victorians so very important with their fascination, and need, for buildings to have the surface richness of a slice of plum pudding. Most important of all I think was the relationship of Venice to its lagoon – the most inspiring example in the world of an artificial city created by humans rising above the waters, using the natural materials of the earth, transmuting them, but never beyond the point where a symbiotic relationship with their origins cannot be felt and seen in the baked bricks and tiles, carved limestone and cut marble of the city. All this was doubled in the balanced reflections of buildings in the canals and lagoon – a balance whose satisfying nature would later be illuminated, after psychoanalytic explanation had permeated art history, by Adrian Stokes's remarks on the union of male stone with female water in Venice.

Ruskin, after *The Seven Lamps of Architecture* (1849), was developing the ideas expressed in the earlier book for a renewal of Gothic architecture, and with it for a renewal of moral and spiritual values in society, that would disengage architecture from what he saw as the ugly material degradation of Victorian buildings. In *The Seven Lamps*, precepts for building well in terms of scale, proportion and the right use of materials were paralleled by the need for architecture to learn from and thereby connect to our past and our forebears, and by the need to see an inevitable relationship between the moral values of a culture and the quality of its buildings.

In *The Seven Lamps* Ruskin had recommended the buildings of past times that he considered to be the most perfect. Venetian Gothic was one of those recommended, alongside French Gothic, north Italian Gothic,

Figure 8.2
Venice: lily capital in St Mark's.

Pisan Romanesque and early English Gothic. Ruskin was now developing his ambitious programme for aesthetic and social change. He had already written about painting; concentrating now on architecture, with its necessarily tight connections to social, political and technological events, it would be a decade before he realized that changes in architectural expression are more often a reflection of society's values than a vehicle for changing them. After the publication of *The Seven Lamps*, *The Stones of Venice*, the giving of many a lecture and his involvement in the building of the Oxford Museum of Natural History, he would move his thoughts away from architectural matters to the naked advocacy of political change. In the 1850s, though, he thought that through architectural and artistic change society could be persuaded by example to change its ways. In words and in his brush with actual building he was to act as ringmaster for a new order.

*

A green reading of Ruskin could start with 'The Nature of Gothic', perhaps the best known part of *The Stones of Venice*. Significantly he begins his analysis like a chemist at work on a mineral:

Now observe; the chemist defines his mineral by two separate kinds of character; one external, its crystalline form, hardness, lustre, etc.; the other internal, the proportions and nature of its constituent atoms. Exactly in the same manner, we shall find that Gothic architecture has external forms and internal elements.

The characteristic or moral elements that he finds are six: savageness, changefulness, naturalism, grotesqueness, rigidity and redundance. From a green standpoint the most important of these are savageness, naturalism and redundance. Venice notwithstanding, Gothic is essentially a northern style:

and we should err grievously in refusing either to recognise as an essential character of the existing architecture of the North, or to admit as a desirable character in that which it yet may be, this wildness of thought, and roughness of work; this look of mountain brotherhood between the cathedral and the Alp;

His account of Gothic naturalism blends a romantic feeling for nature with the scientific spirit of Victorian times:

The affectionate observation of the grace and outward character of vegetation is the sure sign of a more tranquil and gentle existence, sustained by the gifts, and gladdened by the splendour, of the earth. In that careful distinction of species, and richness of delicate and undisturbed organisation, which characterise the Gothic design, there is the history of rural and thoughtful life, influenced by habitual tenderness, and devoted to subtle inquiry; and every discriminating and delicate touch of the chisel, as it rounds the petal or guides the branch, is a prophecy of the development of the entire body of the natural sciences

Redundance, in the sense of redounding with superabundance and superfluity, is shown by:

the rude love of decorative accumulation: a magnificent enthusiasm, which feels as if it never could do enough to reach the fullness of its ideal; an unselfishness of sacrifice, which would rather cast fruitless labour before the altar than stand idle in the market; and finally, a profound sympathy with the fullness and wealth of the material universe, rising out of that Naturalism whose operation we have already endeavoured to define.

However the relation of architecture to nature goes deeper than that. Reading *The Seven Lamps* today one is liable to be maddened by the hair splitting arguments over what is and what is not permissible (e.g. in 'The Lamp of Beauty'), but again and again one responds to the underlying current of feeling that surfaces in the purple passages, in the aphorisms or at the end of a chapter – a feeling of the essential symbiosis of buildings and the natural world.

We are not surprised to read in the first aphorism of 'The Lamp of Power' that 'whatever is in architecture fair or beautiful is imitated from natural forms', but he goes on to assert that there is 'a sympathy in the forms of noble building with what is most sublime in natural things'. The argument builds up to a ringing, passionate declaration:

In the edifices of Man there should be found reverent worship and following, not only of the spirit which rounds the pillars of the forest, and arches the vault of the avenue – which gives veining to the leaf, and polish to the shell, the grace to every pulse that agitates animal organisation, – but of that also which reproves the pillars of the earth, and builds up her barren precipices into the coldness of the clouds, and lifts her shadowy cones of mountain purple into the pale arch of the sky, for these, and other glories more than these, refuse not to connect themselves, in his thoughts, with the work of his own hand; the grey cliff loses not its nobleness when it reminds us of some Cyclopean waste of mural stone; the pinnacles of the rocky promontory arrange themselves, undegraded, into fantastic semblances of fortress towers; and even the awful cone of the far-off mountain has a melancholy mixed with that of its own solitude; which is cast from the images of nameless tumuli on white sea-shores, and of the heaps of reedy clay, into which chambered cities melt in their mortality.

In his next aphorism, concluding a very detailed analysis of light and shade in which the architecture of Venice is never far from his mind, he rises to an even more powerful statement:

The rolling heap of the thundercloud, divided by rents, and multiplied by wreaths, yet gathering them all into its broad, torrid, and towering zone, and its midnight darkness opposite; the scarcely less majestic heave of the mountain side, all torn and traversed by depth of illumined swell and shadowy decline; and the head of every mighty tree, rich with tracery of leaf and bough, yet terminated against the sky by a true line, and rounded by a green horizon, which, multiplied in the distant forest, makes it look bossy from above; all these mark, for a great and honoured law, that diffusion of light for which the Byzantine ornaments were designed; and show us that those builders had truer sympathy with what God made majestic, than the self-contemplating and self-contented Greek. I know that they are barbaric in comparison; but there is a power in their barbarism of sterner tone, a power not sophisticated nor penetrative, but embracing and mysterious; a power faithful more than thoughtful, which conceived and felt more than it created; a power that neither comprehended nor ruled itself, but worked and wandered as it listed, like mountain streams and winds; and which could not rest in the expression or seizure of finite form. It could not bury itself in acanthus leaves. Its imagery was taken from the shadows of the storms and hills, and had fellowship with the night and day of the earth itself.

There is another mode of symbiosis which is arguably just as important and which we encounter in 'The Lamp of Memory' in a discussion of 'the rents, or fractures or stains, or vegetation, which assimilate the architecture with the work of Nature'. As we have seen previously he is quick to bypass the merely picturesque potential of this, but allows,

that it is an exponent of age, of that in which, as has been said, the greatest glory of the building consists; and, therefore, the external signs of this glory, having power and purpose greater than any belonging to their mere sensible beauty, may be considered as taking rank among pure and essential characters;

The consequence of this – 'that I think a building cannot be considered as in its prime until four or five centuries have passed over it; and that the entire choice and arrangements of its details should have reference to their appearance after that period' – links back to an earlier passage in 'The Lamp of Memory' which from a contemporary green standpoint must rank as one of Ruskin's most remarkable utterances:

The idea of self denial for the sake of posterity, of practising present economy for the sake of debtors yet unborn, of planting forests that our descendants may live under their shade, or of raising cities for future nations to inhabit, never, I suppose, efficiently takes place among publicly recognised motives of exertion. Yet these are not the less our duties; nor is our part fitly sustained upon the earth, unless the range of our intended and deliberate usefulness include, not only the companions but the successors of our pilgrimage. God has lent us the earth for our life; it is a great entail. It belongs as much to those who are to come after us, and whose names are already written in the book of creation, as to us; and we have no right, by any thing that we do or neglect, to involve them in unnecessary penalties, or deprive them of benefits which it was in our power to bequeath. And this the more, because it is one of the appointed conditions of the labour of men that, in proportion to the time between the seed-sowing and the harvest, is the fullness of the fruit; and that generally, therefore, the farther off we place our aim, and the less we desire to be ourselves the witness of what we have laboured for, the more wide and rich will be the measure of our success. Men cannot benefit those that are with them as they can benefit those who come after them; and of all the pulpits from which human voice is ever sent forth, there is none from which it reaches so far as from the grave.

A chasm of sensibility separates this passage from picturesque theory. These are sentiments that seem to come out of our time. Setting these alongside his recurring sense of symbiosis – of Venice and her lagoon, of buildings and nature – it is not difficult to discern the idea of ecology lodged in his thinking. Yet it is primarily as a man of the nineteenth century that Ruskin speaks to us: a man who would draw lessons from mineralogy, and commit himself to the building of a cathedral to natural history. It is to this that we must now turn.

9 Ruskin and the Oxford Museum

Certain buildings seem to summarize, in their design and particular circumstances, crucial cultural issues of their time. Not necessarily the best buildings, they have in their siting, purpose, construction, appearance or timing the crystallization of ideas seen faintly, if at all in other buildings. Such buildings may show the direction that design will take; they may shout 'no-go area' for the time being, if not forever; or they may equivocate.

In previous periods many buildings could be seen as equally powerful in their meaning. No single building or small group of buildings was unique, although for me the churches of Steinhausen, Zwiefalten, Birnau and Vierzeinheiligen, together with the great staircase at Bruchsal and the library at Schussenried, contain well enough the Rococo spirit, just as Von Klenze's Kelheim and Valhalla monuments carry the will of the classical revival that was to overcome the Rococo. In the middle of the nineteenth century, at the height of Britain's industrial revolution, there is no such choice of alternatives. Only in the design and the building of the Oxford Museum can the excitement and the dismay of our relationship with nature at the time be seen in built form. In a sense this is the first green building, not because of an attempt to propose technical answers to the conserving of natural resources, or for any expressive humility before nature in the manner of its building. (It would have been grander if there had been more money available.) It was though, from the first thoughts about its inception within the last decade when such a belief among the forward thinking was possible, a building intended to display unity: between faith and science and between humankind and a beneficent nature. That during the short period of its building, the cracks already apparent between such unities widened, makes how the building spoke then through its inconsistencies both truthful and poignant.

*

The Oxford Museum lies north of the main university area. Originally surrounded by meadows it has since become surrounded by other buildings. The first of these was the Pitt Rivers Museum of Ethnography which was built onto the back of the Oxford Museum. Then as scientific activity in Oxford increased additional buildings were (and continue to be) added piecemeal to the site. Only the facade now has free space around it. In the 1860s, on the opposite side of the road, William Butterfield designed Keble College.

Although always called a museum, the building was from the beginning designed as a teaching and research department of the university,

Figure 9.1
The Oxford Museum.

Figure 9.2a–b
Dinosaur in the Oxford Museum.

with the specimens displayed primarily for academic reference, and with limited access for the general public.

In the early 1850s when the university agreed to fund the new building the need for such a centre, even in conservative Classics and Divinity bound Oxford, had become urgent. The growth of scientific studies, and with this the burgeoning university collection of specimens, needed a common home, which they got due to the efforts of a small group led by Dr Henry Acland. Ruskin had been at college with Acland and they had remained friends with shared interests in the arts, sciences and theology. Ruskin at this time had become absorbed by architectural study. *The Seven Lamps of Architecture* had been published in 1849, he was completing the three volumes of *The Stones of Venice*, and was giving many lectures. He had become the most active spokesman of those favouring the study and revival of Gothic architecture. Ruskin in the introduction to *The Seven Lamps* had defended himself against those who might dismiss his views because of his lack of architectural training:

I must be prepared to bear the charge of impertinence which [must] attach to the writer who assumes a dogmatical tone in speaking of an art he has never practised ... I have been forced into this impertinence ... I have suffered too much from the destruction and neglect of the architecture I best loved, and from the erection of that which I cannot love ...

Ruskin must clearly have jumped at this opportunity, through Acland, to influence the design of an important new building. Acland was clearly under the spell of Ruskin's views on architecture so it is not surprising that when the winner of the competition for the museum was announced it should be for a Gothic revival design by the Irish partnership of Deane and Woodward. Benjamin Woodward, who was to take all the design decisions, turned out to be an enthusiastic reader of Ruskin.

A central court for the display of specimens, with a structure of iron and a glass roof, was to be surrounded on three sides by laboratories, teaching rooms and offices, connected by a two-storey arcade around the central court. There was to be a higher portion of this surrounding building to house water tanks for hydraulic experiments. The third (rear) side of the court was to be left clear for future extension. An anatomical yard and a chemistry laboratory were to be positioned to avoid too many smells invading the other departments!

The Oxford Museum's architectural style is Gothic Revival. It is not at all like the earlier playful Georgian Gothick of Strawberry Hill, or the straightforwardly antiquarian approach of a Victorian architect like R. C. Carpenter, who used a consistent Gothic style from one epoch and one country as in the Lancing College Chapel.

It shares a more adventurous rearranging of Gothic with buildings like All Saints Church, Margaret Street, by William Butterfield where the freshness of approach lies in the imaginative adaptation of Gothic forms and motifs, freely planned but consistent in style, to mass-produced, richly decorated Victorian building materials. By contrast the Oxford Museum is as handmade as could be managed; its originality is in what we would now call a collageing of elements from varying Gothic sources, a process that gathers complexity as the nineteenth century proceeds with the range of sources eventually overspilling the resources of Gothic. (The culmination of this process can be seen in buildings like Bentley's Westminster Cathedral where Persian, Babylonian, Renaissance and other modes are bound into a wild unity by a version of Sienese Gothic.) Descriptions of the museum's Gothic language at the time of the competition varied from Belgian and Rhenish to Venetian or Italianate. It was all of these and more. French, English and Flemish sources mix with Venetian, Pisan and Sienese. The abbot's kitchen at Glastonbury was model for the detached chemistry laboratory.

Figure 9.3a–b
The Oxford Museum: a cathedral of science.

Outside, the chromatic stone work is misty and delicate in colouring, the subtle carving around the windows unfinished. The front facade has, as was said at the time, a general air of a Hotel de Ville, an effect that recedes as closer inspection reveals the idiosyncratic and unfinished detail. Inside, the central court's iron and glass structure with its elaborate wrought iron decorations is surrounded by the stone columned and piered two-storeyed arcade which has the carved capitals to its columns and corbels to its piers. The columns were intended to be, and mostly are, each from a different British rock:

On the ground floor are 33 piers and 30 shafts, on the upper floor are 33 piers and 95 shafts. The shafts were carefully selected under the direction of the Professor of Zoology ... in order to furnish examples of many of the most important rocks of the British Isles ...

Around the edge of the court were to be statues of great scientists of past and present. Together with the stone capitals carved into different plant forms and the wrought iron beaten into twisting foliage overhead, the building was intended, along with the specimens on display, to be not just a place of instruction, but to incarnate in its forms the unity of nature and man, of science and faith, of the reassuring enclosure of humankind by the beauty of the natural world. To this end Ruskin, who shrank from the study of dead specimens, wanted the meadows around to be filled with live creatures to complement the live flora in the nearby botanical gardens.

The building was intended to be the secular science-based equivalent of a Medieval cathedral, with the biblical iconography replaced by representation of natural form. Ruskin was clear about the aims of his kind of Gothic revival:

We desire ... to make art large and publicly beneficial, instead of small and privately engrossed or secluded ... to make art fixed instead of portable, associating it with local character and historical memory ... to make art expressive instead of curious, valuable for its suggestions and teachings, more than for the mode of its manufacture.

... all art employed in decoration should be informative, conveying truthful statements about natural facts, if it conveys any statement. It may sometimes merely compose its decorations of mosaics, chequers, bosses or other meaningless ornaments; but if it represents organic form (and in all important places it will represent it), it will give that form truthfully, with as much resemblance to nature as the necessary treatment of the piece of ornament in question will admit of.

... all architectural ornamentation should be executed by the men who design it, and should be of various degrees of excellence, admitting, and therefore exciting, the intelligent co-operation of various classes of workmen.

Ruskin, inspired by the symbiotic relationship of sculpture to architecture in Gothic Venice, most particularly in the sculptured corner and capitals of the Doge's Palace, thought that to approach the quality of such work he would have to involve himself with the workmen, not to act as an enlightened patron of the Middle Ages might who could assume a unity of thought between craftsmen and architect, but to be instructor and provider of their creature comforts. For Ruskin believed that no-one who was unhappy, anymore than anyone who acted

Figure 9.4a–c
The Oxford Museum: capitals with botanical decoration.

immorally, could produce good work. In Woodward's gang of workmen brought over from Ireland he had some men whose traditional skills were probably better maintained than those working in the increasingly industrialized buildings of mainland Britain. Even so the rough designs for carvings were sometimes made by Millais and Rossetti, who with other Pre-Raphaelites had made friends with Woodward:

Woodward brought with him his Dublin pupils, drew round him eager Oxonians, amongst them Morris and Burne-Jones ... the lovely Museum rose before us like an exhalation ...

Ruskin's enthusiasm shows in a letter to Acland:

... I hope ... to get Millais and Rossetti to design flower and beast borders – crocodiles and various vermin – such as you are particularly fond of ... and we will carve them and inlay them with Cornish serpentine all about your windows. I will pay for a good deal myself, and I doubt not to find funds. Such capitals as we will have.

Every morning came the handsome red-bearded brothers O'Shea, bearing plants from the botanic gardens, to reappear under their chisels in the rough hewn capitals of the pillars. The O'Sheas and the other workmen were given a hut which had dining room, smoking room, a reading room with library and a kitchen, with a caretaker to look after them. Most of the men used this as their home, having just a bed in town. A service was held for them each morning and Ruskin himself took them on nature walks and lectured them on art and about their role in the museum.

   Did it make any difference? Many of the carvings are lively and inventive; all are skilfully done. The O'Sheas drifted away from the job towards the end, as the money ran out. They were an ebullient bunch who had clashed with the university authorities, and who seemed to have answered only to Woodward. After his death they went. They had probably indulged Ruskin and Acland's attempts to educate them, while gratefully taking the superior comforts on offer. Ruskin was later to say that he had never imagined that the building problems of the nineteenth century could be solved by 'laying hands on the first bunch of lively Irishmen you had come across'. Of both the O'Sheas and Benjamin Woodward he was to speak with great affection in later years. Whether the treating of the workmen with conscious dignity helped the quality of their work cannot be shown; they had worked as well for Woodward in Ireland beforehand. But as a working out of the principle of ennobling labour by encouraging creativity, and providing decent conditions, the experiment was important to Ruskin as he prepared the way for his move into purely social issues that led to the publication of *Unto This Last*.

Realizing that society could not be changed by advocating a way of building, any more than advocating a particular way of painting, as he had done earlier, and believing that only a happy healthy workman could produce beautiful things, Ruskin was inexorably driven to making plans for social change. Fear of the mob (the riots of 1848 were a jarring memory) as well as pity for the urban poor played their part, but the catalyst for the change may well have been his involvement for the first time with working men in his attempt to inspire the craftsmanship of the museum.

The money ran out before the museum's elaborate programme of carving could be completed and the full range of British rocks could be accumulated (instead there had to be some duplication). The attempt to raise money by private subscription failed to raise enough to complete the series of sculptured scientists. Public interest was insufficient, and Ruskin's ideas insufficiently listened to. (Research has shown that his books sold well only to a small coterie until much later in the century.) In these aspects the building failed to lead the Gothic revival. Subsequently Butterfield, using in his buildings the Victorian industry's tiles, bricks and reconstituted stone, rationally translated from the colours, forms and textures of building materials of the handmade past, showed the Victorians how to build. Only E. W. Godwin tried to follow the Ruskinian example, in the town halls at Northampton and Congleton, where the workmen were encouraged to inaugurate as well as execute their sculptural ideas. The enthusiasm for Italian Gothic was to be replicated all over Britain in the years following in all manner of buildings. Venetian Gothic was prominent among the borrowings, translated usually into factory-produced materials for the columns, capitals and arches. The architectural details almost always had their origin in the colour plates of *The Stones of Venice*, or of the later book by G. E. Street (1855), *Brick and Marble Architecture in the Later Middle Ages in the North of Italy: Notes of Tours*. Ruskin was to rage against the (still continuing) tendency for architects to look at, and use, the pictures while ignoring the text. He complained of having unwittingly produced Frankenstein monsters of buildings, spawned by the illustrations and half-read half-understood quotations from his writings. Later when he was Slade Professor of Fine Art at Oxford he gave up the walk he had grown accustomed to take past the museum, as the hated 'streaky bacon' Gothic of Butterfield's Keble College rose nearby.

Not that it would have been easy for an architect working with Victorian building materials, and with more ordinary clients than Acland to deal with, to do other than just extract what they liked in the way of illustration. The struggle Ruskin himself experienced between theory and practice can be followed most acutely in the matter of iron.

*

Nowhere in the construction of the museum was the conflict between Ruskin's ideas for an organic architecture and the realities and enthusiasms of the time more evident than in the use of iron in the building. The competition conditions had stipulated that the central court of the building should be covered with a glass roof, presumably because of the Oxford dons' desire to have a brightly lit space in which to display teaching specimens and probably also because of an enthusiasm for the new iron and glass structures associated with railway travel. Woodward designed a pointed-arch cast iron structure of heavy Gothic appearance, with decorative wrought iron clipped to the column capitals and the roof interstices. It was as if he had tried to imagine how a Gothic building might be if its aesthetic had been transferred to the material. The metal craftsman and designer Skidmore was employed to make and erect this ironwork. The museum was over-running its parsimonious budget and cuts were called for by the university. Skidmore, whose undoubted skills were to do with decorative rather than structural ironwork, advocated a new lean totally wrought iron structure of exquisite appearance – and inevitable frailty. The steering committee agreed to the change, probably with Ruskin's connivance. Of course when built the inevitable occurred. The structure, when loading up with the timber roof sub-structure and glass tiles, buckled and gently slid floorwards in a tangled heap. Ruskin was absent from the ensuing enquiry. Woodward probably abetted by Ruskin suggested that stone columns replace iron, confining ironwork to the roof structure. This the committee rejected – it would certainly have cost more – and Woodward's original structure was agreed to after an engineering consultant had checked out its adequacy. What we see today is how it was then built, only the wrought iron decorative elements being salvageable from Skidmore's folly.

Iron, made by new processes, was the most important material in nineteenth-century industrialization, in making the new Iron Age. The manipulation of naturally occurring materials would become ever more sophisticated in their transmutation into new man-made forms. Iron, a basic resource of an earlier Iron Age, had in various forms been used in Western culture since Roman times; but its use had been limited because of the small amount available through the laborious processes involved in processing it from iron-bearing ores, the difficulty of removing impurities, and the problem of regulating the carbon to be added to make iron as we know it. (In its pure state it is a soft, silvery-white substance.) Iron varies in its properties according to the amount of carbon mixed with it. Wrought iron is relatively soft, therefore poor in compressive use as in a column, but highly ductile and therefore capable of being turned into complex decorative shapes by heating. Cast iron is hard and brittle with a high compressive strength; it fuses at a lower temperature than wrought iron, making it even more vulnerable to meltdown in a fire.

In the building that was to be an example for its age, that was to act as a practical working out of his architectural ideas of how to build at that time, Ruskin was faced with a problem of how to cope with the use of iron as a major material in the museum. Iron with its metaphoric force and ubiquitous presence in the new Coketowns of England was not, perhaps could never be, a durable, time-honoured and organic material. How could he avoid its use sullying what the museum was to stand for? In 1849 in 'The Lamp of Truth' from *The Seven Lamps of Architecture* the use of cast iron in building is anathema to him and he concedes its use in only the most hidden or utilitarian circumstance:

... true architecture does not admit iron as a constructive material ... the cast iron central spire of Rouen Cathedral, or the iron pillars of our railway stations, and of some of our churches, are not architecture at all, yet it is evident that metals may, and sometimes must, enter in the construction to a certain extent, as nails in wooden architecture, and therefore as legitimately, rivets and solderings in stone; neither can we well deny to the Gothic architect the power of supporting statues and pinnacles or traceries by iron bars; and if we grant this I do not see how we can help allowing Brunelleschi his iron chain around the Dome of Florence or the builders of Salisbury their elaborate iron binding of the central tower. If however we would not fall into the old sophistry of the grains of corn and the heap, we must find a rule which may enable us to stop somewhere. This rule is, I think, that metals may be used as a cement but not as a support ...

He displays a consistent view as to what constitutes an organic material. Iron is not organic because it has been moved away too far from its state in raw nature to be so. Therefore it cannot carry the truth and beauty of the natural world as laid down by God. Instead it carries connotations of human hubris, and potentially destructive power.

In his lectures and writings of the 1850s Ruskin was to praise wrought iron, while becoming silent about cast iron, where earlier he had been abusive. He had stated that a building containing iron as a support was not architecture, yet the museum had to have iron supports to its main inside space. In his impasse he seized upon the virtues of wrought ironwork; he may have influenced the attempt to have an all wrought iron structure. Certainly at the time of the Skidmore debacle he had modified his views on iron in building. He gave a conciliatory lecture in 1858 on 'The Work of Iron in Nature, Art and Polity'.

It is to the earlier remarks in *The Seven Lamps* on Medieval wrought ironwork that he turns in his search to find precedents in nature and in architecture that will bind his theories to the building of the museum without too much contradiction. In relating iron as used by man to its natural origins he observes:

... we suppose it to be a great defect in iron that it is subject to rust. But not at all ... it is not a fault ... but a virtue to be ... rusted for in that condition it fulfils its most important function in the Universe and most kindly duties to mankind ... Iron rusted is Living; but when pure or polished, dead.

After making an analogy between the way that both mammals and iron take up oxygen to live he continues:

the iron keeps all that it gets. We and other animals part with it again ... the ochreous dust we so much despise is ... so much nobler than pure iron, insofar as it is iron and the air.

He goes on to discuss how indispensable iron oxide is in nature, and to enthuse about:

that ochreous earth of iron ... it stains the great earth wheresoever you can see it ... it is the colouring substance appointed to colour the globe for the sight, as well as subdue it for the service of man.

Ruskin then talks of the dirty whiteness of the earth if it were not coloured by the presence of iron, of gravel garden paths taking on the colour of ashes, and of the golden sands of the seashore appearing as a grey slime without iron. He tells of the disappearance of characteristic reds in tiles and bricks of the cosy English village, of the loss of purples from Welsh slates and of the coloured veins from many Italian marbles, should there not be 'ochreous staining'. Then in a direct connection of iron with the life-force of human existence he continues:

... and last of all; a nobler colour than all these ... is mysteriously connected with the presence of this dark iron. I believe it is not ascertained on what the crimson of blood actually depends; but the colour is of course connected with its vitality, and that vitality with the existence of iron as one of the chief elements. Is it not strange to find this stern and strong metal mingled so delicately in our human life that we cannot even blush without its help?

The themes of the argument draw together:

I confine myself ... to its operations as a colouring element ... what I wish you to carry clearly away with you is ... that in all these uses the metal would be nothing without air. The pure metal has no power and never occurs in nature.

Ruskin can now pass on to integrating his hard won respect for iron with his admired and preferred range of building materials. After noting that a material has to be responsive to the hands that work it for it to be suitable for 'the utmost power of art', he maintains also 'that your art is base if it not bring out the distinctive qualities of the material'. Finally iron is allowed to join with his admired marble and wood:

... again marble is eminently a solid and massive substance. Unless you want mass and solidity don't work in marble. If you wish for lightness take wood; if for freedom take stucco; if for ductility take glass ... so again iron is eminently a ductile and tenacious substance ... it is the material given to the sculptor as the companion of marble with a message ... what is solid and simple carve out; what is thin and entangled beat out. I give you all kinds of forms to be delighted in – fluttering leaves as well as fair bodies; twisted branches as well as open brows ... and if you choose and work rightly what you do shall be safe afterwards. Your slender leaves shall not break off in my tenacious iron, though they may be rusted a little in an iron autumn ...

After praising the ironwork of balconies he has seen in the Italian town of Bellinzona he suggests how ironwork could become part of a meaningful architecture:

... let me leave you with this distinct assertion – that the quaint beauty and character of many natural objects, such as intricate branches, grass, foliage, (especially thorny branches and prickly foliage) as well as that of animals, plumed, bristled and spined, is sculpturally expressive in iron only, and in iron would be majestic and impressive ... and that metalwork ... rightly treated might be not only superb decoration, but a valuable abstract of portions of natural forms ... It is difficult to give you an idea of the grace and interest

which the simplest objects possess when their forms are thus abstracted from among their surroundings of rich circumstances which in nature disturbs ... our attention. A few blades of common grass, and a wild leaf or two – just as they were thrown by nature – are thus abstracted ... Every cluster of herbage would furnish fifty such groups, and every group would work into iron (fitting it rightly of course to its service) with perfect ease, and endless grandeur of result.

Ruskin does not say so, but he has in fact described the newly completed wrought iron roof decorations. In so far as possible he has accommodated, even found enthusiasm for ironwork. In decoration it can carry images showing the truth and beauty of the natural world as an equal partner of other materials. But of the real power of cast iron in its ability to assume previously unimaginable compressive loads with so little materiality, and in combination with wrought iron's strength in tension (later combined in the refining of iron into steel) to make possible the great structures of the nineteenth century, on this Ruskin is silent. The central iron structure of the museum cannot be contained within a Ruskinian view, however much it is Gothicized in form and stencilled with abstract decoration at the most appropriately humble level. Ruskin's view of iron construction was shared by many: partly just resistance to the new, partly because of the role of iron as symbol of industrial power, but also because of real problems associated at the time with its use in building. Where Ruskin's view goes beyond prejudice and reaction is in his understanding of the problems then and in the future that the new industrial society needed to face. His reaction to the Crystal Palace, built in the year that the first volume of *The Stones of Venice* was published, shows the mixture of petulance, conservatism, fear and insight with which he regarded what was happening through industrialization to both humankind and nature. Looking at the great iron and glass building and its admiring crowds of visitors, Ruskin saw shiftlessness rather than permanence. (The Palace was a prefabricated structure which had permission from the Queen to stay in Hyde Park for just six months.) The building housed not only exhibits showing the marvels of Victorian technology but all the ebullient vulgarity of furniture design and the like. In the repetitive order of the building itself Ruskin saw the effect of the static modular principles of Classicism as it had become rationalized, moving the expressive aspect of building ever further away from an intimate mimetic connection with the vital life-reflecting forces of nature. And in the huge spaces formed by the new technology, unbounded as they were by the comforting enclosure of masonry, he perhaps felt fear, haunted as he was by the ever increasing knowledge of the immensities of space and time:

Our taste, thus exalted and disciplined, is dazzled by the lustre of a few rows of panes of glass; and the first principles of architectural sublimity, so far sought, are found all the while to have consisted merely in sparkling and space ... I would [not] deprecate...the mechanical ingenuity which has been displayed in the erection of The Crystal Palace, or that I underrate the effect which its vastness may continue to produce on the popular imagination. But mechanical ingenuity is not the essence of architecture, and largeness of design does not necessarily involve nobleness ... as much ingenuity [is] required to build a screw frigate or a tubular bridge, as a hall of glass – all these works are characteristic of our age ... and all deserve our highest admiration but not ... of the kind that is rendered to poetry or to art. We may cover the Bristol Channel with

Figure 9.5
Nineteenth-century ironwork: Viollet-le-Duc, Imperial Church of St Denis.

iron, or the German Ocean with frigates, and roof the county of Middlesex with crystal, and yet not produce one Milton, or Michelangelo.

The practical difficulties of using iron in many situations has not been fully solved. There was the fire problem – the New York version of the Crystal Palace burned down in 1855. Hiding the iron structure in masonry avoided this but allowed the possibility of iron rusting and expanding through damp because of the porosity of masonry. The development of Portland cement to encase the iron would not happen until later in the century. Fire risks were compounded if the building was to be gas lit. The Crystal Palace had not been, and had to close at dusk: the museum was to be. Apart from frequent leakages due to yet imperfect design, the gas was often impure and therefore unhealthy, the impurities blackening the decorations of rooms. Installations were so unsatisfactory that there were suggestions to light interiors by placing gas lights with reflectors to be placed outside windows, and these were taken seriously. From 1840 to the invention of the gas mantel in 1885 such lighting remained smelly and primitive as well as a fire risk.

Iron structures could produce problems involving the metal's high thermal transmission compared to surrounding traditional materials. If large areas of glass were associated with such a structure its general heat loss and gain could limit its suitability for many building uses.

Apart though from the practical snags, there was a disinclination among designers to accept iron as having a large part to play in buildings of more than utilitarian status. Iron was all right for railway stations, temporary exhibitions, even for a palace (as long it was for a black king in Africa needing a prefabricated palace to be exported to him). For the ruling classes such an architecture could only be suitable if you were in transit to another town as in a railway station, or perhaps to other destinations as in a hospital; for your workers as in a factory or for your plants as in the 'ironizing' of the conservatory. For houses, hotels and the like, iron if used at all would need to be well hidden. As part of the slowness to change the materials and designs that were felt appropriate to the expression of hearth and home (concepts that to the Victorians were a central expression of their values), the psychological shock of the appearance of the new materials must have played a role. To a sense of what felt secure in a building derived from the long traditions of masonry and timber construction, the resulting reduction in size of equivalently strong materials made of iron must have been unsettling. Exciting though that might be in the atmosphere of an exhibition like that in the Crystal Palace or in abetting the intrinsic excitements of the railway terminus, it had none of the stability to be expected of buildings for family, club, town hall or even office. As might be expected, Ruskin with his almost neurasthenic awareness expresses this precisely:

Nothing in architecture is half so painful as the apparent want of sufficient support when the weight above is visibly passive; for all buildings are not passive; some seem to rise by their own strength, or float by their own buoyancy; a dome requires no visibility of support, one fancies it supported by air. But passive architecture without help for its passiveness is unendurable. In a lately built house ... three huge stone pillars in the second storey are carried apparently by the edges of three sheets of plate glass in the first. I hardly know anything to match the painfulness of this, and some other, of our shop structures, in which the ironwork is concealed; nor even when it is apparent can the eye ever feel satisfied of their security, when built, as at present, with fifty or sixty feet of wall above a rod of iron not the width of this page.

Ruskin discusses elsewhere recent accidents in the collapse of iron-framed buildings. It is not enough to suggest that the motivation for this is to discredit ways of building that jar with Ruskinian theories. It might be helpful to suggest a potential modern equivalent to the mid-Victorian view of their new materials. Should the carbon fibre steels now being researched eventually be produced in quantity for constructional purposes, a building, such as Ruskin talks of, would be held up by a structural member as little as one-eighth the width of Ruskin's page. If an equivalent to the Clifton suspension bridge over the River Avon were to be built of such a new steel, the structural dimensions would be similarly reduced. Imagine a walk across this and our apprehensions might well match those of the Victorians facing the problems, and the excitements, of iron.

*

The Oxford Museum was a building that, in its design and the events surrounding it, symbolizes a cultural crisis. An important building in showing how the functional requirements of secular buildings could be accommodated by the Gothic revival, it is important for reasons beyond the arguments about style and function that necessarily preoccupied architects in the nineteenth century. Its uniqueness is in what it attempted, and failed, to express.

The museum was to house the sciences, with all the disruption to traditional views that they stood for at the time, within a university that was a bastion of Classical and Divinity studies. The few dons who studied and taught science were usually clergymen as well. The building of the museum was started twenty years after the geologist Charles Lyell had revealed the true timescale of the formation of the earth's mountains, plains and seas, in flat contradiction of God's word as expressed in Genesis. Five years later, when the building was left unfinished but usable, Charles Darwin finally published *The Origin of Species*, with all that it implied about the parentage of Adam and Eve, the truth of Genesis, and Victorian ideas of respectability too. (A great debate on Darwin's ideas led by Thomas Huxley who was for, and Bishop Wilberforce who was against, took place in the museum's new debating room that year.)

The museum was, then, an actual as well as metaphoric centre for these rupturing conflicts between faith and science; between the idea of a beneficent beautiful nature made by God for the use and pleasure of humans, and the nature red in tooth and claw of evolutionary theory. An intention behind the building was for it to act to help contain a rampaging, technologically armed humankind who were laying nature waste; a problematic proposition when the idea of a beneficent nature was under siege as the prodigal waste and essential heartlessness of natural processes were discovered by science.

It is no wonder that the Victorians, faced with this new raw nature, a scientifically uncovered nature the mental equivalent in its frightfulness to the wild beasts outside the hut or cave for earlier peoples, should so want to domesticate, even miniaturize it. Perhaps at a public level a part of the same containing and miniaturizing impulse permeated the idea of the museum for Ruskin; a way of holding together the tugging strands of new knowledge and old received wisdoms through the images of tamed vegetable nature that, carved into stone and beaten into metal, were to vitalize the building in ways that would hearten.

A public building that in its reminder of the human past through the incorporation of past architectural styles, and of a nature whose presence was tamed – by being turned and polished if of rock, carved in imitation if vegetable, and preserved dead if animal – would perhaps act as intermediary to both the awesome nature of what the research carried on within it might bring, and the true scale and detachment of the natural world towards which that research was directed.

Only in botany, and in the lower forms of life, were the new discoveries not unsettling. There the exploration of the remaining virgin lands and the deep ocean brought exotic new forms of plant and other life to human notice. (It is not accidental I think that so much of mid-Victorian symbolism in design and in paintings focuses on plants, just as the Victorian flower garden places emphasis on the use of individual flowering plants.)

It was destabilizing, although exciting too. A fascinated engagement with the new, mixed with the desire to know the past, is everywhere present in the architecture of this time: in the classical or Gothic enrichments of the iron structures of railway termini or of the Crystal Palace, in the polychrome striating and banding of Victorian buildings which, while having antecedents in Medieval buildings (diligently researched by Pugin, Ruskin, Street, Willis and others), also crucially recalls the fascinating new geological diagrams of strata that graphically tell of the age of the rocks. (We can see this too in the display of columnar British rocks in the Oxford Museum, or in the literally accurate geological strata of the Glasgow house built by James McGowan for a coal magnate, its coal seams correctly placed low at ground-floor level.)

To see such buildings, is to see strata risen from below the earth's crust. Their message, unimaginable to us now, of pain in the revelation of the literal untruth of Genesis, and of human shrinkage on exposure to the timespans of the earth's life, is consoled by the nostalgic clothing borrowed from the more innocent, less scientific ages of Gothic.

Against such knowledge Ruskin struggled. To a Protestant the literal truth of the Bible was more crucial than if he had been Catholic where the divine authority of the pope's word might have helped a little. He wrote of the 'clink of the damned geologist's hammers chipping away at my faith' just as he feared the effect upon him of his vision of the earth 'as a blackened escoriated globe circling lifeless around a dead sun'. Against these thoughts he hung on as best he could to his earlier belief in a divinely provided beneficent nature. Throughout his life he sketched and measured nature, believing like the Romantic poets that by seeing nature clearly, but in Wordsworth's words with eyes that 'half-create what they perceive', an inspired art could be made, as authoritative as the Renaissance had believed neo-Platonic proportions to be: a reflection of cosmic order infinitely more complex and infinitely more truthful. He has described the beginnings of such a process with regard to one small tree:

Languidly but not idly I began to draw it; and as I drew the languor passed away; the beautiful lines insisted on being traced ... more and more beautiful they became, as each rose out of the rest, and took its place in the air. With wonder increasing every instant, I saw that they composed themselves, by finer laws than any known to men. At last the tree was there, and everything I had thought about trees [before], nowhere.

Ruskin had, too, a Medieval sense of the symbols to be found in nature. Like Sir Thomas Browne, whom both he and Acland admired, he could find emotional and moral lessons there. He did so just as readily as an Elizabethan whose society still understood human life as being attached into its appropriate place in the Great Chain of Being. To Ruskin, nature has not just been created by God, it is animated by his spirit. In this Ruskin's pantheism was animistic. Looking at nature he beheld, 'the living inhabitation of the world – grazing and resting in it – the spiritual power of the air, the rocks and the waters'.

Thus when nineteenth-century industry despoiled nature, Ruskin saw blasphemy, and murder. To see ugliness in nature, of the kind that followed despoliation, was for Ruskin to see death. The Christian belief, revealed by the biblical examples of Jericho, Nineveh and the rest, and confirmed by the relics of past civilizations being regularly exhumed by Victorian archaeology, meant that such immoral action would lead to divine retribution; to the destruction of the culture which allowed such things to happen.

10 The Arts and Crafts house

In the 'Nature of Gothic' chapter of *The Stones of Venice* Ruskin moved from a discussion of the virtues of Gothic architecture to an attack upon the exploitation of labour in industry, of its dehumanizing effects and of its implications for design. His comparison of the state of nineteenth century England with the earlier craft-based societies was rose-tinted as far as the latter were concerned, but the essential argument against untrammelled industrialization and its effects on humankind, nature and design was potent:

You must either make a tool of the creature, or a man of him. You cannot make both. Men were not intended to work with the accuracy of tools, to be precise and perfect in all their actions. If you will have that precision out of them, and make their fingers measure degrees like cogwheels and their arms strike curves like compasses, you must unhumanise them.

This image, brought into dramatic visual realization more than half a century later by Fritz Lang in the film 'Metropolis', resonated through late nineteenth-century art and social thinking. William Morris stated 'The Nature of Gothic' to be 'one of the very few necessary and inevitable utterances of the century' and printed it as a penny pamphlet for working men. It was Morris who was to do more than anyone to move the ideas of Ruskin from the critical and theoretical into the practical.

Morris's position was, of course, as riddled with contradictions as Ruskin's. Rejecting the machine for its effect upon those who worked it, as well as for the banal quality of much that was turned out by it, involved rejection of the technology that might provide cheaply for the poor. He was well aware that his hand-crafted products could only be afforded by the well-off. His enthusiasm for the products and society of the Middle Ages led him to seek solutions for the founding of a fairer industrial society in ways based on idealized Medieval structures that were inadequate for the new phenomena of an industrialized society. Like Carlyle, Pugin and Ruskin before him, Morris's dream vision of the Medieval was idealized. Yet just as Morris developed his views of Medieval society to make John Ball the heroic figure of Medieval history, a character who was clearly opposed to the autocratic Abbot Samson of Carlyle's *Sartor Resartus*, so Morris's ideas about design moved from the direct historicism of the Gothic towards new organic and original forms. In looking to the simpler houses, decorations and implements of the past, coupled with a call for action to make the present a less unfair, less cluttered place, Morris broke from the ponderous historicism of the mainstream of nineteenth-century architecture.

Figure 10.1a–b
The Red House, south-east London, designed by Philip Webb for William Morris. Photos: John Farmer.

Morris wanted to bring together a group of artists and friends to recreate a creative idyll, and the need for a family house for himself and his new wife gave him the excuse he needed. In collaboration with Philip Webb the Red House was completed, shocking to many contemporaries but, to Morris and his friends, a positive statement as to how life could be.

It was the only house he was to have designed for himself. The site was an orchard, a cart ride from the railway station from which he travelled into London each day. The house is Gothic in spirit and simple in detail. Constructed of warm red brick with white painted timber window frames and a steep, red tiled roof, the house owed something externally to the houses of Street and Butterfield. The L-shaped plan was designed to be the first two sides of a courtyard but like many of Morris's dreams this was never to be fulfilled. The interior was almost stark by Victorian standards with plastered walls edged with soft red brick around the window openings. The walls were to be decorated with frescoes and the ceilings mainly plain sometimes pricked out in geometric patterns for painting. Hand-embroidered fabrics and tapestries hung in bedrooms and large simple brick fireplaces adorned the living spaces; on one the words 'Ars longa vita brevis' are set, almost a prophecy as Morris was only to live in his 'palace of art' for five years. It was a house to be lustily enjoyed, a young man's house. It is far from perfect, its siting although positioned to minimize the loss of trees had the living rooms face north and the kitchen south-west. It was cold in winter and the windows in the south and east walls which enclose the courtyard light corridors on both ground and first floors. But the accounts of the house from Morris's friends describe the magical qualities and timelessness of the house. Rossetti described it as 'more of a poem than a house' and other writers describe apples dropping into the rooms through the open windows on warm summer evenings.

It is said that the factor which provoked Morris to enter the manufacture of household objects was, as in much of Morris's life, that of necessity. Morris always coupled pragmatism with idealism. Prompted by the impossibility of finding 'appropriate' furniture, and encouraged by the examples of other members of the Pre-Raphaelite Brotherhood, Morris and Burne-Jones designed furniture and had it made up to a basic finish. They then set to work to decorate it with scenes from Morris's poems and scenes depicting Dante and Beatrice. So 'Gothic' was the major piece of furniture, the settle, that it had to be dismantled to get it into their rooms.

The architectural world of G. E. Street, into which Morris had briefly entered as an architectural pupil, had emphasized the designer/craftsman relationship. Street had himself constructed a staircase in one of his architectural projects and encouraged his staff to develop craft skills including fabric dyeing, stone and wood carving and illumination.

'Morris, Marshall, Faulkner and Co. Fine Art Workmen in Painting, Carving, Furniture and the Metals' was formed to offer household furnishings and decorative arts as they might be based on the ideas of Ruskin. It put together the arts and the handicrafts in a sure belief that each would enrich the other. To follow Ruskin it was essential that the means of production should be ennobling. The company attempted to train young men into true craftsmanship and employed boys from a boys' home to be apprenticed into the variety of crafts the firm offered. Never a great commercial success at the time, its products were always too expensive to find their way into anything but wealthy homes. Morris was well aware of its inadequacies in improving the lives of working people and this frustration led him, as it had done Ruskin, to apply himself to social and political reform. His writings and charismatic lectures carried his message to an ever widening circle of young designers.

In attempting to bring into practice the writings of Ruskin, Morris applied himself to the production of household objects. In *Decorative Arts* (1878) he declared:

Our subject is the great body of art, by means of which men have at all times more or less striven to beautify the familiar matters of everyday life.

The manufacture of these objects and their ornament was rooted in the Ruskinian view that all art was derived from nature and that only through the study and understanding of nature could true art be created. For Morris in a discussion of decoration,

... everything made by man's hands has a form, which must be either beautiful or ugly; beautiful if it is in accord with Nature, and helps her; ugly if it is discordant with Nature, and thwarts her; it cannot be indifferent:

If beauty raises the human spirit when found in everyday objects a man might use, how much more does it have the capability of raising the spirit of man when he is able to *make* beauty,

till the web, the cup, or the knife, look as natural, nay as lovely as the green field, the river bank, or the mountain flint.

Although not identified as any particular place, Dickens's description of Coketown in *Hard Times* sets a background for Morris's rhetoric:

It was a town of red brick, or of brick that would have been red if the smoke and ashes had allowed; but as matters stood it was a town of unnatural red and black like the face of a painted savage ... It had a black canal in it, and a river that ran purple with ill-smelling dye and vast piles of building full of windows where there was a rattling and a trembling all day long and where the piston of the steam engine worked monotonously up and down like the head of an elephant in a state of melancholy madness.

In a later lecture, 'The Beauty of Life', delivered 1880 and published in 1882, Morris makes a further extension of the relationship between nature and art. Delivered to an audience in the industrial Midlands, which must have looked close to the Coketown of Dickens, Morris castigates those who profess to love art and collect it whilst ignoring the effects of the processes which generate the very wealth that enables them to indulge their artistic pretensions. Those who 'buy pictures and profess to care about art, burn a deal of coal' says Morris; how can you care about the image of a landscape when you show yourself by your deeds that you don't care for the landscape itself?

Everyone had their own version of the good old days when life was simpler and happier, the buildings in village and town beautiful and functional, echoing in their traditional forms a balanced relationship between humans and the land that they belonged to. Of course in idealizing the past in this way the brutal aspects of living on the land for the rural poor were largely ignored.

In *The Stones of Venice*, Ruskin proposed that the beauty and harmony of Gothic Venice resulted largely from a culture sharing common beliefs. For Morris and those who followed him, Venice was too patrician, too artificial, as well as decaying and enervated under its Austrian occupiers, to be emulated. The major cities of Venice, Paris and London were

Figure 10.2a–b
Letchworth: cottages by Parker and Unwin.

already becoming the dark cities of the European mind where Thomson's *City of Dreadful Night* and Fagin's London might interchange with Hugo's Paris.

For the English Arts and Crafts movement the historical good old days were often the days of Good Queen Bess, the last of the Medieval times or the days of Good Queen Anne, the last period when English traditional construction balanced imported Classicism. As the Arts and Crafts spread each group located their own golden past: for the Scots the baronial manor no doubt inhabited with Walter Scott's great heroes; in central Europe the late Medieval period of Durer and the *landsknecht* tradition with its fluttering banners and beribboned imagery. Yet Arts and Crafts architecture absorbed much more. It absorbed the humble cottage, and deeper, the fascination with childish ways and animal goings-on. It offered doors that solidly protected and door handles that matched the action of the hand and visibly improved with touch over time. It looked at the detail of day-to-day existence and sought to match it with the movement of the sun. When Raymond Unwin, an architect and planner of Letchworth Garden City and Hampstead Garden Suburb, looked at the parallel rows of bye-law housing developed to replace back-to-back slums, he stated what was obvious to an Arts and Crafts designer:

Figure 10.3
Greyfriars, near Puttenham, Surrey.

It does not seem to be realised hundreds of thousands of working women spend the bulk of their lives with nothing better to look at than the ghastly prospect offered by these back yards, the squalid ugliness of which is unrelieved by a scrap of fresh green to speak of spring, or a fading leaf to tell of autumn.
                Raymond Unwin, *Cottage Plans and Common Sense*, 1902

The sun was referred to as the explanation for the horizontal emphasis in his work by C. F. A. Voysey (1915):

when the sun sets horizontalism prevails, when we are weary we recline ... What then is obviously necessary for the effect of repose in our houses, [is] to avoid angularity and complexity in colour, form or texture and make our dominating lines horizontal rather than vertical.

Grounded in the practical study of the folk traditions of construction, this architecture represented a quiet revolution against the assumption that the products of industrialization were superior and offered the only possible future. The recognition of the importance of local materials was not merely an aesthetic or stylistic preoccupation. Local materials incurred little transportation cost and local skilled labour would be available to work them. There need be little fear of materials failing to perform satisfactorily in a given location as they had been tried and tested in that location over centuries. Unusual microclimates had created unusual construction solutions. Using these as models Arts and Crafts designers were renowned for their innovation which was always based on a thorough working knowledge of materials. The attention to detail was often obsessive.

Irrespective of the political ideologies espoused by particular Arts and Crafts designers, all of them had a holistic view of the world. In nineteenth-century design, form had been separated from material, labour had been separated from the rewards of production and had been fragmented into tedious, mindless tasks which even Adam Smith, the founding father of capitalist economics had identified in 1776 as being destructive to the human spirit. The labour of the majority of working people had been divorced from all moral considerations.

Arts and Crafts houses look again now, as they did to early modern movement architects, to show a way forward, not altogether in how they are put together but in the variety of responses they represent to the questions we have to deal with in re-making the union of humankind with the natural world, a union that not only eschews but makes good what it can of the destruction wrought on nature.

Arguably it is not in the great houses of Lutyens or even Voysey that the main legacy of the Arts and Crafts movement resides, it is in the small dwellings that were developed in garden cities such as Letchworth or the early estates of the LCC. In addressing the problems of the small

Figure 10.4a–c
Letchworth: cottages by Baillie Scott. Drawing reproduced by kind permission from *Letchworth: The First Garden City* by Mervyn Miller, reprint published 1983 by Phillimore & Company Ltd, Chichester, West Sussex.

urban dwelling the reinstatement of the relationship between man, his dwelling and the natural world was to be attempted.

In 1898 Ebenezer Howard had published *Tomorrow: A Peaceful Path to Real Reform* which was to re-emerge in 1902 as the better known *Garden Cities of Tomorrow*. Like many works of reform, the idea it expressed was not totally original. As already mentioned, model communities had been developed since the eighteenth century such as those at Chaux by Ledoux. Owen's New Lanark offered a prototype for progressive and humane industrial towns and during the later nineteenth century Lever developed Port Sunlight and the Cadburys their model workers' suburb at Bournville. The London suburb of Bedford Park, designed by Norman Shaw, was created in the 'Old English' style, which although based on traditional vernacular buildings owed less of a commitment to integrity of construction than later Arts and Crafts designs. However the references to an idealized English village were obvious.

The difference between these developments and that of Letchworth, the first garden city, was that Letchworth was to be created to be autonomous and an integration of both agricultural and industrial activity providing all the necessary facilities to recreate life for the working man and his family. The design was a competition-winning entry from two young Arts and Crafts architects Barry Parker and Raymond Unwin who had already completed a housing scheme in New Earswick near York.

Considerable effort was put into landscaping the site and enhancing its natural contours. The existing three villages were integrated into the scheme and as many hedgerows and trees as possible were kept *in situ*. The renewing and enhancing aspects of nature were to be essential ingredients in the layouts of the streets and the design of the individual housing. Sunlight was essential and to maximize the amount entering each dwelling care was taken to avoid overshadowing and plans kept shallow, the living rooms running from front to back. This concern for environmental quality and the simplification of the house plan had been developed in earlier, larger Arts and Crafts houses. Baillie Scott, who was to add some wonderful houses to Letchworth, had developed a much freer internal arrangement in houses such as his own in Douglas, Isle of Man. Large internal spaces could be divided by folding screens and south-facing bay windows brought in sunlight allowing it to move through, exploring the different surfaces throughout the day. Other designers such as Prior developed the butterfly plan, creating a south-facing sun trap and sheltered terrace onto the gardens. These designs, refined on larger commissions, were all to be found in smaller prototype houses built as part of the 1905 and 1907 Cheap Cottages competition. Younger Arts and Crafts designers such as Smith and Brewer, Geoffrey Lucas and Randall Wells all contributed designs as did J. Brodie with an extraordinary precast concrete house.

Elmwood Cottages, a pair of semi-detached cottages in Letchworth by Baillie Scott, show how the small house can be designed to offer the maximum in a limited space and to a limited budget. The main space is the kitchen separated from the parlour by the staircase. This open living space is lit by windows to front and back. The simple white-washed interior bounces the sunlight around and the brick floor and low ceiling give a bright but homely environment. The kitchen range is set in an inglenook and accompanied with the built-in settle lit with its own small window. The daylight can penetrate the shadow of the inglenook and offer a prospect to the outside on a winter's day when the fire is lit and the occupants warm themselves as they read or talk. Other built-in window seats in both kitchen and parlour are provided with the intention that very little loose furniture need be purchased. In the summer the kitchen range can remain unlit as a small fireplace is set in the scullery to heat water and provide simple cooking requirements. The bedrooms nestle high in the roof, each with their own fireplace, the chimneys extending up to become the characteristic markers of the hearth, anchoring the buildings to the ground. The houses sit broadly across the plot, the hipped roof at either end sweeping to within a few feet of the ground. The front gardens to the north have a shared formal square court whilst the gardens are divided to the south, 'to provide the family with at least all the vegetables it requires, if not fruit, whilst its borders would be set with all the old-fashioned cottage flowers'.

Along the same road Baillie Scott's smallest detached house looks almost a doll's house in comparison. As Baillie Scott said in his book *Houses and Gardens*, 1906: 'A small house is a large cottage and not a restricted mansion ... We need large rooms of a small kind and not small rooms of a large kind.' In this house the roof next to the front door sweeps to waist height, convenient for cleaning gutters but disconcerting to the uninitiated. More than any other Arts and Crafts house it sits as a three-dimensional version of the cottages of Kate Greenaway's illustrations.

Figure 10.5
Kate Greenaway, 'My house is red'. From *The Kate Greenaway Treasury*, published by Harper Collins Ltd, © World Publishing Company.

External porches with timber bench seats were placed on the south-west faces of many of the Letchworth houses, 'to enable their male occupants to sit in the sun after returning from work and smoke a pipe'. Letchworth was planned to produce a model community, with activities taking place in the Institute such as educational sessions combined with musical recitals and country dancing. From the centre of town the radial roads and avenues were positioned to afford vistas of the town from the country and the country from the town. Low-density housing, a maximum of twelve to the acre, was the rule although when open spaces are taken into account the density is even lower. The later garden cities such as Welwyn have less coherence and quality than the early, pre-1920 Letchworth. Hampstead Garden Suburb of 1912, was set out on a more formal model, its architecture demonstrating a rather uncomfortable transition from Queen Anne to Georgian. It has undoubtedly fine buildings but probably due to its location within Greater London it has little of the robust quality of Letchworth, despite being only a few years younger.

The effects of the Arts and Crafts house were felt as far west as California where Greene and Greene produced their vast Japan-inspired creations; as far south as Australia where via the Chicago School and Frank Lloyd Wright, architects such as Walter Burley Griffin produced timber-framed villas and suburbs; and across Europe to Austria, and Germany in the artists' colony at Darmstadt. In 1974 John Berger, in *About Looking*, wrote that,

All art, which is based on a close observation of nature eventually changes the way nature is seen. Either it confirms more strongly an already established way of seeing nature or it proposes a new way.

Each variant of the Arts and Crafts house necessarily reflected the nature that surrounded it and was in turn subject to the changing attitudes towards the natural world as they developed in individual cultures. When Herman Muthesius, a Prussian civil servant, studied and recorded *Das Englische Haus* in his three-volume work and exhorted his country-men to face their own conditions as honestly as the English faced theirs, it would have been impossible to see the divergent paths that would look back to the Arts and Crafts as their progenitors. Both the Modernism of the Bauhaus and the Volkisch architecture of the Third Reich would be considered the successors of the English Arts and Crafts movement.

However, as with much of architectural production, what develops with integrity as a coherent realization of profoundly held beliefs becomes misappropriated by others and used as 'style'. Although Morris became a revolutionary socialist, the Arts and Crafts house was developed across the political spectrum as dwellings for both wealthy upper middle class capitalists and social housing for artisans in the garden cities and early corporation housing. Its designers themselves represented the full range of political and social positions from the fiercely traditional Voysey to the socialism and educational zeal of C. R. Ashbee.

In England the movement declined to a style and created the neo-Tudor of the Ideal Homes of the inter-war years. Ribbons of cherry-blossomed avenues spread out from the edges of still expanding conurbations, dotted with fake timbered semi-detached and detached 'villas'. The commuting that had led Morris to abandon his 'palace of art' at Bexley Heath began to choke and kill the very cities that the low-density suburbs encompassed. Pioneer modern architects in the Congrès

Figure 10.6
Muthesius, *Das Englische Haus* (1904), frontispiece.

Figure 10.7
Edward Prior, Kelling Place, Norfolk.

Internationaux d'Architecture Moderne (CIAM) attacked even the garden city ideal:

There are those who seek to turn those disordered suburbs, in which the time–distance function poses an ominous and unanswerable question, into garden cities. Theirs is an illusory paradise, an irrational solution. The suburb is an urbanistic folly, scattered across the entire globe and carried to extreme consequences in America. It constitutes one of the greatest evils of this century.
CIAM papers, 'Athens Charter' (1933)

After the vital moments had passed in which the quizzing and the doubting of industrial progress was best expressed through the language of the Arts and Crafts building, and its functional principles had been adopted in the development of Modernism, the later buildings were only pastiche – essays in a facile nostalgia with the smell of withdrawal, of a holing-up away from what the world outside had become. An element of this, what psychoanalysts call regression, is present in all Arts and Crafts building, but in the early vital stages it is integrated and used as a reminder and a recommendation for the world to become otherwise than it is. In the later buildings there is no such hope, no such urging. Instead they become part of that shoring-up of fragments of treasured memory for private use. Whether they be the semi-detached houses built along arterial roads in the 1930s with their faint echoes of Queen Bess in black and white framing and leaded lights, or the luxurious Tudorish houses that the successful commercial architect Harold Faulkner built around Farnham, they have withdrawn into private fantasy, uninterested in the essential reforms that were grasped as necessary in the contract between humans and nature by their earlier and more thoughtful predecessors.

The ideal of the Arts and Crafts house worked best in the country or as village-like groups within town or city. Either designed by enlightened private owners or public authorities for the ordinary citizen, or for private middle class use, the houses ordinarily upheld an urban view of what country living should be like. Some architects such as Gimson built with more verisimilitude than others. The most interesting built with a basis of sound folk-based principles, but transformed that language by being open to other influences. New spatial perceptions and a use of the defensive walls of childhood and of animal ways transform their buildings into places of everyday, but extraordinary enchantment. There is a challenge in their language to a view of the world that saw technological progress as the only goal of the human spirit and rejected nature and natural forms. Some Arts and Crafts houses became wonderful treasure houses in their relationship to the land and in their furnishings and buildings. They held on to, and expressed most perfectly for their time, what humankind had to hold on to if the new technological civilization was not to destroy too much to be borne. They offer symbolic and psychological lessons for us now about how to build. They do not offer us obvious models for marshalling scarce natural resources. We should look at the symbolism of the inglenook and not its energy efficiency. The inheritors of the Arts and Crafts can be traced through into the twentieth century. The ground rules had been set for the expressive language of an architecture intent on making its contribution towards a more holistic society.

11 The architecture of natural forms

The architecture of natural forms does not of course begin in the nineteenth century under the influence of science. The most elemental house of natural forms must be the cave, a natural shelter usable without the putting together of clay, stones, trees, plants or blocks of snow, a shelter no more developed than the rudest shelter for animals. Folk building as we have seen developed its various traditions through the trial and error putting together of the materials suited to building that were to hand. Such buildings, together with those designed by architects in the industrial period that sought to learn from folk building, were natural in their forms and in their relationship to the landscape, in as much as they used the local materials and obeyed long established ways of constructing buildings and of symbolizing what those buildings represented. In the patterns that decorate folk building, and those buildings that later learn from it, natural forms abound. Plant and animal images mix with more abstracted patterns, many of which represent in stylized forms earthly forms and events.

Through the past ages of architecture too, the forms and decorations derive from other natural forms. From the papyrus, lotus and scarab of ancient Egypt, the dolphin forms of Mycenae, the acanthus and spiral forms of Greece to the structural as well as decorative evocation of tree forms in Gothic, the relationship of natural forms to the way buildings are decorated, and sometimes how they are constructed, is ever present.

Figure 11.1
J. M. Fischer, abbey church at Zwiefalten, Bavaria.

(a)

(b)

Figure 11.2a–c
Zwiefalten, Bavaria: Rococo decoration.

(c)

In later Baroque times the structure can continue the mimicking of nature in the Gothic vault, as in Guarini's 'birds-nest' construction in his Turin Chapel of the Holy Shroud. The overwhelming Rocaille decoration of Bavarian Rococo replicates the teaming complexity of vegetation.

(a)

(b)

(c)

Figure 11.3a–c
Harvest festival at Otterswang, Bavaria.

If one is looking for evidence of a green sensibility expressing itself in natural forms, it is here in abundance. The south German Rococo that was officially condemned and swept away by the force of the Enlightenment and Neo-classicism has in retrospect been celebrated or damned for its sensuality and its exuberance; it has also been seen as a decadent, frivolous last phase of the Baroque. What this misses – as does its frequent unfavourable comparison with its more sophisticated Italian antecedent – is the integral part that it played in the lives of an unsophisticated peasantry; a peasantry whose daily experience of the world of nature, and whose unquestioning belief in the heavenly world that it mirrored, finds expression in the architecture's imagery of fecundity. It is hard to think of a more perfect emblem of this than the Wieskirche, the pilgrimage church in the meadows.

Figure 11.4
Pfullendorf, Bavaria: Rococo decoration.

Through the ubiquitous image of the shell – linking the Virgin Mary with Venus – these churches spoke of rebirth, of springtime. In their abundance of fruit and corn they spoke of harvest. The peasant's experience of the seasons of the natural year was affirmed and transcended, his pre-industrial time sense sanctified by the church's cycle of festivities and pilgrimages. No-one I think has expressed this better than the American philosopher Karsten Harries in his book on *The Bavarian Church*:

One begins to understand why the peasant was so reluctant to give up his religious holidays and pilgrimages. They gave him a sense of security, of being in harmony with the earth and powers that preside over it, that must elude those who have decided to pursue the Cartesian dream of rendering man the master and possessor of nature. This sense of attunement, this trusting turn to higher powers, is indeed the greatest obstacle to all human attempts to better man's lot. The reformers of the Enlightenment were quite right to see in this popular religion mingled with superstition the main obstacle to making Bavaria a modern state. What a waste of time that could have been spent so much more productively.

Taking up the issue of time ('We find it difficult to make peace with nature and time'), he goes on to pinpoint the Bavarian peasantry's very different understanding of time from that of the Enlightenment:

Precisely because he knew about the precariousness of human existence, because of his intimacy with disaster and death, the peasant experienced more strongly and thankfully the miracle of growth and life. The victory that light gained every morning over the forces of darkness, the yearly triumph of spring over winter, which hinted at the Immaculata's conquest of the devil, supported his trust in the final victory over death. Time is now seen as a scarce resource that, like money, must be spent prudently. Inseparable from this understanding is the emphasis on industry, on the glories of hard work. To this rhetoric the peasant was deaf. The specific beauty of the rococo church is inseparable from the fact that it speaks of freedom from the rancour against time.

*

As scientific enquiry delves further into the natural past, it triggers the beginnings of new natural forms, discovered not just by looking around at the natural world as it is, but also as it has been, and as it is when seen under the microscope, through the telescope, under the earth or in the depths of the sea. Such new knowledge, giving impetus to new forms, appears in the eighteenth century both in architectural detail and in the design of whole buildings – in for instance the ammonite capitals of the British architect Wild, and in the projects of the French architect Ledoux where the stylized form of a volcano makes for an image that tells that a building is for making gunpowder. We have seen how this process gathers pace in the nineteenth century when the discoveries of geological strata find their architectural expression in the striation of buildings into polychrome bandings. The Arts and Crafts house, particularly in its fantastic version such as Baillie Scott's treehouse for a Rumanian Princess, carries in its decorations, its structure and its spirit the reminder of natural forms, but they are forms adapted for human use based on long human experience.

Another way of using natural forms surfaces in the late nineteenth century when the curvilinear forms of nature are translated into the shapes of jewellery, household objects, furniture and even architecture. It is the life-force that at root is being expressed in this Jugendstil or Art Nouveau design. The idea of teeming cataclysmic movement in nature engendered earlier in the century by Lyell with his images of mountains in upheaval, and then by the Darwinian view of the prodigious waste and movement in the animated natural world, had been followed by ever more images of the natural world, all of which suggested restless movement, from the flux of organisms seen through the microscope to the emerging awareness of an unseen sub-atomic world of particles in movement permeating all matter, even the most apparently inert. The increasing pace and movement in modern technological societies was seen to be an equivalent process and for a while the discoveries, besides being visually exciting, could be seen in some cases to be ameliorating human misery; microbes when seen could begin to be controlled. Looking at nature scientifically, the way that natural living forms developed fed into design both as object lessons in economy and beauty of means, and in the visual metaphors that they offered for expression of life as dynamic movement, in which to be still was to die.

Natural selection depended on dynamic change, and every new scientific discovery from the bugs in the microscope, the atomic particle, the strange billions of inhabitants of the deep seas to the Heisenberg Principle of Uncertainty (in the measuring of anything at all), reinforced the urge to express movement and thereby growth. In contemplating this new knowledge and the new images it produced, the artist and designer as well as the scientist could be affected by a renewed sense of wonder at the appearance of the natural world. New invention demanded new solutions and some design accommodated the technologically new within natural forms that the scientific exploration of nature had brought to the fore. In this way the deep-sea expedition of the British ship *The Challenger* and the subsequent work on its findings by Ernst Haeckl became, along with land plant forms, the source of the decorations and fittings that accommodated the newly invented electric lamp. The way that plant structures widened and strengthened at their joints were the models for furniture and, in highly rationalized form, for the bentwood furniture techniques of Thonet.

Figure 11.5
Jugendstil decoration at Dresden (entrance for 1899 art exhibition).

Figure 11.6
Guimard, Paris métro entrance.

The impulse towards such forms, easiest to execute in decorative items, posed formidable problems when applied to furniture and more particularly to architecture. The Rococo style that had earlier embraced asymmetrical complexities of form had remained almost exclusively an interior mode, at least in its most convoluted forms. The Rococo church or house had always a reticent boxy outside, leavened only by curvy window shapes and trompe l'oeil painting of the facade. In the Jugendstil or Art Nouveau house both inside and outside express growth and metamorphosis. Victor Horta's house in Brussels is based in form and decoration on the newly found shape and movements of the human spermatozoa. Horta's interiors, to quote Vincent Scully, 'create an environment of flux and becoming'.

Guimard's Castel Beranger in Paris has a wider repertoire of natural forms, of butterflies, plants, sea creatures and seaweeds, as have his less elaborate métro stations. In Barcelona Gaudi used images of the sea in the Casa Mila, of the forest and again the sea in the Parc Guell, and of Gothic reinterpreted through organic forms in the Sagrada Familia. In these as in Jugendstil buildings in Munich and Vienna the natural forms of sea, cave or stylized forest are expressive fantasies, exuberantly using natural forms without the quietening influence that northern folk building exercised on the Arts and Crafts movements.

It is most striking in Gaudi. The mountains of Montserrat, their cliffs and crags, are plain to see in the Sagrada Familia. In the Casa Vicens we have the palm fronds of the Moorish world, in the Parc Guell a wealth of marine forms evoking the nearby Mediterranean. Lava flows and sea-scoured rock and seaweed abound in the Casa Mila. It's not just the profusion of imagery that is important: it is the way in which architecture and natural forms merge, particularly in the facades of the Sagrada Familia, reminding us of Ruskin's powerful feelings about cathedrals and alps, Gothic vaulting and northern forests.

In neither these wild buildings nor in the Arts and Crafts movement were natural habitats transposed directly into architectural ideas; always there was paraphrase and invention. Disenchantment after the Great War had to happen before it could be suggested seriously that the right place for humankind might be an animal burrow.

(a)

(b)

Figure 11.7a–b
Gaudi, Casa Mila, Barcelona.

After the slaughter in that war, the possible detachment of humans from the savage and brutish aspects of nature became harder to assume. Trench warfare, experienced by hundreds of thousands, fixed the necessary image. Afterwards the French built a long super-burrow, the Maginot Line, fit for humans, equipped for work, sleep and play; while artists thought about the future in ways that reflected upon recent human behaviour, evoking burrows and other furtive spaces that, however thick-walled and deep, gave no protection, indeed themselves expressed insecurity. Such was the nature of German Expressionist space.

The sometimes sentimental empathy with animals at a time of renewed wonder at the appearance of the natural world, with human life showing signs of becoming more comfortable through social and technical progress, was no more. The excitement of the never before seen

Radiolaria from the sea, of time-lapse photographs of plants bursting into bud, and of the vitality seen in the growth and renewal of life, which gave impetus to Art Nouveau and Jugendstil, was replaced for some by a need to express the feeling that humans needed, and deserved, not a primitive hut but a rude animal burrow.

Figure 11.8
Gaudi, entrance to apartments in Barcelona.

Part Four
Modernism

In introducing this part of the book, a number of points need to be made. Its alternative reading of Modernism between the wars gives prominence to strands of architectural thought and practice that historians often marginalized (Expressionism) or ignored (English cottage housing). Its reading of the Modernist mainstream highlights features that can be legitimately claimed as evidence of a responsiveness to nature in its fullest sense – the nature of Einsteinian space-time. That such a cosmic sensibility may not be readily communicated to the occupants of buildings – and that even the directly experienced realities of light and space may not compensate for the loss of contact with what most people understand as nature – does not totally invalidate Modernism from a green standpoint. The dominant metaphor was an 'opening up' of the plan, sections and form of the building, for functional reasons but also as symbolic act: towards the sun, towards the horizon, or out to the stars, in search of the future. In its attempt to make an architecture of more than utilitarian function, a bridge was attempted between humankind and their immediate natural world: in the ideal of a transparency (of glass) between the inside human spaces of a building and the outside world of nature, in the pushing apart of the towers of the visionary city, and in lifting these too above limitless green spaces.

However, these could also be seen as weakened variants of the post-Great War dreams of Bruno Taut for an architecture of shimmering glass laced across the High Alps as an ecstatic affirmation of man, nature and peace. Now rehabilitated as an alternative mode of the modern movement – almost, though not totally, eclipsed by the International Style for a time – the Expressionism of this visionary architecture probably contributed more to the continued presence of a green sensibility between the wars.

Ideas about an organic architecture, seen metaphorically as an organism with a necessary relationship between its parts like that of natural organisms, and involving the use of natural 'alive' materials and 'organic' rules in the way they are put together, derived from the previous century, as Frank Lloyd Wright, who admired Ruskin, would have acknowledged. Together with a strengthening through psychological theory of his ideas about the horizontal and its importance in an organic architecture, Wright's personal inventiveness with modern materials at the time of the mid-western dustbowl eluded confrontation with the wrecking of nature.

In Britain too among some modern architects such ideas began to percolate through in response to the work of painters like Nash and Piper. But the English cottage housing from 1917 to the mid-1920s is important as part of an English rejection of Modernism – partly through ignorance, partly through antipathy – which needs to be taken seriously. A critical stance in relation to the modern movement and its machine-age technology is a recurring feature of this book. Here, in the years before the International Style began to affect British architecture, saner, greener attitudes prevailed.

12 Geometric and crystalline forms

A building, composed as it is of inorganic materials, can be thought of as living in only a metaphoric sense, unless a concept like the Great Chain of Being is held to, where all matter is live from the rocks to the angels. All earthly species of organic life have their appointed places on the Great Chain – from insects above the rocks to humans below the angels. To our modern senses the inorganic can live only through the perception and imagination we bring to bear, in how we see or order it. With the Great Chain of Being under rational dissection by the European mind, it was possible in the eighteenth century to carry the Renaissance neo-Platonic belief in mathematical order further into the idea that the order of the cosmos was expressible through geometry – through abstracting the apparently confusing and multifarious face of nature to reveal, like the heavenly order described by Newton, a value system of preferred geometric forms. The underlying mathematical ratios of Renaissance building were thereby supplanted by more overt geometric forms in which pure geometry would give the highest earthly reflection of order. Basing the most perfect harmony on the apparent shape of the planets, the sphere was reckoned by Ledoux and Boullée the most pure form followed by the other prime shapes of cube, cone, pyramid and so on.

Few buildings can carry theoretical ideas perfectly. It is easier in some buildings than in others but almost all are, unlike other art forms, intended for use, and function usually compromises dogmatic forms. The buildings that expressed best these ideas were often unbuilt, even unbuildable, projects like Boullée's spherical monument to Newton and Ledoux's underground cemetery or his House for the Rural Guards.

An essential difference between rational and Romantic ways of seeing, and representing the human condition, had lain in the attitude towards symmetry as an expression of order. In the last unrevived buildings of Classicism – the Baroque – the symmetries of form and plan were crucial to its coherence. In the postscript to this style – the Rococo – a unique balance between symmetry and the asymmetries of Rocaille ornament was achieved. In turning away from this to the formal purities of Neo-classicism, symmetry again came to dominate, reflecting both an earlier simpler Classicism and the symmetrical order of Newtonian ideas about the Universe.

A purely functional problem arose in that the increasingly complex and technically complicated buildings of the industrial period were difficult to plan within the gridlike symmetries of Classicism, however brilliantly the rationalizing of the classical tradition had been done by Durand and what became known as the Beaux Arts method. Engineers, forging a new discipline that added iron, then steel to the repertoire of structural materials, initially dealt casually with the question of style if at all. Faced with new demands and new materials, they had by experience and trial and error to understand how to handle these new materials.

Eventually tables and other data became available but even then, hunches or inspirations would formulate solutions – and in this approach natural processes were observed. Smethwick's watching of the wave forms crashing against rocks led him to the curves of the Eddystone lighthouse; Paxton found in the Victoria Lily's ribbed leaf structure, and that of other leaves, the model for the ribbed glazing systems at Chatsworth and the Crystal Palace (a process that Nervi and others in the twentieth century would emulate). This process, so evident later in the development of flight, was present in other design areas such as the development of bentwood furniture by Thonet, and represented a practical, rational application of the detailed perceptions of nature that at amateur as well as professional levels permeated Victorian society.

As systematic analyses of the way that materials and structures behave took the place of instinctive and traditional understanding, so the appropriate forms came to include the advantages of repetitive elements in mass producing parts of a building as well as in their planning. So, with echoes of the grid planning of the Beaux Arts, the grid and the module became essential tools. This idea, poetically rendered and taking on the space and time continuums of the new sciences as well as the new communication systems of the modern world, came first in the shift of Mackintosh and of Hoffmann's circle as they moved from the realistic natural forms of Art Nouveau into ubiquitous use of gridded perforated artefacts, and inevitably less tidily gridded would-be buildings. These gridded forms were of such simplicity, such sophistication, such neutrality that the poetry they undeniably had would have difficulty as a future language in coping with the full messiness and vitality as well as the tragedy of human existence.

The visual interest in geometric order was stimulated by the exploration of crystalline forms which, as part of research into the chemistry of matter, were quite well understood in the later eighteenth century. The regularity of crystal structures, the diversity of forms possible through the distribution of their equal parts, and the geometric laws which seemed to govern their formation, reinforced ideas that nature was best reflected by man through geometric order. By the next century investigations of organic nature had caught up. In the maelstrom of news that the mountains had moved and that live species had developed in shocking ways, static concepts like the idea of geometry reflecting nature had lost emotional ground, although they remained increasingly crucial for rational design. (An industrial culture was inevitably geared to mathematics and the forms it engendered.) Now, stimulated by theories about atomic structure, there were developments in the understanding of crystal behaviour. X-ray research had confirmed that crystals grew by the addition of identical units. The idea of life in crystals, albeit unlike organic life, that grew by addition rather than by parturition, added tenuously to the imaginative linking of the inorganic and organic. Haeckel, whose work on Radiolaria was so influential on the development of German Art Nouveau or Jugendstil, drew no rigid distinction between the inorganic and organic worlds and tried, by drawing a parallel between the growth of crystals and the development of cells, to establish their affinities. By 1917 D'Arcy Thompson in his massive summary

Figure 12.1
Crystals of iron pyrites and barite.

of organic growth, *On Growth and Form*, included a sympathetic glance at crystal structures although they were outside the scope of his book. He noted that the endless variations in snow crystals were based upon one single form – Plato's 'One among many'. The skeletons of Haeckel's Radiolaria show similar patterns of variation. It is in snow crystals and Radiolaria that the greatest affinity between the inanimate and the animate is to be found.

Glass was to be a key material in modern architecture. New forms developed from the conjunction of interest in crystal structures and glass, which was then becoming available in larger pieces and more varied forms. Its role in dissolving of divisions between inside and outside, important to the International Style, is discussed in Chapter 13. German Expressionist architects began to use glass somewhat differently, not as an unseen intermediary, but as a replicator of crystal forms, cutting it into sections and integrating it into reflective, faceted structures like Bruno Taut's 1914 Cologne Glass Pavilion, where running water and colouring of the glass enhanced the crystalline effect. Paul Scheerbart, in his generally very practical book *Glass Architecture* published in the same year, proclaimed that our culture could 'rise to a higher level' by building with glass,

which lets in the light of the sun, the moon and stars, not merely through a few windows but through every possible wall, which will be made entirely of glass – of coloured glass.

Figure 12.2
Taut, Glass Pavilion, Cologne Werkbund exhibition 1914.

Coloured glass 'is bound to give nature another hue, as if a new light were shed over the entire natural world'. He wanted to test the possibility of 'the crystal room illuminated by translucent floors'. Coloured glass could only be good for the human psyche; it would make 'homes into cathedrals'. Towns must have towers, whose lights will turn night into day; architects must create enormous brilliants ('the diamond effect'). Glass towers would even be built deep in the sea. 'The new glass environment will completely transform mankind'.

In the desire for peace following the Great War, German architects again used crystal forms in their utopian architectural ideas. Taut, inspired by Scheerbart, proposed crystal-like cities of glass to be strung across the valleys and mountain tops of the Alps – a pacific architecture aptly made of glass for a people who 'living in glasshouses would not [want to] throw stones'. He developed aspects of Scheerbart's vision in his own *Alpine Architecture* (1919). Taut, Gropius and a number of other architects were at one time linked by a utopian correspondence, 'the glass chain'. In the mystical utopian visions of these architects we thus find glass and crystalline structures merging imaginatively with the wider realm of inorganic nature and the cosmos. Glass 'admits the light of the sun, of the moon, and of the stars'. Gropius wrote in the Bauhaus manifesto of 'a building like a crystal symbol'. Hans Poelzig filled Berlin's Grosses Schauspielhaus with glass stalactites and Mendelsohn built an observatory for Albert Einstein. Mies's early glass skyscraper designs used glass in a way that was more visionary than functionalist – though that is a distinction that should not be made too glibly.

Taut's *Alpine Architecture* is a collection of visionary sketches with often lengthy captions. Part 1, The Crystal House, transports us to the crystal house in the mountains, through 'a gorge spanned by arches of heavy coloured glass'. Part 2, Architecture in the Mountains, proposes a crystal mountain with its rocky summit converted into many-faceted crystalline forms, while 'the snow-domes in the background are covered with an architecture of glass arches'. Snowfields in regions of eternal ice and snow would be 'built over and decked with embellishments in the form of planes and blocks of coloured glass – Mountain flowers'. ('The execution', adds Taut, 'would most certainly involve unheard of difficulties and sacrifices, but would not be impossible'!)

These are constructive, though understandably febrile, attempts to transmute the bestial below-ground experience of the trenches, and the depressing evidence of human stupidity and cruelty they had revealed. In these crystalline spaces, their coloured glassy domes filled with sparkling light, the crystals, emblems of the rock-bed of the earth, are transformed. People inside, instead of being embedded in the surrogate crystals as if in the rock-bed (as soldiers were in the trenches), are lifted above that, and from earlier earth memories. Back at the beginning of time the first rude huts, cut halfway into the ground, and the first inhabited caves are evoked by the crystalline metaphor, while transformed by this lifting upwards into the clear air and sunlight. That the ground as tomb is ever present in the German mind at the time can be seen from the parallel Expressionist activity of exploring the spaces inherent in organically derived forms like the burrow. In these organic forms the implications are unequivocally despairing of human loss and human alienation from the natural world. The forms replicate the trenches and what they stand for. Optimism and constructive thoughts, although outlandish, have moved from organic imaginings to the more resilient, immutable forms of the inorganic.

Figure 12.3
Taut, 'Alpine architecture'

13 Modernism and the International Style

The modern movement or International Style was defined in 1931 by the famous exhibition 'The International Style: Architecture since 1922', organized by Henry-Russell Hitchcock and Philip Johnson in New York. This showed and shaped a growing consensus about what constituted modern building. In the architecture of the previous ten years that was on display, the thick walled, solidly roofed building rooted to the ground was abolished. Instead there were buildings whose volumes were enclosed by the thinnest possible walls and roofs, whose large glassy areas dissolved the boundaries between inside and outside, as effectively as minimal partitions and unobtrusive structure allowed inside spaces to flow into one another.

These buildings represented the culmination of developments which were under way by the turn of the nineteenth century. Advances in science and technology led to the curbing of disease, the X-ray, anaesthetics, aseptic techniques and the modern operating theatre in medicine; to the generation of electricity; to the beginnings of telecommunications; to the modern ship, the car and the aeroplane.

Although many new buildings were already guided by functional technical considerations – American skyscrapers, many factories, and almost all buildings were modern in the sense that it was difficult to avoid using the products and methods of an increasingly mechanized building industry – the expressive aspect of important buildings did not reflect the radical new forms brought about by technology. The new approach to architecture took up the imagery of progress. The car, the ship, above all the aeroplane and the operating theatre, became sources for the language of the new architecture, both in how their materials were put together and in their overall look. The Futurists' exploration of movement in modern life and modern inventions was absorbed (more than in Futurist architectural projects) by Mendelsohn's images of fantastic surging buildings that he drew when in the Great War trenches. These in suitably damped-down and usable form were absorbed in the streamform aspects of the International Style. In Holland the didactic drive for a new language produced neo-plastic ideas and their resolution in the buildings of the De Stijl movement where space was defined by uncompromised rectangular planes, the colouring limited to white, black and primary colours. Russian architects expressed their technocratic materialist revolution in the soaring forms of buildings whose mass high above the ground was supported without equivalent mass below.

This radical diversity from the first quarter century, a speeded-up inverse of the many historical styles employed during the nineteenth century, was trimmed down by Hitchcock and Johnson into its common factors which might make a new, unifying 'International Style'. Up until the nineteenth century an architectural style had always, so it seemed, encapsulated a 'spirit of the age'. With a careful selection of images exploring volume over mass, functional organization, repetition rather than symmetry, the machine-made over the natural, glass walls, balconies, whiteness, the International Style pointed the way forward.

However, it was Le Corbusier's work that largely defined what became the International Style. A series of houses he designed in the 1920s culminated in the Villa Savoie where the idea of the house as a 'machine for living' attained its final formulation. The interior of the Villa Savoie aestheticizes the functional purity of the operating theatre, its external appearance is of a grounded aeroplane, its pilotis (free-standing columns) barely keeping the building in contact with the ground. It is a twentieth-century realization of Ledoux's House of the Rural Guards, that spherical house which neither sat on the earth nor was yet capable of physically lifting off but which metaphorically pointed to this ambition.

Le Corbusier was able to build houses that did rise off the ground thanks to reinforced concrete. Drawing upon his early experience of working for the leading engineer/architect Auguste Perret, he designed the Dom-ino House in 1914, a reinforced concrete frame system which exploited the new material's tensile strength to eliminate loadbearing walls. Not unlike Laugier's primitive hut, Le Corbusier's drawing of the Dom-ino House emphasizes columns and roof. But whereas the eighteenth century primitive hut implied ideas of protection and shelter, Le Corbusier's is simply a frame awaiting the assembly of mass-produced components.

His first projects to put a body on this frame he called Citrohan house 1 (1920) and Citrohan house 2 (1922), the name an obvious pun on Citroën. W. Taylor's principles of scientific management and the success of Henry Ford's model T were much in the news, and Le Corbusier aspired to produce a house as economic, readily available, and as efficient as a car.

From our standpoint today it is hard to grasp the sense of innocence, beauty and liberation that the machine offered to someone like Le Corbusier in the '20s. The machine and mass production had been equated with ugliness and squalor since the 1851 Great Exhibition, and whilst serious efforts had been made to bring together art, design and industry, there remained that long-running moral rejection of the machine begun by Carlyle and Ruskin, and carried on by Morris and the Arts and Crafts movement. However as the twentieth century got into full swing it became clear that the machine would not go away. The Great War did show the enormously destructive power of the machine which prompted a post-war artistic response of pacifism and hoped-for new beginnings. It is in this context that Le Corbusier's ideas and projects need to be understood; he was trying to take the machine in hand artistically. This idealistic project is demonstrated on almost every page of his hugely influential book, *Towards a New Architecture*, published in 1923. The book opens with a chapter entitled 'The Engineer's Aesthetic and Architecture' in which Le Corbusier points to the positive contributions engineers had made to modern progress which he contrasts with 'the cult of the home':

But the cult of the house has remained the same for centuries ... Engineers fabricate the tools of their time. Everything that is to say, except houses and moth-eaten boudoirs.

The book is, however, more than simply a radical, ahistorical, utilitarian tract. At the heart of the book is a section called 'Eyes which do not see' divided into three parts: 1. Liners, 2. Airplanes and 3. Automobiles. His argument is that there is a new spirit evident in these machines and that their beauty and harmony results from engineers working logically with strict regard for economy and physical necessity. He illustrates this section with photographs of ship's decks redolent with associations of fresh air, sun and sea, biplanes as fragile as butterflies, beautifully streamlined and sleek cars which he compares to Greek temples. It is on the page where he juxtaposes a view of the Parthenon with a side view of a Delage Grand-Sport that his point is truly made. Just as the Greek temple found its perfect form by processes of development and selection guided by geometry, so, says Le Corbusier, has the modern car. Since the discovery of Greek temples by Stuart and Revett, architects had tried to explain their beauty largely in terms of subtle proportion. But Le Corbusier followed the engineer Choisy, whose influential histories of architecture stressed form, mass and construction. The Greek temple became seen as a type – a particular building form that had been developed to a high pitch of art from a rude timber prototype over many generations of adjustment and improvement. Le Corbusier saw the same process at work in the development of machines such as the automobile, his photographs emphasizing them as assemblies of distinct geometric forms. He called his readers' attention to a similar process at work in craft-produced things such as pipes, violins, bottles, plates, things he called 'objet-types'. Le Corbusier was proposing that there existed a process of mechanical selection just as there is natural selection. Architects were bidden to draw upon the evolution of machines in making the new architecture.

To understand the deeper meaning to this we need to backtrack a little and consider Le Corbusier's youth. Charles-Edouard Jeanneret (as he was before reinventing himself as Le Corbusier) was born and raised in La Chaux-de-Fonds, a small town in the Jura region of Switzerland bordering France. He entered the town's School of Applied Arts in 1900 where he studied the art of engraving associated with watchmaking. Somewhat surprisingly, in the light of his later adulation of the machine, his earliest art was a form of painting where natural motifs dominated. He had come under the influence of his teacher L'Eplattenier who was interested in developing a regional art. In the young Jeanneret's painting the predominant aspects of local nature, mountains, rocks, pines, etc., are abstracted and re-combined in a manner reminiscent of other forms of European Jugendstil art. L'Eplattenier was a great admirer of Ruskin whose writings he introduced to his pupil which he in turn found inspiring, liking his anti-materialism in particular.

Underlying L'Eplattenier's teaching seems to have been a neo-Platonism which left its mark on Le Corbusier. Seen first in the young student's paintings where abstraction and rhythm attempt to grasp the underlying essence of natural forms, this neo-Platonism shaped his whole attitude to the machine and machine production. Hence his emphasis on geometry, the wheels and circular headlamps of cars, the mathematically orchestrated curves of mudguards and the aerodynamically calculated sweep of an aeroplane's wing. From a book that greatly affected his thinking at this time, Schuré's *Les Grand Initiés*, he found Pythagoras to be the initiate of most value to modern man because of his scientific spirit. But seen from this point of view, science is not empirical but abstract and *a priori*. Just as Pythagoras postulated ideas,

Figure 13.1
Le Corbusier, Villa Fallet, La Chaux-de-Fonds, Switzerland.

Figure 13.2
Maison La Roche, Paris.

essences and number beneath the directly experienced natural world, so did Le Corbusier, a process he later extended to his understanding of the machine-made world. Perhaps it comes as no surprise then that his first house built in La Chaux-de-Fonds when he was just twenty is a stone and timber, steep roofed adaptation of a regional farmhouse, just

Figure 13.3
Villa at Garches.

as his first house to be built following the Dom-ino project was a rational white box on pilotis.

The La Roche–Jeanneret houses (1922; now the Fondation Le Corbusier) are a pair built on a tight, awkward, back-garden Parisian site that severely cramped his first attempt to build the new ideal. Only the living room of the house for M. La Roche is lifted off the ground. Nevertheless its white curved wall dominates the entrance approach so his intention is announced. Le Corbusier's next house, the Maison Cook (1926) at Boulogne-sur-Seine is emphatically the house as machine. Lifted up on pilotis, the only contact the building has with the ground is the entrance hall, its form a direct quotation from the nose section of a Farman Goliath biplane (illustrated no less than six times in *Towards a New Architecture*). The house is entered through a door at the side, just as is the Farman whose wings have been lifted up here to form the roof of the house.

The next house in the series was a Villa at Garches (1923–27) that takes almost literally the cropped image of the liner *Acquitania's* rear pleasure deck, also illustrated in *Towards a New Architecture*. The villa itself was first illustrated in carefully composed photographs showing the owner's car pulling in from Paris, as if suggesting that thanks only to the machine, the new captains of industry could retreat from the city to the country at the end of each working day and inhabit this appropriate fragment of a ship's bridge or ship's deck beached here in the midst of nature. Machine, mass production, nature, all are reconciled.

A sketch Le Corbusier made for the Villa Savoie (1928–31) strikes just such a lyrical chord. The house, a pure white box raised above the crest of a hill on its pilotis, appears as some unearthly machine poised for lift-off, an impression reinforced by the ship's bridge-like strip windows and control tower-like forms above. The house as machine is lifting off from, or landing upon, a scene of arcadian nature across which the car, brought into harmony with nature through mechanical selection, is free to traverse.

Perhaps an ambivalent note creeps in when we explore the interior. After leaving the car and the shadowed world beneath the belly of the house/machine we enter the first floor living quarters from a ramped promenade which cuts through the centre of the plan. From within the clinical world of the house and from on the terrace, we see nature through the strip windows, perhaps imagined as if from the windows of a fast moving car, or alternatively as if from First World War protective bunkers. In either case we are distanced from nature, cut off from direct contact with it. Raised above it like the new aviator, we become objective surveyors of the landscape rather than steeped in it, body and soul.

In a dramatic drawing illustrating his 'Five points of the new architecture' Le Corbusier demonstrates the advantages a building like the Villa Savoie has over a traditional building. The latter, drawn as a negative image dominated by black, is shown stuck in the ground, with cellar (dark and damp), relatively small holes in the walls for windows, plans necessarily repeated floor above floor, and capped by a pitched roof. The new house in contrast, lifted above the ground on its pilotis, allows nature to run beneath the building; the frame allows windows to be as wide as wished, placed where desired to illuminate the house; and the roof has become a roof terrace, an unshadowed world on which gardens can grow luxuriantly.

It was such a symbiotic relationship between the new architecture, man's creation, and nature that underlies Le Corbusier's development of this 'machine in the garden'. If his overblown rhetoric in support of the machine analogy itself tended to overshadow this aspect, then the International Style exhibition completely eliminated it. Concentrating on style, image, construction techniques and an aesthetic of pure rationality, the International Style disseminated a monstrously truncated version of Le Corbusier's ideal which in any case was probably beyond the reach of anyone not equipped with a similar poetic and painterly engagement with nature. Exactly the same process occurred when his ideas on town planning became widely adopted.

Although Le Corbusier is well known for his advocacy of skyscrapers and motorways as the basis of city planning his first housing project was decidedly 'cottagey' – just like his first house. A little-known project from 1917 for about forty houses at St Nicholas d'Aiermont, Normandy, shows the dominating influences on his thinking about groups of buildings to be Raymond Unwin and the garden city, garden suburb movement, as the historian Mark Swenarton has pointed out. This was not built and Le Corbusier's ideas underwent a complete metamorphosis but nevertheless, just as for the individual house, nature remained an underlying ground in his radical proposals for the human habitat.

He first collected his thoughts on this subject in the book *Urbanisme* published in 1924 (translated as *The City of Tomorrow*). The first chapter is called 'The Pack-Donkey's Way and Man's Way'. 'Man walks in a straight line because he has a goal and knows where he is going', says Le Corbusier, whereas, 'The pack-donkey meanders along'. European

Figure 13.4
Villa Savoie, Poissy.

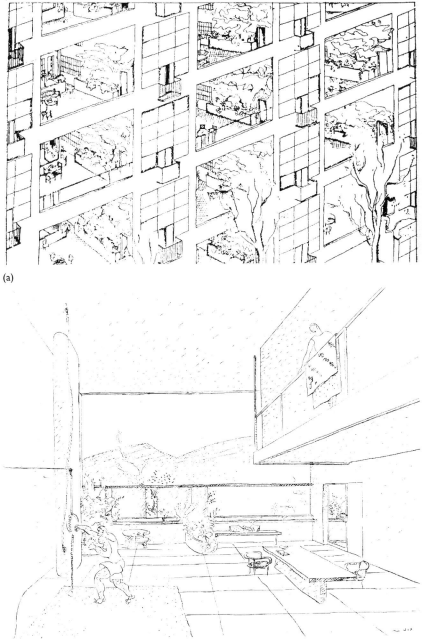

(a)

(b)

Figure 13.5a–b *The City of Tomorrow*: block of dwellings on the cellular system with hanging gardens.

cities were legacies of the pack-donkey into which the arrival of the motor car had brought chaos 'like dynamite flung at hazard into the street, killing pedestrians'. (He reproduced a cartoon from *Le Journal* showing a traffic jam captioned 'Heartrending farewells of the father of a family about to cross the street in front of the Gare de L'Est'.) The great city, by which he means the rapidly expanding industrial city, is barely fifty years old, and he points to the American grid-iron cities for models of urban order, geometry and the right-angle being all pervasive.

However, he does not propose emulating the American city with its chasm-like streets between dense buildings blocks. After a polemical tour through statistics, classification, analyses of the growth of traffic, its movement and a chapter in praise of 'our technical equipment', he closes the book with a description of his 'scheme for a contemporary city of three million inhabitants'. Sixty-storey, cruciform plan office buildings occupy the city centre which is linked to its surroundings by geometrical systems of 120 feet wide main traffic arteries and interconnecting minor roads. Industry is zoned away from the commercial centre and the housing which takes the form of twelve-storey buildings with setbacks or with 'hanging gardens' looking on to immense parks. The caption beneath his plan for the new city aptly summarizes his aim: 'The heavy black lines represent the areas built upon. Everything else is either streets or open spaces. Strictly speaking the city is an immense park'.

He drew a number of perspectives to illustrate how the corridor-street of the traditional city would be replaced by flowing open spaces across which cars would speed, in which people would find repose amongst the trees, amongst which fragile biplanes would flit. The traditional corridor-streets, he wrote, were 'full of noise and dust and deprived of light'. Le Corbusier's new layout in contrast, 'enables us to introduce trees into our city', and 'aesthetically speaking, the proximity of geometrical forms of dwellings to the picturesque forms of vegetation produces a much-needed and satisfying combination in our urban scene'.

Near the beginning of the book in a chapter entitled 'Order', Le Corbusier had introduced his argument for this coexistence of nature and geometry in terms which drew upon his neo-Platonism. Man, he writes:

created by the universe, is the sum of that universe, as far as he himself is concerned; he proceeds according to its laws and believes he can read them; he has formulated them and made of them a coherent scheme, a rational body of knowledge on which he can act, adapt and produce.

He goes on to say that this understanding has put man, not in opposition to the universe, but in harmony with it. Above this sentiment he illustrates roughly made, circular primitive huts. He then moves rapidly on to the proposition that,

Nature presents itself to us as a chaos, the actual scene which lies before our eyes, with its kaleidoscopic fragments and its vague distances, is a confusion ... but the spirit which animates nature is a spirit of order; we come to know it.

From this he concludes that 'we therefore reject appearance and attach ourselves to the substance'. By this he meant geometry. With a Rousseauesque phrase he said that 'When man is free his tendency is towards pure geometry. It is then that he achieves what we call order'.

It is from this curious mixture of neo-Platonism, Newtonian mechanistic science, and pure megalomania that Le Corbusier projected his utopia in which size and geometry determined the dwelling to be neither the cottage nor the primitive hut surrounded by nature, but twelve-storey high blocks of flats. However, his overriding concern in the design of the flats was to organize the accommodation around a space open to sun and air with tremendous views across great tracts of nature. This double height balcony he called a 'jardin suspendu' in his 1922 project for 'Immeubles-villas' (which were evolved in connection with his plan for the city for three million). Le Corbusier's drawings for the exterior of these apartment blocks are either axonometrics drawn as if from a great height emphasizing the vast areas of ground given over to nature,

Figure 13.6
L'Esprit Nouveau pavilion.

or close-up views showing nature spilling out from the balconies. His interior views depict either a similarly verdant nature or the inhabitants working out on the balcony against the backdrop of a splendid landscape. The prototype built as the Esprit Nouveau Pavilion at the Exhibition of Decorative Arts, Paris (1925) he even sited to embrace a living tree in the balcony.

This pavilion exerted a huge influence on the International Style with the white, abstracted forms and machine-produced components readily copied. But Le Corbusier's broader vision of the machine in the garden, implicit in the individual house and explicit in his town-planning, became similarly absorbed in the burgeoning international scene exclusively in its rational aspect. At the founding meeting of the Congrès Internationaux d'Architecture Moderne (CIAM) a declaration was made that 'rationalisation and standardisation' had to be design imperatives. In town planning this developed under the banner of 'Neue Sachlichkeit' (New Objectivity). The third meeting of CIAM in 1930 discussed 'Rational Methods of Site Planning' where purely rational principles of optimum orientation for sunlight were proposed, simple rows of tall buildings accepted as best, the distance between them determined by mean sun angles. This had the same effect as the International Style exhibition of disseminating a set of formal and technical principles applied piecemeal in or around the edge of existing cities rather than Le Corbusier's deeper, all-embracing, potentially green city.

We have seen that the separation from the ground, whether in the skyscrapers on pilotis in Le Corbusier's city for three million project or in the Villa Savoie, detaches human building from the earth's surface, not for the functional reasons of getting above the water level or snow line as in folk building, but in order for the building metaphorically to fly, to separate itself from that which is earthbound. It is both an optimistic, confident gesture – and also one with its share of hubris. Coupled with transparency, with the glass window wall barely separating inside from outside – seen most completely in Mies Van der Rohe's

Barcelona Pavilion and his Tugendhat House – the gestures point two ways. Compared to the earthbound building there is a delicacy of contact with what's outside, an openness, a metaphoric defencelessness, that some may see as connected to the pacific intentions of the post-Great War generation. If the health-giving properties of sunshine and fresh air which fundamentally underwrite the design of these buildings is added to the raison d'être of these modern city open spaces, then these early modern buildings seem to point to renewal, though of a different kind, of union between the human and the natural. On the other hand a detachment from what is outside can happen when viewed from life inside a space which is artificial in its materials and its technical systems, beyond the possibility of earlier cultures. The human progress of the man-made away from its earlier, tighter connections with the natural was as necessary as it was inevitable given the increasingly scary information about the workings of the natural.

The nineteenth-century industrial cities had produced a jungle-like world where micro-organisms thrived with disastrous effects on its inhabitants. The only available initial response of retreating to the garden suburb was now complemented by the remedies of science – 'Physic or Surgery' in the title of Le Corbusier's penultimate chapter. In England, for example, the Russian émigré Berthold Lubetkin proposed the Finsbury Plan to clear away the dark, fetid Victorian streets, courts and alleys, replacing them with Corbusian housing blocks surrounded by open space such as the Spa Green Estate, centred upon the white, light, off-the-ground Finsbury Health Centre (1938). From the perspective of the dark Victorian city an extreme position of science against nature easily arose, just as Freud, for example, set the new science of psychology against the dark side of the mind: 'Against the dreaded external world one can only defend oneself by some kind of turning away from it, ... with the help of a technique guided by science, going over to the attack against nature and subjecting her to the human will'. And architects who moved commonsensically away from naturalistic forms, were moving constructively away, too, from the confusions and desolating implications of the new proofs of the chance disinterestedness of natural processes.

While technology was making for practical as well as spectacular inventions which inspired modern architects, the pure sciences as well as bringing benefits were unanchoring the mind's view of the world with their dizzying insights into the nature of space, time and matter. This too the new architecture reflected. The International Style house, open to space through its wide windows, with its free-flowing inside volumes, was, as Giedion later grasped, the metaphor for a modern view of space and time as it had come to be understood. His book *Space, Time and Architecture; The Growth of a New Tradition* built upon the aesthetic foundation laid by Hitchcock and Johnson to suggest that the spirit of the new architecture was inevitably of its time. Arguing that perspective and hollowed out interior space were now being replaced by 'hitherto unknown interpenetration of inner and outer space', he likened this to Cubism's depicting of objects simultaneously from several points of view. Both the new art and architecture he saw as equivalents to Einstein's replacement of solid matter acting under gravity with the gravitational field concept of a space–time continuum curved in the vicinity of matter, matter itself conceived of as fields of energy rather than atoms and subatomic particles. The glassy minimalism of the new architectural construction validated, in its invisibility and therefore its immeasurability (metaphorically speaking), the new attitudes towards matter. A close-up gaze through the glass walls looking either way – outside in, or inside out – confirmed the looping, paradoxical, unconfirmable boundaries of twentieth-century being.

Such buildings, images of progress and a modern sense of being, had a deliberate disinterest in the particularities of climate and society, and thereby from the functional and symbolic ideas of place. Instead these modern buildings took on the expressive aspect of machines. Often sophisticated and chic, they were not that amenable to the messier aspects of human living and not always that comfortable either. After all, after the car, ship or aeroplane journey ends you get off – or with luck survive the operating theatre – to resume living in a less extreme ethos.

Some, such as Alvar Aalto, withdrew from the International Style – in Aalto's case after designing one of its most successful buildings. He saw that Finland was not the place to build thin-walled glassy buildings with flat roofs, surfaces stuccoed over to achieve a 'machine-like' finish, windows set flush with the wall in imitation of aeroplane detailing. The tough climate and the traditions of timber construction ruled it out unless buildings were to be maintained with the regularity and precision of cars, and have similarly short lives. He wanted too, he said, to design buildings that would age into magnificent ruin, a wish that would later affect Le Corbusier's buildings as well as his words. Frank Lloyd Wright had long thought this way; his buildings were not part of the consensus that grew around the International Style. The abstract, Platonic white style of that movement, had tugging at its didacticism from then on, the organic ideas of Aalto and those like him, as well as the alternative modern example of Wright. The impulse behind the Arts and Crafts movement had joined Modernism.

14 Organic ideas in modern architecture

It has become difficult to know quite what the word organic means when applied to architecture. Confusion reigns. In architectural circles it has been seen to be synonymous with the buildings and writings of Frank Lloyd Wright in particular. Some connect it to others like Hans Scharoun whose freer geometrical approach was just acceptable despite the developing consensus about modern architecture that produced the International Style of the 1930s. To some the attitudes and subsequent buildings of Alvar Aalto and those who followed his lead are organic. Aalto left the rigid doctrines of the International Style in favour of a more regional approach that favoured building durably, and the need to reflect the imperatives of climate and tradition. The spikiness and the burrow-like qualities of German Expressionism were organic in feeling too, although poles apart from the sunnier creations of Frank Lloyd Wright, or even those of Aalto. Even within the confines of modern architecture in its pioneer days, organic as a term was being asked to do too much.

Moderns who would not have thought of themselves as organic in a Wrightian sense did use organic metaphors to show the logic of what they had done. Le Corbusier used biological analogies to explain that his buildings and city plans worked like the functional relationship between the parts of the human body, or like the development of tree and plants. Discussing buildings in such a way by organic or biological analogy had its origins back in the nineteenth century. In the development of Modernism, reaching back to functionalist ideas in the nineteenth century, organically derived notions of form following function had helped allow the stripping away of superfluous ornament and the jettisoning of rigid Beaux Arts planning. Helped initially by Gothic revival ideas that preferred Gothic forms, in part because of their relatively free compositional possibilities as opposed to the symmetrical rules of Neo-classicism, Modernism moved to the idea that a building's form is necessarily generated by ideas of fitness and economy – the idea of form generated by function not by style. It thus adopted the idea of Gothic-inspired forms being more functional because they were more flexible.

In theory, although not always in fact, the modern organic architect differed greatly from the mainstream of Modernism, enough really to have little in common. Organic theories had sources not only in science but in poetic thinking too. Earlier on in science these moved from the religious-based to the open mindedly scientific. Buffon's *Histoire Naturelle* of 1769, taking literally the Genesis account of the Fall, had seen the development of species in terms of degeneration. Buffon though had set out the idea of an evolutionary process that he felt must have originated from a single type (in which he was broadly correct). The idea of evolution as a dying fall was later scotched by Lamarck who stated that evolution was a progressive, improving process provoked by the stimulus of adaptation to environment. As Peter Collins pointed out in his *Changing Ideals in Modern Architecture* (1965), the idea of the organic, as architects were later to discuss it, was first articulated by Buffon:

... he was the first scientist to distinguish correctly between the 'vegetative' and specifically 'animal' parts of animals, whereby an animal can be regarded simply as a vegetable organism endowed with the power of moving from place to place. Thus 'organic life' has come to mean, for architectural theorists at least, the sum of the functions of the 'vegetative' class; for all living organisms, whether plants or animals, possess them to a more or less marked degree.

Buffon's contemporary Linnaeus had suggested that plants should be classified according to inherent characteristics determinable in a museum. Von Humboldt, like Buffon, opposed this and thought, like Lamarck later, that they should be classified according to the climates in which they were found:

Being of a romantic and aesthetic disposition, he sought a system of classification through the impression made by landscapes when simply looked at by the ordinary observer. Contending that each latitude possesses its own characteristic natural physiognomy, he eventually differentiated between certain vegetable types according to the impression given of their form as a whole ... Darwin naturally took Von Humboldt's doctrine considerably further by contending that Nature had selected *those forms, which were most suitable for the environment in which they were situated ...*

The idea that natural selection orders the forms of organisms to suit a particular environment has obvious parallels with how folk building came to be seen, its forms and ways of doing things determined through the opportunities and limitations afforded by particular places and climates. Functional forms came to be seen as derived from a process analogous to natural selection. As these evolutionary ideas were being formulated, Coleridge (1818), following the German Romantic philosophers, was setting out a concept of the organic, as opposed to the mechanistic:

The form is mechanic when on any given material we impress a predetermined form, as when to a mass of wet clay we give whatever shape we wish it to retain when hardened. The organic form on the other hand is innate, it shapes as it develops from within, and the fullness of its development is one and the same as the perfection of its outward form.

This is much the same as Wright says in 1914:

... by organic architecture I mean an architecture that develops from within outward in harmony with the conditions of its being as distinguished from one that is applied without.

The 'conditions of its being' to Wright, and the 'innate' quality to Coleridge, are dependent upon a particular place in the world, an environment that determines, or helps determine. Wright's buildings and his writings drew together these threads to stand at the centre of

(a)

(b)

Figure 14.1a–b
Two of Wright's 'prairie houses' in the Chicago
suburbs: the Ward Willits house (a) and the
Coonley house (b).

ideas of an organic tradition in modern architecture. His mentor Louis
Sullivan had in his buildings combined a tough-minded functionalism
with an idiosyncratic feel for naturalistic ornament that seemed to grip
the building here and there with its twisting vital forms. The idea,
important to nineteenth-century thought, of the movement, the physical

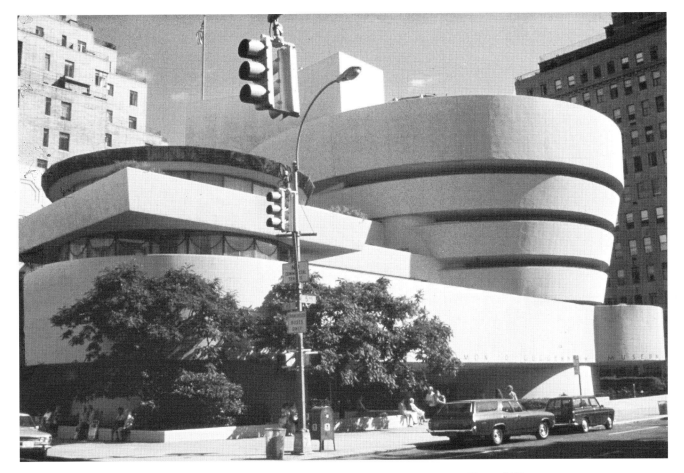

Figure 14.2
Guggenheim Museum, New York City.

actuality of life force, inherent in living things, was given imaginative impetus by thoughts of the struggle to adapt and change in the processes of evolutionary development. This is made manifest in the ornament of Sullivan's buildings, as in the Art Nouveau and Jugendstil buildings of Europe. Wright was to express the vitality of life, so apparent in Sullivan's ornament and, eventually, to make it inherent in the structural forms of some of his buildings.

His first buildings, theoretically influenced by Ruskins's writings and those of Emerson, as well as by the Arts and Crafts movements in Europe and the United States, were in the Chicago suburbs. These houses with their open interpenetrating spaces, overhanging eaves lines with their extreme horizontal emphasis, go well beyond the equivalent reinterpretation of vernacular forms to be seen in Europe at the time by Arts and Crafts designers. True progenitors of modern space making, they show Wright to be responsive as well to the new para-scientific probings into the psyche in their conscious use of the horizontal line, with all that conveyed in the psychological speculation of the day in terms of harmony, passivity, an expressing of contact with the earth, and the feminine qualities of the home. This eagerness to assimilate modern thought is part of what makes Wright a modern in contrast to a more conservative Arts and Crafts architect like Voysey (who when honoured as a prophet of Modernism in 1943, angrily refuted the idea). Wright's talent for the siting of a building, and the innovative use of natural materials, and his inventive structural sense developed further the scope of organic ideas. His later buildings, before his last crazed 'Disneyland'

Figure 14.3
Falling Water, Pennsylvania.

phase, are at their most magical in strong natural settings. It is wrong though to see his architecture as a countryside or wilderness genre, a variant of Modernism that just turns its back on the city, on urbanism. Wright hated our cities as they were, although he built brilliantly within them, often using natural forms as inspiration in such buildings as in the lily pad inspired structure of the Johnson Wax Building or the spiralling drum forms of the Guggenheim Museum. In the city his buildings, while sophisticated, do not integrate, they are not calm; instead they are generally noisy intrusions into the city as it is.

In his buildings in the landscape though, he gave architectural form to the American ideal that the good life means joining the settler at the frontier, at least in spirit. His houses present a modern reinterpretation of the idea of the frontier house, energetic in their incorporation of the elemental in materials and structure and in their eager hugging of the landscape, yet accepting the softness of modern American ways of life in their incorporation of the latest technological comforts. In the assertive yet sympathetic way they sit in the American landscape, awash with goodies, they are however very much the inheritors of the white man's way of imposing himself upon nature, rather than of that other way represented by the red man and his tepee.

In Wright's masterworks like Falling Water and Taliesin West (his own house), buildings of the modern industrial age sit in an ancient landscape. They are fully of the present in form, yet resonant of the ways of the past in the materials that give their forms substance. Falling Water as its name implies is a house whose rooms are cantilevered out over a waterfall. The walls are natural stone, there is much glass to interconnect the woods and the waterfall with the interior, and the enormous cantilevers are of reinforced concrete. The effect is to transform the landscape around into a beautiful backdrop to the arresting building. In the more hostile desert landscape of Taliesin West the building crouches on the desert floor, its form less dominant in the context of the open desert panorama. It appears to grow naturally out of the ground, its organized boulder walls petering out into the random boulders of the landscape. Inside the abstract forest of structural roof timbers is a

Figure 14.4
Taliesin West, Arizona.

modern equivalent to the architectural tree forms from the Western architectural past, from the roof-tree of the primitive hut to the stony equivalents of the Gothic cathedral. Inspiring as they both are, these buildings of Wright carry the seeds of one of the problems of the crisis we now have to face but also suggest one way of helping towards the solutions. A time-honoured attitude that sees nature as an endlessly providing resource eventually led to buildings that express modern man's oneness with nature. Falling Water integrates its old and technologically advanced materials, its forms and its natural surroundings into one another. But taking too the experience of twentieth-century comfort into the heart of the bush and building over a waterfall is to show who is boss, as well as to appreciate what is being bossed. A century and a half earlier Ledoux had dreamed up a similarly commanding building for the Director of the River at his Royal Saltworks project at Chaux. Then the idea of a house for the controller of the river remained a paper fantasy, unbuildable without reinforced concrete. In this century it gets built as a weekend pad for a wealthy family at a time when material command over nature had become the more commonplace – no longer aspired to but realized. Wonderfully inspiring as it is, Falling Water carries in its forms and its siting the seeds of a problem that ideas of the organic have to face. Wright's own Taliesin, workplace and house, tucked down for survival in the harsh desert climate, perhaps has more to offer us as we put together a green history in terms of how to make buildings that express integration rather than domination of the natural world.

The same could be said of some of Aalto's buildings, the Villa Mairea for example. Designed in 1938 it was much influenced by Falling Water which received great publicity in Europe at this time. Seen through the Nordic forest, the Villa Mairea looks like a white, International Style house overlaid with timber extensions, granite cladding, with the essential strip windows filled in to be replaced with wooden, projecting bay windows. On approaching closely, the white walls are seen to be lime-washed brickwork and a rustic porch is supported on clumps of thin timber columns.

Inside, the abstracted, free-flowing space of the International Style is transformed to that of a forest clearing. A line of thin poles beside the stair feels like a screen of trees; metal columns, scattered in twos and threes, are bound with rattan which looks like the bark of silver birch trees. Large windows in the rooms and nautical handrails give the house a modern feel, but the tree-like columns, the slate and bleached beech floors, pine ceilings and stony fireplaces combine to give the house a sophisticated primitive intimacy; a reinterpretation of a traditional home for the forest.

Figure 14.5
Aalto, Villa Mairea, Finland, interior.

Bruce Goff, whose work is often associated with that of Frank Lloyd Wright, started his own practice in the late 1930s. His work, initially clearly influenced by Wright, also demonstrates his ability to absorb and reflect upon many of the giants of Expressionism such as Mendelsohn and Taut and Modernist designers such as Neutra. Through his long but not always successful career Goff continually explored and experimented with geometries and materials. Always following Wright's tenet that individuality must be developed, nurtured and celebrated, he brought to each commission a genuine intent to allow his clients the opportunity to create an environment which was a natural expression of their values for 'the continuous present':

The past is gone, the future is not here, but the present is continuous. The Bavinger House, earth-bound as it is, is a primitive example of the continuity of space for living ... it is not a 'back-to-nature' concept of living space. It is a living with nature today and every day, continuous space again as part of a continous present.

Goff, *Forty-four Realizations* (1970)

The spiral of the Bavinger house, designed in 1950, is so obviously a form derived from nature but also through the mystic geometries and pattern making of human minds. The materials are combinations of raw and processed; the spiral copper-clad roof hangs from steel tension cables which also extend to support a suspension bridge linking the house across the shallow ravine within which it is constructed. Massive stone walls, constructed of sandstone boulders from the site, rise with the spiral from 2 metres to 15 metres as the spiral tightens in on itself.

Figure 14.6
Bruce Goff, Bavinger house, Oklahoma.

The centre point of the logarithmic spiral is taken by the mast, rising above the walls and roof to hold the cables. The entire ground level is a rocky water garden of pools and luscious planting. The relatively small living areas are set on circular platforms, themselves suspended from the roof structure accessed by a staircase which follows the tight centre of the stone spiral. These are set as a regular spiral allowing them to erupt through the stone walls at high level to provide a glazed studio, filled with light as the culmination of the upward journey. Secondary copper-clad drums are fixed to each platform to provide storage and the only visual division of space is by opaque curtains which might be run round circular frames above the platforms if privacy should be required. The interior is lit by a glazed gap between the rough vertical stone spiral walls and the suspended copper and timber roof. This drops light down the vertical stone walls dramatizing the texture of the walls, a technique so beloved of the eighteenth-century grotto builders. The positions of the few windows in the exterior walls were finally determined during construction as the house was built by the unskilled labour of the Bavingers themselves and student helpers. More than any other modern house, the Bavinger house has the direct expression of a home that a child might imagine building at a smaller scale. It could be the home of one of Barrie's 'lost boys' or a shelter constructed from combinations of materials from shipwrecks, despite its location in woodland in the most inland state of the US. It is a tree house, hanging from its artificial spine the shading and protecting roof under which nature itself can also hide and flourish.

These buildings of Wright, Aalto and Goff are, though, handmade for the few, and one at least marks a stage in increasing material indulgence that has spread farther and wider alongside poverty and deprivation in our times. On their isolated plots they are brilliant interventions into a natural setting. They would have a different context though if they had been buried within Wright's projected Broadacre City. Following Emerson's call in the nineteenth century for every American to have an acre of land for himself to keep his independence and his contact with the land, Wright conceived Broadacre City to achieve something like this for every citizen. It was to have a network of roads linking low-rise houses to regional shopping malls and commercial centres. It was in fact a Wright-designed ordering of what was already, but chaotically, happening across the States, a seal of approval for the suburb. For if everyone has land around their building, then society becomes suburban, even eventually in a country as big as the States. More land is absorbed than in tighter ways of living, and more energy in communicating and travelling. When the problems of housing huge populations are confronted, the choice is between a Broadacre approach and that of denser city living: country lungs for everyone and no wilderness left, or tight city cultures that lose contact with the seasons and the night sky.

Many questions arise. Would a Taliesin or a Falling Water work for those who live in it as well if surrounded by masses of other buildings, even if of a low density? Does the suburb work for people as a way of living, and what does its corralling and taming of nature do to the possibility of any real wilderness being left? Were the draconian and seemingly fascist implications of Sant Elia's Futurist cities or Le Corbusier's city for three million worse starting points for dealing with the problem of housing huge urbanized populations than the idea of a near worldwide suburban alternative? Which is the more realistic starting point for a planet whose resources, and whose remaining wildernesses, are on the brink of more despoliation than we fear it can resist?

15 England and Modernism I

In buildings by Voysey in the 1890s, Pevsner tells us, England came nearest to the idiom of the modern movement. But British ascendancy in the last years of the nineteenth century was not to be followed by the dawn of Modernism in our still partially green and pleasant land: 'For the next forty years, the first forty of our century, no English name need here be mentioned'.

The context of this remark was his *Outline of European Architecture* first published in 1943. In the pages that follow one English name does in fact get a mention, that of Charles Holden who designed Modernist London underground stations. Of Lutyens there is nothing; Parker and Unwin rate half a dozen lines, culminating in the damning of 'the whole conception of the garden city and the garden suburbs' as 'an escape from the city itself'.

There is an extent to which Pevsner is right: England did in the main reject the path towards Modernism in the early years of the century. And in the 1920s Sir Reginald Blomfield, a founding editor of the *Architectural Review*, was to diagnose the dangerous new continental virus 'Modernismus' as something to be resisted vigorously. Ruislip-Northwood District Council resisted it by the refusal of planning permission; and there were denunciations from within the architectural profession in terms (now scarcely believable) of a Jewish conspiracy. None of this makes happy reading.

There was however an alternative tradition to the reinstated Classicism for which Blomfield spoke: a tradition which derived partly from the Arts and Crafts movement and partly from the picturesque planning of the Viennese Camillo Sitte. This is the garden city and garden suburb movement as it developed in the hands of Barry Parker and Raymond Unwin. And while both the Arts and Crafts movement and the garden city/garden suburb ideas influenced developments in Europe in the first third of the twentieth century, what we find in England is a distinctive and parallel development that perpetuates those trends without developing into Modernism.

The combination of picturesque planning and neo-vernacular design emanating from Parker and Unwin was not the only strand in British housing in the war years and the 1920s; there was also a neo-Georgian style emanating from the Liverpool School of Architecture, which accepted many of the principles of the continental modern movement – standardization, mass industrial production, etc. – but took the view that the English Georgian style was a totally appropriate embodiment of these principles. (Le Corbusier himself was to point out a few years later that the classicism of Versailles was likewise a perfect example of mass production.)

(a)

(b)

Figure 15.1a–b
Hampstead Garden Suburb, north London.

What the picturesque neo-vernacular and the neo-Georgian had in common was their focusing on the cottage. The neo-Georgian style picked up the threads of an urban tradition; but in other respects the schemes emanating from both schools of thought were equally anti-urban in their emphasis on cottages and gardens rather than on the urban planning that characterizes Vienna, Amsterdam and the later work at Frankfurt. However rich in human values and meanings we may find the social housing of Vienna and Amsterdam, their apartment blocks are unequivocally urban in concept – as are the low-rise satellite towns of Frankfurt's Nidda valley when the early influence of Raymond

(a)

(b)

(c)

(d)

Figure 15.2a–d
Housing for munitions workers at Well Hall, Woolwich.

Unwin had receded. By contrast the geometrical development at Dormanstown by Stanley Adshead, Stanley Ramsay and Patrick Abercrombie, all of the Liverpool School, is as much a village with its market square and semicircular green as any of the picturesque layouts of Parker and Unwin – notwithstanding the Liverpool School's criticisms of the 'romantic' anti-urbanism of the latter.

That said, it is certainly in the Parker and Unwin tradition that we find the most striking manifestations of a green sensibility in the first half of the century. At New Earswick in Lanarkshire (1901), a company village in the nineteenth-century philanthropic tradition for Rowntrees the chocolate manufacturers, neo-vernacular cottages look out on a green. Letchworth Garden City (begun 1903) and Hampstead Garden Suburb (begun 1907) display the principles that Unwin was to lay down in *Town Planning in Practice* (1909): no more than one-sixth of the land to be built on, giving between ten and twelve houses per acre; the use of footpaths and minor access roads ('carriageways') to reduce the need for thoroughfares, and lining of the wider roads with trees; and the inclusion of greens as well as squares. Visual variety could be achieved by setting houses back from the road, giving the road curvature, arranging houses round greens, varying their positioning and orientation at intersections, and taking full advantage of topography. Hampstead benefited from the hilly site, and there are wonderful views of the heath extension.

Unwin was much in demand in the war years when the need for a social housing programme was discussed. However, the first housing resulting from the war itself was a garden suburb for munitions workers in Woolwich – the Well Hall estate designed by Frank Baines for the ministry. A shortage of shells on the Western Front brought about this imaginative example of working class housing, now a conservation area (as is Roe Hill in Hertfordshire, another of the twenty-six schemes produced for munitions workers during the war years).

In terms of planning, Well Hall (1917) followed the principles of Parker and Unwin. Developed to both the east and west of Well Hall Road – the larger eastern half climbing up the side of a hill – it has a green in each half, plenty of trees, generous gardens, footpaths and minor access roads, and a picturesque handling of the main road system so that the vista is continually changing. What makes Well Hall even more distinctive is the variety of materials and styles used. There is brick, tile, slate, stone, timber, and a range of vernacular styles using projections, gables and dormers. The sense of being in an old English village remains strong to this day.

When the post-war government began to build its 'homes fit for heroes', the need for standardization made the lavish variety of Well Hall economically unacceptable. But it was to the development of the 'standard cottage', rather than any of the modes of standardized dwelling unit being developed on the continent, that post-war architects directed their energies. A concern to remain true to Ruskinian ideals of individuality and craftsmanship remained allied to the overriding social need, and in practice a number of different standard cottages could be produced using standard components.

A good example is the LCC Dover House estate in Roehampton. Here we find whole streets of identical cottages some of which are quite frankly 'boxes with lids' – the result of cost-cutting in the later stages of the development. But other streets have cottages of different size and shape (a government report published in November 1918 had specified five types); there are cul-de-sacs, crescents and greens; and the setting back of the terraces on sections of Dover House Road gives space and vista. A central square and circus reflect the neo-Georgian ideal of the Liverpool School; a more rural Arts and Crafts influence shows in houses whose roofs come right down to floor level, and in the dormer windows that characterize some roads.

It is interesting that Pevsner, in his Buildings of England series, notes a number of examples of 1930s LCC flats by the architect G. Topham Forrest, while ignoring this very substantial estate at Roehampton. He also ignores the housing at Well Hall. Buildings like these, and even the cost-cutting schemes that followed them, were not conceived as 'machines for living in' or 'minimum existence dwellings'; and though steel frames had been used at Dormanstown, and a concrete system was introduced by the LCC at the Castelnau estate in Barnes, the English housing of the war years and the 1920s typically provided its tenants with a friendly environment of traditional building materials. Above all, the wartime munitions worker and the returning serviceman and their families were provided with cottages, not with apartments in a superblock. In all these respects English practice diverged from the most celebrated achievements of continental Modernism.

This is not to denigrate those achievements, or to misunderstand the desperate urgency that drove architects in directions that England was largely loath to follow. England did at this time reject Modernism, about

(a)

(b)

Figure 15.3a–b
Dover House estate, Roehampton, south-west London.

which there was widespread ignorance well into the 1920s; but it had a valid alternative solution to the housing problem, rooted in its own vital traditions – traditions which had not only influenced continental Europe in the first years of the century but were also matched in the post-war years by such little known European alternatives to the Modernist mainstream as Hubert Sellier's cité jardin at Suresnes near Paris, and the Rosenhugel pioneers in Austria.

When at the end of the 1920s and the beginning of the 1930s, the excitement of international Modernism began to make itself felt here, it was not in social housing but in houses for an intellectual and artistic élite who were able to appreciate and pay for them. Only after the Second World War, when the new towns perpetuated little more than the basic planning principles of the garden city, then was the English vision of the cottage and garden suburb eclipsed by the Corbusian vision of a city of towers. At their best the towers and slab blocks could provide sunlight and air space, parkland and communal amenities, in an urban context; what they could not offer was the human scale, intimacy and natural materials of the 1920s cottage housing.

Part Five
The second return of the primitive hut

The first two chapters of this part of the book deal, partly at least, with the two main movements in British architecture in the period following the First World War. Both involve a going to ground – the new humanism deriving directly from Scandinavian 'back-to-nature', while the new brutalism reflects the bunker mentality of those parts of Europe that had experienced and/or were threatened by war. These can be seen as two modes of a second return of the primitive hut that has occurred in our century.

Building oneself a bunker can also be seen as building oneself an ark. Bunkers are very much of an era; arks have more universal, more mythic connotations (as Julian Barnes showed so powerfully in his novel *A History of the World in 10½ Chapters*, published in 1989). The ark remains a powerful image for those who are concerned today with the threat and avoidance of ecological catastrophe: the Herb Greene House is an ark, and the Autarkic House again picks up the theme in the final chapter of this section. Green architecture now comes centre stage, and is given the prominence that our situation dictates.

If the first return of the primitive hut was a return to nature motivated by a dissatisfaction with artificiality and excess, with social injustice and religious wars, the second return was fuelled by humankind's survival instinct. The science that once liberated man has produced a technology from which we in turn must liberate ourselves – harnessing it to save the earth and not destroy it.

A house which showed how to reconnect modern lives to the natural world, that did not trivialize contact with nature, would have to display more than Scandinavian architecture did, or could in 1947. For most the realization had not yet dawned that the human future as well as social and technical progress was inextricably linked to learning to live within our planetary resources and to look after other lives than those of our own species. The problem would first be posed in the urgent terms of domesday weaponry. Later would come the data showing that all those cola cans, car fumes, plastics products, CFCs for harmless refrigerators and the rest of the products, added to ruthless exploitation of the remaining forests and seas, would be an equal, though longer term threat.

Then in the development of sufficiently green houses, it might not matter too much what they looked like, except that publicizing the issues through appropriate visual forms might help. The priority would be to invent strategies for survival involving a holistic approach to the natural world, while hoping urgently that the social and political changes necessary for planetary survival could be made in time – a matter, whatever might be hoped or desired, that is outside the medium of architecture to implement.

16   England and Modernism II

By the end of the Second World War, the International Style had changed considerably from its earlier self. In European countries at war almost no civil building took place, although in Britain as elsewhere plans were being made. Before the war the effects of northern weather were already causing some architects to modify the white style prescribed in the 1929 New York exhibition. The rusting of inadequately galvanized windows and doors, the difficulty of preventing water entering walls which were inspired by the detailing of aeroplanes, the problem of flat roofing in wet or snowy areas, the overall degeneration into seediness of white-style buildings unless continually maintained, were practical reasons for change. Architects who did not hold to the organic ideas of Wright, and who had nothing to do with those who were simply reproducing versions of traditional building, were realizing the centrality of climate, materials and siting in design. Aalto's earlier initiative was being followed.

There were less tangible reasons too. As war had approached nationalist sentiment increased both in Fascist countries and in the democracies. Use of the trappings of the Roman and Holy Roman Empires in Germany and Italy, and of Nordic myths and ideas of the Volk in Germany, had cultural parallels in the British and Scandinavian rediscovery of their past traditions. Architecturally this led in England to Moderns becoming aware of their roots in the Arts and Crafts as well as in pioneer engineers, in the Georgian terrace house and the picturesque landscape as well as in French Rationalism. In Scandinavia similar reconnections were made. Before the war started, the neutralizing of national characteristics in the name of aesthetic and social progress, inherent in the International Style, was failing. (Parallels could be found in the ideas for constructive communication in words through Esperanto or Basic English, in art through either the search for a pure abstract language like that of the architectural white style, or in searching for the unconscious and the archetypal as in Surrealism.) The fact and practice of war overtook such theoretical niceties. The idea of order being expressible through pure geometries broke, and the surface realities of warfare overtook and made trivial the fancies of Surrealism. The variety of experiences and the chaos thrown up by war changed people. How could architects not be excited by the visual changes wrought by bombing if at home, or by the exotic buildings they encountered if posted abroad, or by the contradictions imposed upon pre-war modern simplicities like the idea of form following function, if like many designers they were put to designing camouflage? The machinery of war itself provoked technical and aesthetic change, an issue which I shall return to.

Outside the war zones building continued, in Latin America with sinuous and exotic forms of Modernism smothered by jungly plants. For Europe though, and particularly for Britain, it was Swedish building that was to become the most important influence. Frank Lloyd Wright, an isolated figure to Europeans, was admired, but his inventive buildings were perhaps too personal, his buildings and their setting too alien – and luxurious – to invite much emulation.

In a 1947 issue of the *Architectural Review*, then by far the most influential British architectural magazine, a description of a new Swedish house appeared. Like other coverage of modern buildings from Scandinavia, it was distinguished by a text which proclaimed that the building was typical of 'The New Empiricism', but more importantly for architects, who are (or rather were) more likely to be held by an arresting image, there was such an image in the photograph at the head of the text. A small blond nearly naked child, arms upraised to the sun, stands with his back to us. Beyond him is a pool disguised artfully as a pond. Other children play around their seated sunbathing parents on the other side of the pool, around which stands a low shallow roofed house. The house is modern, the windows, the sunblinds and the general appearance tells this, but it is not a modern house that recalls an aeroplane or ship. Planned along the sloping contours of the site, its relationship to the surrounding birch and spruce trees looks spontaneous but a little too perfect to be so, just as Repton's improved picturesque landscapes a century and a half ago would have done. This house, inside as well as outside, is modern, but has not lost contact with the Swedish past. A key influence here is the summer house, later their permanent home, that the Swedish painter Carl Larsson built for himself and his wife in the 1890s at Sundborn in central Sweden. Adding rooms of various shapes and sizes, mainly remarkably small, to an existing simple timber cottage, Larsson was consciously following the practice of English Arts and Crafts architects in letting the house grow over the site. The Markelius house is Larsson updated, a modern house, learning from the Arts and Crafts past, connected – just – to the first primitive hut, and what that stood for by way of renewal through contact with nature; it gives the feeling that a house can be beautiful if in such circumstances it is just

Figure 16.1
Markelius's house, Sweden, as shown in the *Architectural Review*, December 1947. Courtesy of *Architectural Review*.

Figure 16.2
Larsson house, Finland, interior.

Figure 16.3
Royal Festival Hall, London.

sensible, the designer's imagination working on the materials, landscape and setting of the building.

More perhaps than the grander concepts of Aalto's houses (from which it learns much), this house explains well the leaning of British architects after the war towards Scandinavian design. Here was a Nordic culture, untainted by perverted Nazi doctrine, designing modern buildings in a northern climate that was responding to the needs of a social democratic welfare state such as Britain had voted to become. We can see now that its ideas would not transfer easily, for Scandinavia was underpopulated and relatively under-industrialized compared to crowded industrialized Britain, but British myth still held to the idea of Britain as a pastoral paradise, which like the illusion of being still an imperial power, no longer accorded with reality. The example of this house though, built by the architect Markelius for his family, and of other houses and of whole towns like the new town of Vallingby, where the idyllic was less apparent, provided the main inspiration for British post-war Modernism. All over Britain houses were built, at their best in the woods of northern myth, and whole new towns too, following the example set by Nordic designers.

The wider effect on English architecture as a whole in the next decade was immense. Social democratic Sweden provided a model for the new Labour Britain, in the form of a visibly more humane architecture and design that could be welcomed and celebrated as contemporary. Its highpoint was to be the 1951 Festival of Britain, its monuments the Festival Hall and Coventry Cathedral.

The 1930s in England had ended with international Modernism finally making a breakthrough on a wider front. The period 1936–39 saw Frederick Gibberd's Pullman Court in Streatham, and Berthold Lubetkin's Highpoint I and II in Highgate as well as his Finsbury Health Centre. If it had not been for the Second World War there would surely have been a growing volume of buildings such as these. The war, as we have seen, brought a shift in architectural thinking, with patriotic and conservationist sentiments creating a climate of awareness of national

Figure 16.4
Ralph Erskine's house at Lissma, Sweden, as shown in the *Architectural Review*, June 1947. Courtesy of *Architectural Review*.

tradition that was to culminate in the *Architectural Review's* 'Townscape' articles of December 1949 and January 1950. Pevsner and J. M. Richards, the apostles of Modernism, were editors of the *Review* at the time and clearly identified with the revived cult of the picturesque. A commitment to pre-war Modernism allied to the new enthusiasm for picturesque planning would point the way forward. Coming as they did two years after the *Review's* photograph of the Markelius house (together with one by Ralph Erskine who was then working in Sweden), with 'The New Empiricism' having now generated another catchphrase, 'The New Humanism', these articles served to consolidate an expanding body of architectural thought.

It was in housing that all these ideas came together. The context was an LCC estate that Pevsner was to praise for its picturesque planning but which split the profession down the middle. At the Alton West estate in Roehampton the Corbusians of the LCC Architects' Department came nearest to realizing the dream of towers in a park – though a more immediate influence was Le Corbusier's great Unité block outside Marseilles. But at Alton East the hard left faction produced a mixed development of socialist realist housing that included low-rise buildings characterized by their 'people's detailing'. There was talk too of a William Morris revival which prompted James Stirling's exasperated outburst: 'Let's face it, William Morris was a Swede!'.

One has only to compare the houses at Roehampton with their Swedish predecessors to see what has been lost in the interaction of the Nordic inspiration with the indigenous mix of socialist realism, Modernism and the picturesque. Charles Jencks's characterization of the style – 'pitched roofs, bricky materials, ticky-tacky, cute lattice-work, little nooks and crannies, picturesque profiles all snuggled within a cardboard-like rectitude' – says it all. It was empirical and humane but it was a compromise not a fusion.

The often uninspiring buildings that resulted here and elsewhere from an amalgam of ideas that had produced a building as successful as the Festival Hall needs some explaining. There were many factors,

Figure 16.5
Low-rise housing at Alton East, Roehampton, south-west London.

among them the dilution of such ideas in the new setting of British industrial culture, the comparative lack of money and materials and the inadequacy of the designers. But out of an increasingly confused language of mixed industrial and traditional materials, and of prefabricated and traditional ways of constructing buildings, that led often to tacky compromises, can be seen the problem that a house like Markelius's addressed no more than its less successful British successors. In an industrial society geared to growth and endless expansion, contact with the natural, except through the artificial, like on film, or in zoo or garden, would become ever rarer. What you don't know about is difficult to miss. If contact with the natural is everlastingly shrinking, the images and metaphors of that necessary contact inevitably degrade. The slightly earlier mythmaking of Britain as an Edenic paradise expressed by British artists like Vaughan Williams in music, Powell in film, or Nash in painting, was not pursuable convincingly after the war in the socially intertwined activity of architecture, even when this derived from Scandinavia. There, rural myths and Modernism could hold together for a little longer; the British, without yet coming to terms with it, were by then substituting suburbia and its natural fringes of friendly countryside, and not just preferring it (like Betjeman), but mistaking it for the wild. Because the thinking behind the new towns, and of the British followers of Markelius's revivification of Larsson's house (itself a recall of the primitive hut) was essentially suburban, the resulting buildings lost much of that ecstatic connection of sun, nature, and a humane comfortable way of life. In Britain, in what became of the new towns and despite a few ventures for the middle class like the Span estates, ideas of community atrophied, as did the essential Swedish empathy with the wild. It was, rather, the tamed that characterized British design, eventually reducing the connection with nature to the symbiotic cord between garden centre and that private plaything, the suburban garden. The social dimension was gone, and the empathy between little humans and nature in that Swedish photograph confined to a degree that warps.

17   The ark makers

Increasingly effective military technology, and human stupidity, had led the supposedly cultured nations of Europe to kill millions of each other's citizens in the Great War. The area of land in which the fighting took place was however comparatively small, especially on the Western Front where most of the casualties occurred within a three-mile strip of France and Belgium. There as elsewhere they were usually military casualties. By contrast, in the Second World War the growth of air power with the indiscriminate blitzing of cities and the repressive nature of German and Japanese occupation, meant that many civilians were directly affected. They experienced instant ruination of their buildings, and they had similar experiences as they sheltered from the bombs above or under ground to those of the military when they were in their bunkers. It was from the confined metallic spaces of aeroplanes, ships, tanks and other vehicles that men attacked, but their command headquarters and the defences would be behind reinforced concrete if there had been time to construct it. Military lines were protected by bunkered fortifications. Before the war the French had built a linear underground concrete city, the Maginot Line, complete with hospitals, restaurants, cinemas, sports halls and connecting electric rail links, along the German border. As war progressed and the Germans were on the defensive they strengthened two bunker lines in the west, the Atlantic Wall and the Siegfried Line. Whether a German soldier in a gun emplacement bunker on the Atlantic Wall or a civilian in a city concrete shelter, or if British in a military pillbox or a street shelter (or that peculiarly British DIY alternative, the Anderson shelter), both soldiers and civilians experienced confined spaces with thick walls securing them from possible onslaught.

The First World War had seen air battles take the form of medieval combat complete with duels, chivalry and legendary individuals fighting over a mythic landscape and a just cause. Biggles, the popular creation of Captain W. E. Johns, spread this picture of aerial warfare. London and other British cities had been bombed by Zeppelin airships and biplanes, but these raids were sporadic affairs during which bombs were dropped overboard from the gondola of the Zeppelin or the open cockpit of the plane. The results of these usually solo raids were startling in their effects but had only a limited impact – both physically and upon the imagination.

This perception changed after the Fascist air attacks of the Spanish Civil War such as the raid on Guernica, the subject of Picasso's great mural. The horror of these raids by German dive-bombers raised the question of how many would be killed and injured in another war, if that should come. An extrapolation from Great War figures of the number of casualties caused in relation to bomb tonnage dropped produced alarming predictions of hundreds of thousands of victims should German bombs come raining down on British cities. Following these events and such speculations, the aeroplane became more of a fearful image and less a source of enthusiasm for a new machine age.

It was a change that can be traced even in the work of Le Corbusier, whose utopian optimism held at bay as much as anyone could the threats posed by his beloved air-machines. In 1922 he illustrated his 'Plan for a Contemporary City' by perspectives that show peaceful biplanes circling dreamily like butterflies amongst the tall buildings. But for his Ville Radieuse project of the mid-1930s flitting butterflies have been replaced by drawings of bombs falling on the widely spaced tower blocks of the new city. Le Corbusier attempted to give added credence to his architecture by its supposedly bomb-resistant qualities.

The Second World War brought the fear of the aeroplane and bomb to everyone. Nowhere in Britain or Europe was safe. It was the blitz on London and other cities, experienced in itself or through the newsreel films, that imprinted the devastating impact of aerial bombardment on the psyche. But unlike the RAF's almost total destruction of such German cities as Dresden, the Luftwaffe's bomb damage was limited in extent. When the rubble-filled streets were cleared and unsafe buildings shored up, another order was superimposed upon the destruction. Among the still standing ruins and the bulldozed heaps of rubble could be seen the geometrical order of serried rows of basements amid the rectangular and curving lines of streets. The ruins of London, where shops had been reduced to a brick ground plan, looked like those of Pompeii to Cecil Beaton, Graham Greene and others.

Henry Moore's drawing 'The Farringdon Road' shows a similar scene where a bomb crater had exposed a basement to the street. Moore found himself 'strangely excited by the bombed buildings, still more by the unbelievable scenes and life of the underground shelters'. The impulse to go to earth came as the air raids began. The half-buried Anderson shelter in the garden was a response borrowed from the First World War

(a)

(b)

Figure 17.1a–b
Drawings by Henry Moore of people sleeping on the London Underground during the Second World War: (a) 'Pink and Green Sleepers' (1941) and (b) 'Tube Shelter Scene' (1941). Courtesy of the Henry Moore Foundation.

and not all that secure. In the East End of London, where the raids became heaviest, the search for protection led to the people sheltering in the deep underground stations of the Tube system. It was Kenneth Clark's inspiration in commissioning Henry Moore to draw the scenes in the Tubes that was to give this nightly life underground its most distinctive portrayal.

The simplest of Moore's sketches are drawings that record more or less realistically the positions of the resting and sleeping shelterers and their surroundings. Some show how human dignity can hold up under stress. Others transform these images in differing ways suggesting figures lost or spectral. Yet others, looking like medieval effigies, metamorphose into drawn versions of his earlier reclining sculptures where archetypal ideas of women's fertility and an eternally regenerative sheltering landscape resonate. It was this possible transmutation of fear and destruction through the agency of the sheltering earth that excited Moore. The son of a miner, Moore had experienced the protection of trenches whilst at the front in the First World War, a background which helps explain the particular nature of his own art. Now with cities in ruins he sensed the possibility of a new civilization arising from the collapse of the old order, a civilization where the protective, nurturing attributes of the earth would be given proper place.

This perception was reinforced by vegetation sprouting everywhere amongst the ruins. It was most notable where destruction had been greatest, the bombed German cities. In her novel, *The Black Laurel*, published in 1947, Storm Jameson vividly described the nightmarish scene:

Sprawling pyramids of dust, of shattered brick; the skeletons of buildings leaning over ossuaries of splintered stone and dust ... acres of reddish dust. Carcasses of tanks, burnt-out cars. The torn out megalithic bones, corroded by fire, of a railway station. Perspectives only of ruins.

In his later study entitled *Berlin 45 – The Grey City*, Richard Brett-Smith noted the invasion of the ruins by nature:

Shrubs dirty but determined and weeds, grass and wispy flowers forced their way up through stones and masonry, and among rusty iron and steel. The greenery of the ruins was forlorn but it throve mysteriously and lavishly.

Just as he noted nature's survival so he remarked upon,

the almost unbelievable way in which people managed to live in some of these ruins. A new race of troglodytes was born, one or other of whom would pop up from nowhere, periodically, at one's feet among rank weeds and rubble.

Again and again the response to the aftermath of war seems to have been of surprise and even shock. Out of the ruins of mankind's shattered dreams of civilization sprang new life and with it new hope. It is almost as if it needed a war of the magnitude wrought by machines of devastation to remind mankind of the Romantic truth of nature's eternal power of regeneration. But there had been other shocks which struck deeper blows to the psyche and perhaps prompted the post-war architectural response to be rather different from simply rebuilding in the same manner.

As the war neared its end two profoundly important events occurred. One was finding the death camps of the Nazis, the other the dropping of the first atomic bombs, an event compounded in the following years by the development of more devastating nuclear weaponry from the hydrogen to the cobalt and neutron bombs. The gas attacks feared before the war had not happened, nor had bacterial or other chemical warfare, but atomic bombs had been developed and used. Some grasped immediately that this meant for the first time that humans if they so wished, or if they made a big enough mistake, could destroy not only themselves, but the rest of the natural world.

An opposite view could be taken. The bomb had stopped the war in its tracks, maybe it would stop all war. The use of atomic power for peaceful purposes made some feel optimistic. At a popular material level 'atomic' took on the implications of a new age, of a better future. Vacuum cleaners, central heating boilers, all kinds of powered things were called 'atomic', and most powerfully of all the new minimal swim wear was called the Bikini, after the place where the bomb was being 'improved'. The shapes of the atomic age, the pressure vessels, the diagrams and models explaining the unseen processes became incorporated into decorative forms. In that last incarnation of International Style architecture in the 1951 Festival of Britain, models of atomic reaction were a leitmotif in both the buildings and their furnishings. Levity and assumptions of atomic progress could not be sustained though, by all, or for long. Architecture was to be affected by other ways of looking at what was happening, when after the euphoria as war ended, the memory of experiences undergone and the events that had occurred were turned over in the mind: of life in the bunkers or shelters, of the pessimism brought on by the evidence of human cruelty, and above all by the changes to come caused by the bomb.

The destructive force – unimaginable before 1945 – of the first atom bombs was to jangle the time scales in the imagination. The feeling that a sort of instant fossilization had taken place began to form following stories from Hiroshima that told of the shadows of humans, disintegrated by the blast, whose outline had been etched into the concrete and stone of the city. These were man-made equivalents to the natural cataclysm at Pompeii where the hot lava of erupting Vesuvius evoked the processes of fossilization in the footprints, even bodies, of the fleeing populace, caught and preserved in the rock. But the magnitude of the destructive power seen in the ruins of Hiroshima bore no comparison. Yet in a curious presaging of James Lovelock's 'Gaia' theory, whilst human life might be totally destroyed, reduced to a shadow by the bomb, nature would recover. Just four and a half weeks after Hiroshima's bomb this was the scene described:

Over everything – up through the wreckage of the city, in gutters, along the river banks, tangled among tiles and tin roofing, climbing on charred tree-trunks – was a blanket of fresh, vivid, optimistic green: the verdancy rose even from the foundation of the ruined homes. Weeds already hid the ashes, and wild flowers were in bloom among the city's bones.

Even if the benefits of the atom were to outweigh the risks, the burden that had to be borne was enormous. With the invisible additional threat from radiation beginning to be known, no one involved could be carefree. Pulling the wrong switch, whether in power station or rocket silo, would have consequences beyond the unleashing of any previous power source. In the power stations, aside from the weaponry, the fuel rods were corralled in lead and the thickest of concrete enclosures. Even for this peaceful use so much protection was needed. Against this power and the massive effort, physical and intellectual needed to contain it, the architecture of the Festival, light, purposely insubstantial, felt inappropriate: just as the late Baroque must have felt two centuries earlier to those facing a new order, which demanded of them a reassessment of fundamentals. In architecture that review turned again to the past, and to the primitive, this time not for revivifying progress, but for ideas of how to hide-out.

The new modern, yet ancient, language of a way of building in concrete that Le Corbusier called Brut after its deliberately rough shuttered surfaces, had been anticipated by painters and sculptors as well as by the defensive architecture of the war and the protective cocooning of atomic power. Moore, for example, began a series of room drawings that took up the themes of shelter from his Tube sketches. The first were single cell-like enclosures in which are disposed forms derived from his earlier sculpture. The rooms have rough-textured walls with windows like the lookout slits in defensive pillboxes. Later in the series family groups of figures stand as if about to leave the rooms, which now have greater spatial complexity, their walls patterned as if with the board marks of shuttered concrete that Brut was later to propose as a proper backdrop for civil life.

Le Corbusier himself had hinted at the change to come in his Petite Maison de Weekend. Designed in 1934, just three years after the Villa Savoie, it is the antithesis of that house as flying machine. Here is earthy, rough brickwork, a vaulted concrete roof pulling the interior space down to earth, grass on the concrete roof, and the genesis of this new architecture shown as a concrete-framed primitive hut amongst the trees of the garden. Civilians having suffered from the now obsolete power of high explosive had surely to have the highest possible protection against the new power. This remained reinforced concrete, thicker than in the recent past and with lead, water- and air-conditioning as added refinements against contamination. In this architecture, soon called the New Brutalism, these ingredients appeared in varying configurations in a generation of buildings which, particularly in Britain, spoke of an impulse to build with illogical heaviness and with materials of extreme dourness.

The first brut buildings of Le Corbusier were different from this, the brut concrete and heavy forms leavened by modern evocations of Provençal folk tradition, the patently archaic craftsmanship and the symbiotic relationship between these buildings and the ancient forms of Mediterranean pre-Hellenic culture. The two linked houses, the Maisons Jaoul (1922–24), that Le Corbusier built in the Bois de Boulogne are the most obviously related to war-time shelters. They are family houses whose forms can be seen as wrested from the imagery of the air-raid shelter, to be made sufficiently commodious for comfortable family living. Using the same forms and constructional techniques as the Petite Maison de Weekend, these are more defensive in appearance, the solidity of the rough brick walls and the massive concrete horizontal bands prevailing over the freely punched-out window panels. The interior is full of light but all surfaces are heavy with texture: rough, flush mortared brick walls, board marked concrete and clay tiles on the low vaulted ceiling. From within this earthy enclosure we cautiously peep out. Badger's conversion of those abandoned basements within the Wild Wood comes to mind when thinking of the psychological shift Le Corbusier made in moving from those elegant exposed pre-war houses to the cruder but snugger and tougher forms of the Maisons Jaoul.

Figure 17.2
Le Corbusier, Maisons Jaoul, Paris.

(a)

(b)

Figure 17.3a–b
Unité d'Habitation.

The Maisons Jaoul are air-raid shelters with their insides scooped-out to accommodate domestic life, but a life that is protected by the totems of defence – solidity, the reminder of certain forms, a sense of impregnability – against the psychological threat of a warring peace. The two houses share an underground car park which has the connotation of a residual deep shelter. This air-raid shelter of a house is lifted above ground and opened up to be only nominally, psychologically defensible but it has this deeper shelter immediately convertible into a physically safer space.

It is quite possible that the building of the Atlantic Wall by the Nazis after the fall of France acted as a catalyst for the change in Le Corbusier's architecture. Although his attitude to materials had changed before 1939 – as can be seen in his paintings as well as the Petite Maison de Weekend – immediately after the war the appearance of his buildings is transformed by this radical use of rough concrete and massive forms. In the late 1940s and early 1950s after the terrible war, Le Corbusier seized upon the image of the bunker as he had seized upon the image of the aeroplane in the 1920s.

His first project after the Second World War was the Unité d'Habitation in Marseilles where he translated his urban theories of high-rise living into the new brut vocabulary. In a family house this was one thing; in a gigantic collection of 337 apartments quite another. The idea of protective strength is made apparent by suppressing all the fragile, user-scale elements such as windows and doors. These are set back deep within the building shadowed by the thick concrete frame and brise-soleil (sunbreakers). Rather than reading the building as a hollowed out container of human activity, we instead see it only at the sculptural scale more like a Greek temple with its surrounding colonnade.

Seen from afar, massively rising above its surroundings, it may have this implication, but it could not be removed from its role as a honeycomb of human occupation. Each apartment has a double height living space that looks out to the mountains and the sea. With the section Le Corbusier contrives spaces of deep withdrawal from the balconied living space of sun and air like those of his city for three million. The brise-soleil not only manipulates the scale of the building and gives a sense of muscular protection, but also casts shadow into the interior. This marks that shift in his view of the house as an open machine for living in, to the more complex protective, post-war response. Le Corbusier began to explore a reciprocity between darkness and light as the basis of the sacred, an exploration which found final expression in 'Le Poeme de l'Angle Droit'. In this illustrated prose poem he shows how the dark fecunding earth and the warm sun are the reciprocal forces at work in natural growth. It was probably in some such way that he imagined post-war human psychological life would renew itself within the massive protective concrete carapace of the Unité.

The building is lifted above the ground by muscular columns, and is capped by an artificial landscape of sculptural forms. Hoisted to the very top of the building the men, women and children can come from their dim communal streets in the heart of the building to play like gods, at least in altitude. With the surrounding town screened by high solid balustrades and the roof terrace on a level with the surrounding hills, these ordinary humans are metaphorically where only the heroic aviator had formerly kept company with the birds – and the gods.

But it was Le Corbusier's use of rough, board-marked concrete that caused such a stir. The young James Stirling, expecting the machine aesthetic, noted with discernible shock the rough, crude concrete construction of the Maisons Jaoul: 'technologically they make no advance on medieval building'. Banham also struggled to make sense of this changed use of concrete at the Unité, observing how Le Corbusier exploited 'its crudities, and those of the wooden framework to produce an architectural surface of rugged grandeur that seems to echo that of the well-weathered Doric columns of temples in Magna Graecia'. In quite the opposite spirit of his earlier striving for a machine-like finish, Le Corbusier now used rough sawn boards for the shuttering that left the concrete with fossil-like impressions of the grain and knots in the surface. Le Corbusier came to see concrete itself as a kind of 'natural' material analogous to stone for it was constituted literally from material as old as the earth itself.

Cast into the base of the building (with perhaps Hiroshima in mind) are sunken reliefs of Le Corbusier's modular man, his reinterpretation of the mathematically unified figure of the Renaissance ideal man. Le Corbusier's figure stands erect, one arm raised in a pose reminiscent of the Cerne Abbas giant incised in the Dorset chalk. The arm is heroically raised in defiance – the figure speaks of knowing the grimness of the present, but also of a need for humanist transformation that would forge a language of reconstruction and hope.

His other major buildings from this period, the Chapel of Notre-Dame-du-Haut at Ronchamp, and the monastery of Sainte-Marie-de-la-Tourette, use the same vocabulary with the forms adjusted to meet their religious purposes. The thick battered south wall at Ronchamp is perforated with slits and embrasures just like a bunker. But the slashing

Figure 17.4
Notre-Dame-du-Haut, Ronchamp, south-eastern France. © Archiv Burkhard-Verlag, Ernst Heyer, D-45138 Essen, aus *Baukunst unserer zeit.*

horizontal slit between the soaring roof and wall is in total contrast with the crouched homogenously connected roof-to-wall junction of bunkers. It is like that of a bunker unseated by bombardment, the reinforcing rods in the concrete barely holding the structure together. This redeployment of the forms changes the meaning. Light pours in the slit between roof and walls (which are not military grey but pacifically white). The slits and holes in the wall are filled with coloured glass to light the interior as a house of God, as the first Christian churches had transformed pagan temples of earlier times. The cave-like interior is further metamorphosed by the slit between wall and roof which, in the dark interior, strikes a line of light as if a high horizon. For twentieth-century man, so recently given over to destructive activities, this metaphoric conversion of bunker to chapel yet retaining the idea of the earth's protection and regeneration was a heroic achievement and heroically appropriate.

In other hands than Le Corbusier's though, with the added regularity that more mechanical forms of concrete construction gave, the folk traditions of ancient building, redolent of the primitive hut, made way for a way of building literally similar to its military bunker and civilian shelter origins. In 1967 an anonymous contributor to *Architectural Design* remarked that the 'forms and finishes of military installations are being used for the most hallowed of new buildings – cultural and civic centres. Throughout Europe and even in America architects are setting up their own culture bunkers'. This phrase entered popular speech in Britain where it referred in particular to the culture bunkers on the South Bank; the Hayward Gallery, the Queen Elizabeth Hall, and later the National Theatre were designed in variations of Brutalist style. With the Royal Festival Hall remaining as a major achievement of the Festival of Britain, the South Bank has a group of buildings that show the dramatic change from late International Style to the New Brutalism derived from Corbusian brut. The Hayward Gallery is the earliest, most crudely assembled of the group in its forms and details, while the National Theatre, the last to be built, projects a no less powerful image notwithstanding its greater refinement. The metaphoric toughness of the bunker

(a)

(b)

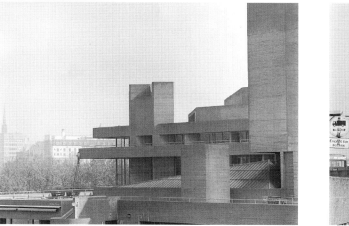

(c)

(d)

Figure 17.5a–d
'Culture bunkers' on London's South Bank: The Queen Elizabeth Hall and the National Theatre.

hangs over all three, parts of the Queen Elizabeth Hall appearing almost literally like images from Hitler's Atlantic Wall.

In these South Bank culture bunkers the process of change that overtook Corbusian brut becomes apparent. Here brut has become northern Brutalism, its dourer tonalities the expression of northern Romantic impulses. The forms of this group of buildings, and of the concrete walkways that wind asymmetrically around them, feel like an abstracted landscape – a craggy northern landscape – modelled in surrogate concrete. Perhaps in its conception it was also hoped to evoke the rocky outcrops of a northern landscape as had the sculptures of Henry Moore. But as it now appears these northern, picturesque connotations are grubbier. For me, as for many, it has on a grey day an openly forbidding military character.

The imagery of fortress, in its modern form of bunker, is carried by both the maze of external walkways which are like some trench-linking systems brought above ground into view, and by the seemingly random-shaped, crouched and massive forms with their associated air inlets and vents which it is easy to imagine feeding the fortified undercrofts below. These buildings, insofar as their actual function will allow, do replicate the command posts, observation points, shelters and gun emplacements of the Atlantic Wall.

Figure 17.6
James Stirling, Ham Common flats, south-west London.

In the Hayward Gallery, unlike the other two buildings that are constrained by the need to provide large spaces for theatre and concert hall, is a maze-like warren that continues the feel of bunker into the interior. Variously shaped spaces with raw concrete walls and coffered concrete ceilings are interrupted by seemingly arbitrary, constricting bottlenecks and unexpected changes of level. Space does not flow from one volume to another with any ease and after repeated use, even for an architect trained to see these things, it is difficult to comprehend the sectional and plan forms of the building in relation to the site. I have not yet been to an exhibition that has overcome the feeling that this art gallery has been converted from a military bunker.

All over the country, town halls, hospitals, office blocks, housing and car parks were springing up, substituting vision slits and firing loopholes for conventional window shapes whenever possible. The grey of concrete in a variety of poured and precast finishes, left with shutter marks, bush-hammered, or faced with a variety of stony aggregates, seemed mandatory. There seemed to be much agreement that surfaces should be hard, very hard, and a willingness to settle for only surrogate versions of nature in the city – of which those aggregates and board-marks were the most subtle and the most enduring that could be expected.

Where brick or concrete blocks were used as the main material rather than concrete, architects adopted the treatment Le Corbusier had applied to the Maisons Jaoul – perhaps recalling also the flimsier British pill-boxes constructed of brick and concrete. Stirling and Gowan's Ham Common Flats are the best known example of this, if rather less defensive in appearance than their precursors. But in the similar language of the Cambridge School of Architecture extensions, the bunker connotations appear in a tougher version that does away with the frail plywood spandrel panels of the Maisons Jaoul in favour of more defensively workmanlike slits for windows. All over Europe these bunker-like images proliferated: the Ingolstadt Theatre by Hard and Marie Haner, the Canton School, Schaffhausen and the extraordinary fortress-like church at Betlach by Walter Förderer, to mention but a few.

It was in the large housing estates where this style was adopted that the paradox of providing such a form of shelter became most keenly felt. In the largest housing estate of all, Park Hill in Sheffield, the long cranked lines of interlocking blocks of flats set in a bleak landscape look on the architect's plan like the trench lines of some fortified position, an appropriate ground base to the grim imagery of these flats. Solid, heavily-built concrete bulkheads against surprise attack, these buildings should have allowed people to feel secure. But the more fortress-like, the more hostile was the popular reaction. Their bunker-like aesthetic conveyed the impression to people that they inhabited some of the hardware of the military's recent past.

Reyner Banham had remarked that Le Corbusier's 'concrete work at (the Unité d'Habitation) Marseilles started as a magnificent ruin even before the building was completed'. Just like Badger, in the ruins of one order, perhaps it was possible to construct another life. It was such transformation of defensive imagery, in which the building voluntarily lays down its arms, anticipating its own sundering, that marked the great skill of Le Corbusier. Few other architects grasped this, hence only a very few Brutalist buildings could resist popular disapproval – Aldo van Eyck's Orphanage in Amsterdam, and some of the work of the Swiss Atelier 5 being examples that would pass the test.

The fundamental transmutations made by Le Corbusier had changed the necessary imagery of the deep shelter, bunker and atomic pile, by reminding us of the enduring architectural past and the resources to be found in folk traditions in their relationship to nature, while still showing awareness of the perilous present. From Ronchamp and the Maisons Jaoul to James Stirling's Flats at Ham Common was a short journey in time, but a long one in terms of a shift from hope to, well, stoicism at best. All these, together with so much other housing built over the succeeding ten years or so, are literally primitive huts. They shelter their inhabitants in the strongest way, both actually and expressively from the dangers of their age and place. They show what many thousands of houses in both Europe and America were actually like, as behind their average facades they housed the newly-dug fallout shelters and emergency foodstocks. In their relationship to natural forms they recall – Le Corbusier's strongly, others more faintly – the response of earlier elemental cultures to the natural world before technology changed things so much. In the reduced microscopic surrogate nature of their concrete, aping stone and suggesting just the presence of basic life-forms on its surfaces, they tell of bare survival if what they fear comes to pass. For these houses are primitive huts, but made ready as arks: waiting for the waters to fall, before normal open life can be resumed.

18 Savage present, savage past: the Herb Greene Prairie House

Just as the Oxford Museum seemed to draw together so many strands of mid-nineteenth century thinking, so does Herb Greene's Prairie House for the mid-twentieth century. Greene was taught by Bruce Goff and built this house for himself and family on the prairie outside Norman, Oklahoma in the American mid-west. I want to discuss it at length for it draws upon that organic tradition running back to Wright, but also it responds to the fear of nuclear apocalypse and to specifically American concerns with the vanishing wilderness.

In the *Architectural Review* the house was described as being like 'a wounded buffalo'. It was most commonly called the prairie chicken house. These descriptions follow Greene's own remarks – in his book *Mind and Image* he says the house has a conscious mother hen image and that he sees this image as an archetypal variation of our need for security and reassurance in our shelter. He adds that the hen image acts to restrain and counter the presence of pain, 'inescapable in life', which is symbolized by the drooping wounded head that dominates one end of the house.

However, to see the house as a brilliant summation of Oklahoma School ideas of the time, or even as an archetypal image of human shelter holding at bay mortal problems expressed by the contrapuntal play between chicken and animal imagery, does not to me exhaust the full implications of its complex forms, which in a general way talk also of nature and industrialization and in a quite specific way of its particular time and place – that of the American mid-west of the 1960s.

This strange house has wooden constructional effects that suggest some fusion of Red Indian, American colonial and north European traditions. It is not at all like the neat balloon-framed and nailed saltbox houses of the early east-coast settlers and it only hints at a connection with those houses' equivalents on the western range. Not evident either are the heavy effects of the earlier western frontier log cabins. Its air of impermanence and something about its roof apex and roof slopes recalls the Red Indian tepee, its predecessor on the prairie, but it entirely eludes the rational constructional symmetry of the tepee. Within the modern organic tradition it most resembles work by Greene's mentor, Bruce Goff – particularly his random shingle roofing technique which, in its turn, recalls the earlier American work of Bernard Maybeck – and in Europe, of course, the buildings of Gaudi.

The controlled anthropomorphism of buffalo and hen in this house seems more like the dragon cult stave churches of Norway than anything else I know, whose dragonish suggestions in their overall forms continue through to their architectural details. Functional junctions of their roofs

(a)

(b)

(c)

(d)

Figure 18.1a–d
The Herb Greene Prairie House. Photos: Herb Greene.

and walls act symbolically as folds between dragon carapaces and flanks. The shingle covered roofs act as scaly skins and roof ridges have a spiny effect. The shingles of Greene's house, though, are not the small chevroned scales of stave church dragon cult. Instead Greene uses heavily graded shingles, many of plank length. Close up the surface abstractly suggests featheriness with the junctions between the planes of the building abstractly suggesting the forms of feathery wings, tail and body. But seen from a distance the shingles merge, the surface texture flattens, featheriness recedes and this change is echoed in the ambivalent profiles of the building. It seems to become less chicken and more buffalo from a distance, with recognizably bowed wounded head.

But the external images of the house contain more than this. A skeletally supported canopy connects to the house's bulk and the canopy's

Figure 18.2
Airstream Trailer: painting by Ralph Goings.

roof climbs to become a louvred grille containing air conditioning equipment and flues. These are not like the porch, canopy or flues of traditional buildings whether stave church, saltbox house or frontier shack. They are elegant versions of the kind of permanent accretion that gets built onto that modern western tepee, the trailer home. Such things sprout around and on trailers that become permanently sited homes. A walk around the building, and there, peeping through between feathery flank walls, is an aluminium window with rounded corners and fluted sheet aluminium panel below it. It is tackier than the back of the Airstream, America's best known trailer made familiar by Ralph Going's painting. But the window is trailerish, a piece of the machine-for-living-in that technology actually made. Discreet trailer-like windows and spandrel panels can be spotted elsewhere in the building. The hint is of a house machine within an anthropomorphic shell, technology within nature.

Adding another range of organic metaphors to that of chicken and buffalo, we might take a clue from the insect-like effect of the canopy legs, and think in terms of insect metamorphosis, to see the trailer machine elements as a coming chrysalis that is about to slough off its nearly spent caterpillar skin. There is a sense of the shingle-covered forms being nearly spent, both in the overall forms particularly of the head, and in the detail of the collaged shingle 'feathers' which ambiguously evoke decay as well as tell of the missing and broken feathers to be expected from the ups and downs of chicken life for a mother hen.

On a Cornish beach I came across a ruined boat where shipwreck and time had produced in the planking similar effects to those of Greene's new shingle 'feathers' – as indeed would any old fence after a storm. A symbolism of decay is in the skin of this house and is a part of its message.

The elegiac sympathy with which the organic forms are handled contrasts with Greene's peremptory tacky way with the machine elements: it confirms his organic bias, his romantic sentiments, but the house implies to me no simple rural escape into the forms or ways of past tradition. If that were to be, the forms would convey the unequivocal confidence in white past and white future of the typical Frank Lloyd Wright western dream house. Besides denying by its forms any simple continuity with the immediate rural past, this little house takes up the question of the relevance of classical tradition. There is a window, a glazed eye, in that dominant wounded head form. It is a large Palladian window placed where the intended symbolization of pain, and by implication of death, is most acute. The window, because of its context, implies disconnection with Classicism. Its use as a dying or dead eye – no longer seeing a way ahead – pungently reverses the optimistic symbolism of the eye to be found in the eighteenth century in the revolutionary classical architecture of architects like Ledoux. Instead, Greene's eye architecturally echoes Scott Fitzgerald's use of the 'unseeing eyes of Dr T. J. Ecklenburg' on the sign that presides over the waste land between Jay Gatsby's house and the city. Greene's unseeing Palladian eye in the mortally wounded 'head' looks instead over the outdoor factory of an artificially fed prairie which had once been dreamed of as an earthly paradise.

A classical Palladian window of this kind is a reference point, an icon even, for Greene's contemporary Robert Venturi in many of his projects including the house he designed for his mother in Pennsylvania. The uses to which Venturi puts this kind of window vary in intention from wanting to produce a frisson of (ironic) nostalgia as in his mother's house, to a jokey pointing out of the troubles that can occur when architects try to achieve classical purity of form and plan. In one of his saltbox revival houses of 1966, Venturi puts a lavatory where it can be partly seen through the house's main Palladian window – which is what you might just see now in one of Palladio's Vicenza originals, as whether it is old buildings that are converted or even new building, modern plumbing and other services can jar ideas of architectural purity.

In Greene's house there is none of that, only the impossibility of reworking classical idioms in a serious way. The placing of the Palladian window infers that it is as dead as makes no matter, or alternatively can only stand for death or atrophy. Given Greene's cast of mind as seen in this building, the classical tradition is tainted with a Ruskinian suspicion of representing an attitude of mind that is responsible, however distantly, for our present machine-age inhumanities. Greene's use of such a motive shares with Venturi a sense of nostalgia but is without Venturi's feeling for the possible re-interpreting of the classical through the use of irony. To Greene the Palladian window is an object of beauty from the past, sadly irrelevant now. W. H. Auden's poem 'New Year Letter' seems expressive of Greene's view and makes clear its separation from that of Venturi: 'The special things begun by the Renaissance have now been done'.

In the outside forms of this house then Greene tells us of tradition under threat, with the new remorseless in its takeover. The inside living spaces enrich and clarify these themes. Venturi's houses adapt the high architectural past to the present by constant reference to pop art techniques of wit, irony, greatly enlarged scale, and Oldenburg-like transpositions of material. In Greene's Prairie House there is wit in the handling of the forms, but no irony. Inside his house trailer-like elements are not permitted. No critical or ironic device could, I feel, for Greene ameliorate the not-to-be-lived-with banality of its aesthetic. Instead Greene's interior is organic with shingle-covered walls and roofs, its floors and staircases are wool carpeted except where function demands ceramic tiles, and these are handmade. The interior is anthropomorphic in texture and the spaces are as if carved out by an animal's body to make its burrow. These free-form curved spaces are Expressionist in the way that they twist and warp. There are simultaneous memories of the angular Expressionism of the interiors in 'The Cabinet of Dr Caligari' and of the feeling for rounded Expressionist burrows in Frederick Kiesler's Endless House. But this Expressionist disorientation, both angular and curved, is held back in Greene's house by its consoling surface textures and natural furnishings. Also in this interior an American Way of Life takes place and whether this is a matter of happy parties or of hominy grits for breakfast or of the downs as well as the ups of family life, such activity must deflect, if only by its almost surreal incongruity, the suggestion of plain terror in the interior forms.

The view of the open prairie seen through the elegant Classicism of the Palladian window from the carpeted, furred and shingled interior confirms those aspects of the interior which suggest shelter, comfort and security. It is however only necessary to imagine Greene's consoling surfaces replaced by the mucus-like textures of Kiesler's journey into Kafka's Burrow or by the hard-edged Dada collages of Dr Caligari to see how near this interior is to an Expressionist scream.

The inventive architecture of Frank Lloyd Wright's middle years was a paradigm to American architects working, however loosely, within the organic tradition. Bruce Goff's use within this tradition of mass produced, sometimes scrap, industrial bits and pieces made the connection tight between this organic tradition and the increasingly machine-based facts of mid-western life. To Greene, younger than Goff, the machinery is less novel, more ordinary. His openness to the increasing plight of traditional values compel from him a house whose forms expose stress. The moment felt and expressed by Greene is of European and east-coast angst reaching his view of life in the American mid-west.

The multiple levels of meaning can now perhaps be connected. The wounded image seen from the distance crouching on the prairie is a monument to the destruction of the buffalo and his hunter the plains Indian. Its closer-up resolution into hen provides symbolic as well as actual shelter, the splayed feather skirts of the building making explicit the connection with earth and with earth mother. The play between images of chicken and buffalo can be seen in another way. The wild buffalo gives way to the domestic animal, the chicken. But mother hen nowadays is not allowed to look after her own – battery machines have taken over. We are back to those discreet trailer elements and their pervasive significance. And so the building tells of brash new technology which the trailer symbolizes, threatening to sweep away humanist architecture, ecological balance, old ways of living. The trailer machine is to be seen as emerging from a cultural endgame with previous traditions as represented by the decaying wooden house forms. The idea of the machine as potential destroyer is confirmed by the vertiginous interior where the idea of machine as house is refuted, but where the organic and the traditional is shown racked by the fear and the effects of our machine age.

Greene's house is as crucial a development within the organic traditions as was Venturi's house to Postmodernism. Venturi gathers fragments of Classicism and the commonsense vigour of early settler building plus other things that appeal, and he launders the mixture for re-use. Greene, by contrast, looks atavistically back to an earlier America:

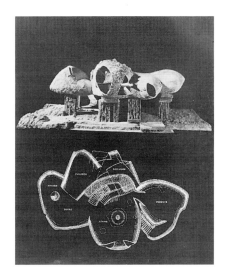

Figure 18.3
Kiesler, Endless House project: experimental dwelling of the 1960s.

to the more settled ecology of buffalo and tepee before the advent of settler and dustbowl. His passing elegy to Classicism in the Palladian window floats within this larger concern. By a mastery of form and texture his vision is given wide mythic force. The building ponders, in miniature, the gains and losses of man's evolution from the archaic past to the rushing present. It is a reinterpretation of the experience of the primitive, avoiding emotional distancing through irony, or a too-literal use of sources. Instead the house evokes, in the aspects which intend this, what the habitat of pre-rational man must have been like to himself.

Since Rousseau a way of imagining the experience of the primitive has been through memories of childhood, that is through our earlier primitive selves. In Herb Greene's house childhood is remembered, and used to help express his adult concern with what it was like to be earlier, much earlier, in the human race. His house echoes those childhood 'pretend' houses of our early games like the first made of sheets and raised knees when tucked up in bed, or other later houses made of driftwood on the shore, or of wood and string in hedge, tree and backyard. Wherever it is, the 'pretend' house that got built had to glean its materials from its surroundings.

The mid-west rural dustbowl of the inter-war years, we can see now, was one of the dress rehearsals for future large scale ecological disaster. Greene was a child in depression America. His adult house, a flapping chicken/buffalo shack on the prairie, is grounded in the wrecked and decaying shacks made familiar to him and us in movies like *The Grapes of Wrath* and *Of Mice and Men*, realizing their essence through the unique act of building a childhood 'pretend' house.

Elegy to the past and allegory of the duel between man and himself in his handling of machines and nature – these are issues implied by the forms of the house. But its architectural power transcends my extraction of such meanings, and this is another way in which Greene differs from Venturi whose didactic buildings usually have the meanings offered in literary description and where the written idea can sometimes be stronger than the architectural effect. His statement is made indissolubly and eloquently through his architecture for you and I to clearly see. The house's forms are ambivalent, the message is of conflict. Is it optimistic or pessimistic? Greene's realism about the decay of living traditions seems to infer that any hope of regaining balance between man's technology and nature, has to come from what the chrysalis of the trailer age will eventually metamorphose into. I think that to Herb Greene the chrysalis could become a wonderful butterfly – a machine age of sense and balance. His subsequent work seems to confirm his essential optimism. It is more likely to be others, often Europeans like me, who would point out that butterflies don't last long, or that chrysalids don't always last out the winter to become butterflies at all.

In those nuclear times the possibility of a real or mythic Paradise was overtaken by the need for mythic places of possible escape and survival. Only to those who did not see the situation clearly was there any possibility of real shelter in the face of nuclear apocalypse. Nuclear shelters were too ineffectual and too few, their reality was constricting and just too nasty for them to act as actual, let alone imaginatively acceptable refuges from the threat of destruction. In the States imagination had to invent new retreats elsewhere, for some with the help of drugs or religion. One of the more material ideas, looking back at such cultural inventions over the past decades, has been to take up the old ideas of a Golden West, before depression, before the despoliation of settlers, and

Figure 18.4
'Christine's World': painting by Andrew Wyeth, evoking the American mid-west dream of Greene's childhood.

remake of it a last frontier in the west behind which the imagination can shelter from the threat of holocaust, and where the company of Indian and wilderness can provide solace. In place of white settler cabins and townships as centres of order is the Indian tepee. On this imaginary frontier only Thoreau and his kind of white man can stand, ashamed, with the Indian. Other white men and their settlements stand for destruction and a savagery that is worse than that of Indians, a savagery that is our own and a way of thinking that eventually produced the inventions of Los Alamos. On this frontier the Indian and those of us others who are ashamed enough connect in mutual grief – as well as in enjoyment and engagement with the wild. It is not just a frontier of escape but also of confrontation with the essential. Indian society and its natural surroundings were broken up by our forebears just as now our society may break under nuclear war or ecological disaster. There is no escape on this imagined frontier, only solace and perhaps renewal.

For above all Greene's house is a last house, a stricken symbolic object on the prairie after eco-disaster or even nuclear white-out, a crystallization of our worst imaginings, insisting through its forms on the inevitability of an atavistic regression in any survival after apocalypse. Such a last house looks back to the architectural tradition of the primitive hut – to the hermit's cell in the picturesque garden of the eighteenth century – and forward to the unavoidable primitivism of a post-apocalyptic future. Such themes whether of last man, last house or last town obsess our time, of course. In 1968 Jean-Luc Godard made the film *Weekend* the end of which showed Europeans returning to a cannibal life of tom-tom, cookpot and campfire. Its cowboy and Indian frontier trappings show typically how widespread such American Western connections are for such nightmare themes.

If Herb Greene's Prairie House catches something of the anguish of the Cuban missile crisis, now that the cold war has been replaced in our nightmares by global warming perhaps the time has come round again to respond to its message.

19 Green trials

As the immediate threat of nuclear destruction began to subside and the cold war settled down into frosted stand off, a new and even more insidious threat was identified. As a biologist, Rachel Carson had concerned herself through the 1940s and '50s with the detailed observation of the biological world and its relationships. Unlike the usual science textbooks her writings described the poetry of the observable relationships between the micro and macro natural worlds. In *The Sea Around Us*, written in 1951, she described taking a species of flat worm into the laboratory for further observation:

Twice each day the Convoluta rises out of the sand in the bottom of the aquarium, into the light of the sun, and twice each day it sinks again into the soil. Without a brain, or what we would call memory, or even any very clear perception, Convoluta continues to live out its life in this alien place, remembering, in every fibre of its small green body, the tidal rhythm of the distant sea.

Rachel Carson wrote *The Silent Spring* in 1962, the year of Herb Greene's house. This time her poetic prose was used to describe the fearful prospect of a world without birdsong, without the background humming and ticking of the insect world. It described how those animals with apparently the most advanced brains and memory banks, the human race, reorder their natural environment through the indiscriminate use of pesticides.

After the relief of the Bay of Pigs incident and the apparent progress of the civil rights movement, the USA and most of Western Europe had new hopes dashed with the death of the 'young' John F. Kennedy. This and the tragedy of the death of Martin Luther King so shortly after his heartstopping 'dream' speech together with the subsequent death of Robert Kennedy in a televised assassination, began to temper the optimism of the post-war generation. More than anything the involvement of the USA in Vietnam from 1965, resulting in the full scale draft of young men for active service, transformed many clean cut American teenagers into radical activists. Television brought the sights and sounds of Vietnam into homes on a daily basis. These were not sanitized newsreels, the juxtaposition of helicopter gunships and thatched huts was telling. The massive US technological input into Vietnam seemed, to some, to reinforce science and technology as the harbingers of doom. For others it created a crisis of confidence in science and technology. How could such a massive technological input be failing to deal with a relatively underdeveloped foe? Science was out of control, progress was accelerating the world into the abyss despite being unable to 'deliver the goods'. In parallel, NASA sent up mission after mission. In 1967 *Apollo 8* sent back its pictures of earth from space. This image was to transform our perception of the planet: it was indeed a spaceship earth and from a distance the greens and blues of nature showed it to be unbelievably beautiful.

Some of the children raised on the excitement and optimism of space exploration and science fiction turned against the technological future offered. By the late 1960s the spring of campus riots and civil rights demonstrations led on to the 'summer of love'. Half a million young and not so young people crammed onto Yazgers Farm at Woodstock, and to 'camp out on the land and set your soul free' (Joni Mitchell) became a prime objective. For the many for whom this event was more than a pop festival, the texts and the ideas were already in place for them to develop. The beat poets and writers such as Ginsberg and Kerouac had documented their physical and spiritual journeys. A growing number of scientists began to question the imperative of greater production through chemical and technical intervention. The pursuit of property and commodity was replaced by the pursuit of experience.

The work of anthropologists such as Claude Lévi-Strauss found itself into the curriculum of architectural schools. Rudofsky's *Architecture without Architects*, as we saw earlier, explored traditional dwellings with a new view and demonstrated the clarity of function and structure in such buildings and the total integration of lifestyle in three-dimensional form. The primitive hut, albeit in examples from Swaziland and Central and South America was back at the centre of a new branch of architectural enquiry.

Post-war austerity in Britain gave way to the 'swinging '60s' and the youth culture emerged not only as a new social and economic force but also as an increasingly vociferous political one. For those who had found so much excitement in the Saturday morning episodes of Flash Gordon or the *Eagle* comic's Dan Dare, a new kind of technological vision was emerging. The intelligent, even robotic building was one of the new visions. The house as 'machine for living in' was taken beyond even the newest technology by groups such as Archigram in the 1960s. In Walking City (1963), giant self-contained living pods, their forms derived from a combination of insect and machine, were proposed which would roam the cities. They would be autonomous but potentially parasitic in that they could 'plug in' to sites of experience to exchange occupants or renew their energy sources. The stable, fixed city was dead. A future of light, movement and superexperience was within reach.

In Japan the Metabolists proposed megacities, such as Ocean City by Kikutake in 1962, who expressed the two elements of his city as the permanent and the temporary. Kenzo Tange had spoken in similar terms:

The structural element is thought of as a tree – a permanent element, with the dwelling units as leaves – temporary elements which fall down and are renewed according to the needs of the moment.
        Kenzo Tange, *CIAM '59 in Otterloo*, Oscar Newman, ed. (1961)

Space City by Isozaki (1960) and the Helicoids project for the Ginza area of Tokyo by Kurokawa (1961) created visions of a high density, high speed future. Reyner Banham refers to 1964 as 'Megayear', when megalopolis and the megacity had captured the imagination of designers everywhere. It seemed possible that the 1914 Futurist cities of Sant'

Elia and the Metropolis of Fritz Lang's film of the same name were to be the blueprint for the future.

For the children of Woodstock, the fixed city was also dead but for them it offered pickings to be transformed into alternative villages inhabiting the semi-desert and forest areas rejected by 'civilized' society. The work of the anthropologists was used as pattern books for building. *The Dome Book* became the technical manual for some of the alternative communities. It offered a fusion of the high technology of Buckminster Fuller and the low technology of the Mandan Lodge of North America and the Yurtas of Central Asia. Traditional materials such as earth, canvas and timber were suggested along with urethane foam and plates of metal cut from abandoned automobiles. Drop City was one such experiment. Bizarre joint ventures arose like the WOBOL, the WOrld BOttLe produced by the Heineken beer company. The flat sides of the bottle could be cemented together to be used as bricks. A product was therefore to be produced for a single primary use, holding beer, which would then be salvaged for reuse for a totally separate longer term function as a building material.

As a reaction against the globalism of the International Style and the manic propositions of megacity, 'genius loci' came back into architectural parlance. Orientation and maximum use of 'free' natural energy

Figure 19.1
Housing for alternative living :illustration from *Dome Book 2* (1971).

Figure 19.2
Alternative living: underground press.

were used to develop building forms, and the creation of microclimates became a new area of architectural study. For those who chose to live an alternative lifestyle in either rural or urban areas, the development of independent energy sources from wind, sun and water was essential. The necessary interest in such technologies disseminated through alternative publications such as *The Dome Book* and *The Whole Earth Catalogue* revealed that scientists had been stealthily researching such possibilities for years, albeit within military establishments, technical institutes and universities.

Solar energy as a potential source of both direct and indirect energy supply had been researched from early investigation in the eighteenth century. A common architectural form designed to use solar energy was the conservatory, so beloved of middle and upper class England and America. Other solar inventions such as water heaters, solar engines and solar house heaters had been produced and successfully used throughout the late nineteenth and early twentieth centuries.

In the 1920s and '30s the movement to health and welfare in European housing included considerable work on solar housing and solar communities. Simple white modern movement houses were set at precise distances to maximize the penetration of sunlight, with roof terraces offering further opportunity for occupants to soak up the sun. This formalizing, even regimenting of the early ideas of the garden city designers eschewed the spiritual, historical and physical aspects of an architecture derived from and in tune with nature, replacing it with a functional relationship with the sun and fresh air.

Much of the work on alternative energy production was in the form of designing devices to harness natural energy sources. In America research into the use of solar energy for domestic heating had begun in the 1930s. In 1938 a team of engineers at MIT was set up with a then substantial grant from a philanthropist with an interest in 'the vast stores of energy in sunlight'. The flat plate solar collector was developed to use the heat from the sun to heat a secondary medium, e.g. water, and transfer this for use as domestic heating. Initially these were designed to be placed on the south face of a roof at an optimum angle, which would be varied depending on the latitude of the site. Vast quantities of water are pumped either through a myriad of small bore copper tubes in the collector or down a blackened surface under glass, to be stored in a vast underground, heavily insulated compartment sunk beneath the house. Although technically satisfactory the system is relatively uneconomic with fossil fuel prices remaining relatively low. Considerable capital outlay is required for a relatively small financial saving if the system is to be used to provide all domestic heating needs. As a supplement to other forms of heating or if used in association with heat pumps it is still in use in many energy-conscious designs. Further research using air as the heated medium rather than water continued, this time funded by the military, as the threat of fuel shortages resulting from war became a possibility.

Following the Second World War research continued, testing a variety of options. Solar walls, storage of heat in sodium sulphate solution and storage in crushed rock were all investigated. What was emerging was the 'look' of the solar house: large monopitch roofs on shallow elongated rectangles with one wall of almost floor to ceiling glazing. These simple angular buildings often with glass covered roof and walls certainly made a break from the fussy chalets of suburban America or the pure rectangles and cubes of international Modernism. Yet few mainstream architects were interested in these prototypes and the work remained, until the 1960s, almost exclusively within the technology faculties of universities or research and development departments of military or commercial organizations.

The next developments in solar energy were spurred on by a variety of disparate perceived needs. The electronics industry expanded as low-cost electrical power became available to almost all American and European homes and enterprises. Utility companies were urging consumption to such a point that in the 1950s American scientists predicted that the projected increased consumption in energy use would lead to a fuel crisis in less than thirty years.

The destructive power of the atomic bomb, so devastatingly demonstrated in Japan, could apparently be turned to the provision of a limitless supply of electricity, and following the Suez crisis Europe too turned to the atom. However it soon became clear that nuclear energy too was fraught with unresolved problems. With electricity accepted as the dominant form of direct power supply the time had come to look for alternative, safer means of power generation. Meanwhile at NASA, it was apparent that satellites and space vehicles would require independent power sources if they were to be viable. Above the atmosphere, the sun could be fully utilized but its radiation must be transformed into electrical energy. The solar or photo-voltaic cell was developed. Initial forms were prohibitively expensive for use in buildings, due to the metals used and the high degree of processing required. As with many technologies, as production increased so costs decreased but their use for domestic supply still presented the problem of power storage in batteries for use on cloudy days, even yet to be fully resolved. With these developments the highest of technologies were deployed involving the use of chemicals and minerals whose by-products themselves would be found to threaten other areas of the natural environment.

The history of wind power is similar to that of solar power. For thousands of years man had used the power of the wind to provide mechanical power. Corn was ground, water was pumped and ventilation was provided long before the industrial revolution. The building forms created to enclose these mechanisms developed alongside the traditional buildings. The white-washed, canvas-sailed windmills of the Mediterranean and Aegean grew naturally from the native building stock just as the timber smock mills of Suffolk and the solid tower mills of Lincolnshire attune with the clapboard cottages and brick houses that they rise above. The modern agricultural windpump of the Kansas cornfields has become a homely image of simple technology, at human scale, set in vast acreages of corn.

These basic wind machines were developed in the inter- and post-war years for electrical generation rather than motive power. The experimenters ranged from multinational corporations through military establishments to alternative 'hippie' communities. One such experiment was the Savonious rotor, a horizontal wind machine, explored using materials ranging from machined precision parts to salvaged oil drums cut in half and set on old automobile wheel bearings. The technologies developed reflected whether the power was to be used for the needs of a single dwelling or small local community or, as vast wind farms, to act as major generation sources for large numbers of consumers some distance away. Certainly these latter versions have not been developed as part of any tradition or theory of architecture. They are raw technology, alien to their setting, apparently unresponsive to all of the natural world except that which they harness.

(a)

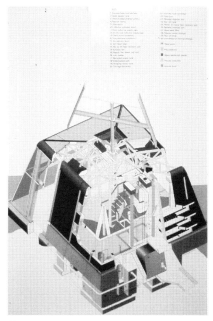

(b)

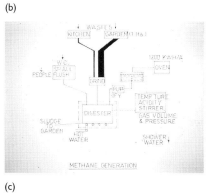

(c)

Figure 19.3a–c
Autarkic House. Photos courtesy of Nona Pike.

In the development of architectural theory and form, the technical advances in power generation and environmental control have either remained 'add-ons' to forms that have been derived from other histories, or have become dominant determinants denying either the need or the aspiration for connection with an architectural past. In the 1970s a group at Cambridge University School of Architecture led by Alex Pike ran a research project into the design of a self-sufficient house. Unashamedly utilizing all the latest technological developments in wind and solar power they sought to create a model dwelling which could provide the lifestyle appropriate to the late twentieth century with minimal need for external support. Named evocatively the Autarkic House, it used a combination of high technology and locally available resources. These included solar collectors for heat and to provide distilled drinking water, and space heating boosted by direct sunlight via solar gain through full height glazing to three sides. Electrical power was to be provided by the wind from a rotor on the roof and methane generated from sewage disposal was to be used for cooking. The sturdy masonry north wall acted as an insulating wall and an internal garden; the full double height was to provide both food and oxygen from plants. Although this project was only developed to a one-tenth size model from which computer simulations were made, it is representative of attempts to weld together new technologies to create an environmentally responsive architectural form. Seen alongside films such as *Silent Running* and *2001*, science fiction visions of technology utilized to protect man and whatever was left of nature from ultimate destruction, the Autarkic House may well be seen as one of the important predecessors of the hi-tech response to environment favoured by Richard Rogers in his 1995 Reith Lectures. The irony is of course that much of the destruction envisaged has been wrought by the misuse of the very same technology.

The self sufficiency of the Autarkic House and the other experimental dwellings of the 1970s has echoes of the ark. It is the ultimate house as machine for living, its entire form being derived from a functional and technological analysis of human need. Instead of a house made by hands and hearts it is a house made by heads, where when human evaluation capacity is exhausted, computing power is substituted to provide reassurance that the artificial environment is functionally matched to physical needs: 'We are not eco-freaks. We are trying to establish a firm theoretical framework before we start building hardware.' Alex Pike, *Evening Standard* (15 March 1974).

The problem of economy being linked to the scale of production and the expediencies of the retention of commercial and political power have meant that there has been considerable resistance to the fully autonomous house. Until very recently, the monopoly of utility companies and the indiscriminate use of public health legislation has restricted the ability of the individual to generate power and deal with human waste and have the ability to live an independent existence in all but the most remote locations.

Recently, by far the greatest technical interest in housing has been in energy conservation as opposed to energy generation. Considerable emphasis has been placed on the retention of heat in cool climates and the restriction of heat in hot climates. Many traditional dwellings had developed extremely effective ways of modifying climate and, while some researchers and designers looked to these for both inspiration and evaluation others looked to the development of new materials to provide superinsulation possibilities. The discovery that building mass, either earth, stone or concrete, could be used as a good climate modifier took many designers back to forms reminiscent of traditional dwellings. Some, like Arthur Quarmby in England and Soleri in America nestled their houses underground or into the sides of hills, a modern 'Moley's house' with plumbing and lights. Others developed the monopitched solar house to include thick walls on one side set at varying orientations depending upon whether the problem was heat loss or heat gain. Most designers however added the new materials such as foamed glass, urethane foam and glass fibres as additional layers hidden within the building fabric. The designer's aesthetic aspirations remained unrestrained by these additions, but they served to provide the client with the advantage of lower fuel bills and a token gesture towards environmentalism.

By the late 1970s building legislation in Europe required higher levels of insulation in all new buildings while campaigns were run to encourage owners of existing housing to insulate lofts, reduce draughts and buy double glazing. The fright of the oil crisis in 1973 and the volatility of some of the oil producing areas encouraged governments to be seen to cut down on energy wastage. Disruptions in other fossil fuel supplies such as coal and the growing realization that resources were really finite added to the requirement for higher standards for insulation and attempts to develop more energy efficient appliances and products. This passive approach to energy conservation rather than a radical approach to rethinking building design and production is still the main thrust of governmental policies.

The radical, vast scale proposals of Buckminster Fuller in schemes such as Tetrahedral City (1967) and Cloud Structures (1968) developed with NASA, in which mile diameter solar powered spheres full of thousands of inhabitants endlessly circled the earth, have been relegated to the status of the visionary designs of Ledoux and Boullée. But their agenda was pragmatic:

If we develop efficient use of technology we could live well within our annual 'income' of wind and water power sources, but such efficient design strategies

to conserve resources would reduce the 'money making' spending of the global 'savings account' that is basic energy economics today.
Buckminster Fuller, interview with Michael Ben-Ali, *AD* (December 1972)

The designers who had looked at the work of the anthropologists and the traditional buildings of the developing world were not overtly aiming at green design in terms of energy efficiency or precise climate modification. For them the attraction was the holistic nature of traditional building in which physical, spiritual and environmental needs were integrated within the greater context of social groups and structures: 'The environment cannot become healthy or alive, until we begin to conceive the process of using a building as a creative, reparative activity.' (Christopher Alexander and Max Jacobsen 'Specifications for an Organic and Human Building System', *The Responsive House*, MIT, 1974).

Through the 1970s publications such as *Architectural Design* in the UK tracked the environmentally aware experiments and prototypes. Other general publications such as *The Ecologist*, edited by Edward Goldsmith, and *Resurgence* spread the gospel of green to the converted. Schumacher's *Small is Beautiful* remained the seminal text for all greens.

Here and there, in Scandinavia, Germany, North America and the UK there remain buildings from this early period which use alternative energy, recycle waste and use materials chosen for their green values. Frei Otto's own house in Germany was completed in 1970, a sparkling glass green house sheltering a series of smaller units set in a wooded site. The imagery of many green houses built since seems familiar, reminiscent of that or earlier times but lacking that vitality. New difficulties have intervened. The pace of technical change has quickened further and for the most thoughtful, the perceptions of nature have also changed, away from the apparant inexorable logic of Darwin. New scientific speculation abounds, which has its parallels in literature, and which is difficult to handle with optimism for those unarmoured by a belief in one of the old faiths or unable to engage in New Age mythologies.

Herb Greene, whose own house for his mother has already been described, was assistant to Goff on the Bavinger house and other

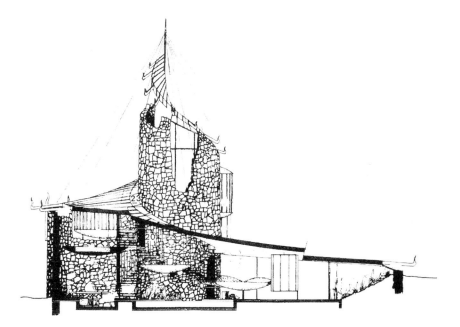

Figure 19.4
Bruce Goff, Kenshiku Planning Centre, Tokyo.

(a)

(b)

Figure 19.5a–b
Frank Gehry, American Centre, Paris.

projects. Only ten years separate the houses but even so Greene is the next half generation, responding to the 'constant present' of his personal experience. Other American designers such as Frank Gehry can be placed as sucessors to the free forms of Goff and Greene. Although far more involved in urban context, Gehry's work demonstrates an ability to trawl back through personal experience to develop what appear as mutant forms initially but which can be read as forms evolving and generating, themselves derived from and responding to the external environment within which they are attempting to establish their unique existence.

In the Solar Research Institute, Stuttgart, Gunther Behnisch plays with the possibilities of the monopitches of consistently angled solar collectors. More consciously formalist in plan, this is at least one of the few buildings that attempts to include the technology of alternative power generation in a free form, crystalline composition. The forced gesture of the red painted steel tube which extends aggressively from the ground to pierce the complex roof projection on the north of the building and skewers the building like an incorrectly aligned sun path diagram, belies its otherwise pragmatic character. Its qualities of a temporary structure are appropriate to the research institute and it demonstrates how the technical components can be dominated by the architectural programme rather than forcing designers and users into the 'blinding grids' that Ruskin had predicted.

More overtly intellectual in their programme and sharing much of the technology of the high-tech branch of the late moderns, practices such as Co-op Himmelblau in Europe are building their sparkling, spiky constructions. Now placed under the banner of Deconstruction, Co-op Himmelblau and other designers like Gehry have sought to express and in a sense celebrate the massive disjuncture described in the work of contemporary philosophers such as Derrida and Barthes. Although derived from extraordinarily complex working methods and concepts, these buildings can be interpreted as also mirroring the more complex theories from physics known to us in popular terms as chaos theory.

Chaos theory and Deconstruction appear to me to be aspects of the same thoughts, the one in science, the other copycatting first in literature and now in the visual arts. An urge towards the use of violently disrupted forms in buildings that has developed since the 1960s, and brought to memory again the Futurist and Expressionist art of earlier in the century, is accompanied now by Deconstructionist explanations. The impulse towards such forms is as strong as that which prompted the spread of Brutalism. It has to be taken seriously, beyond its obvious decorative connections, like the revival in graphic and furniture design of attenuated versions of the 1950s (in itself interestingly stringily neurotic) in the work of Philippe Stark. The forms are reminiscent of the art of Schwitters whose Merzbau took three-dimensional form as he built them: asymmetrical and awkward to inhabit, they take over, even bulge through the houses in which he lived. As developed now by architects like Himmelblau and Gehry, the resulting buildings with their disordered order, their lack of formal hierarchies of form, look to be frozen chaos, curiously mimicking the way that modern buildings, made of large components unlike traditional buildings, disintegrate when explosives or other agents collapse them into ruin.

The Neo-classical forms of the eighteenth century were a language based upon harmonious geometry, underwritten by the order of the cosmos as it was then perceived. After the challenge of the Romantics, the same Cartesian perception of the geometric order was repeated in the formal assumptions of the International Style, renewed by the reference to the necessary functional and geometric order of machinery. The latest abstract architectural language, whose resulting buildings look as if parts of the International Style have been shuffled by a lunatic, shows how far our concepts of order in nature have had to move from those of Newton, and now quite possibly Darwin, with all that involves for the arts, mirroring as they do the human situation.

Deconstructionist buildings are an intuitive visualization of how new science perceives the nature of nature. It seems to have within it too a cry of rage, or perhaps petulance, that the idea of humanity at the centre of things, of slippage from the Great Chain of Being and its pantheistic successors cannot be held to if ultimate issues are tackled by those who

Figure 19.6
Co-op Himmelblau, Red Angel wine bar, Vienna.

Figure 19.7
Terry Anderson's house, northern Idaho. Reprinted from *Fine Homebuilding*, courtesy of The Taunton Press, 63 South Main Street, Newtown, CT 06470.

have inherited the rational scientific traditions of the Renaissance. Auden's words ring true, 'the special things begun by the Renaissance have now been done'.

It would however be a mistake to see buildings like those of Gehry, Himmelblau or Domenig as totally unconnected with environmental issues. Their language breaks with the gathering of memories of the humanist past in the later modern buildings of Venturi and Stirling, where the classical past is integrated into personal architectural languages of a Proustian character, showing glorious past forms in their nearly final incarnations. In the apparently chaotic, in fact complexly organized forms of Deconstructionist buildings there is, as well as ruing over the human situation, an opening up away from the legacy and pressure of the Western tradition. There are other ways of ordering space besides those devised by settled Western man. Because of the disordered (by Cartesian criteria) warping and twisting they open up pragmatic, transient ways of making space. The forms seem meaningful, as Brutalism did a while ago, as if in making a transition between two mutually exclusive orders, like leaving the desert island on a risky raft structure. A shift in the patterns of living is indicated, opposing ideas of the settled, the heavily rooted. These buildings show, at the least, that there is no turning back, the burden of knowledge cannot be shed.

There must be a constructive agenda which deals with the here and now of the environmental crisis affecting the earth and which joins architecture to the effort of keeping the earth in working order. However much the metaphysical crisis afflicting humankind appears to worsen, a looking for solutions rather than a listing of complaints is required. The aspects of Deconstruction that mull over truthful but inevitably nihilistic ideas, and the gathering of memories that takes many guises, must move over and be sympathetic backdrops, to the essential activity, which is to address with vitality and urgency the immediate and long-term future.

Part Six
Where we are now

20   Towards a green audit

Just as the architects of the twenties never found the entirely simple and inexpensive 'house per se', so, the form of the 'natural' house has still to be found today; not surprisingly, since only few architects are searching for it anyhow.

Otto Frei 'The New Plurality', *World Architecture* (1989)

This final chapter is concerned with the idea of a green audit. As we have seen there is no conclusive definition of what 'green' means. The works discussed have however either explicitly or subliminally referenced themselves in relation to nature. Our relationship to the natural world has been brought into sharp focus in the last thirty years by both the anticipation and experience of environmental damage and disaster. At the macro level of global and governmental assessment, environmentalism and sustainable development have come into common usage. At the micro level of individuals adopting 'green' attitudes and lifestyles we can see a continuity of the movements from the nineteenth century through to the 1960s and into the current breadth of action from green consumerism to radical alternative communities.

The weight of depressive speculation is towards the impossibility of a better future, or of any future at all. Whether the threat is from war, economic collapse or ecological disaster, all readily corroborated if the documentary material is studied, architecture, the social art, which builds for us to live now, has to shake itself free. There are good signs.

Making an environmentally sound building by choosing suitable materials and ways of putting them together involves more than having ideas about which resources are scarce or unrenewable. A holistic attitude towards the balances within nature is needed. The practical problems are great, from defining what in nature is inviolate, to sorting through the increasing mass of environmental data. This in turn is framed by political and social issues, that architects and their buildings can affect marginally at best.

There appears to be a real reordering of thought as we approach the millenium, with science itself leading the way. The Cartesian logic which led to the development of ever more specific and defined specialist disciplines is being challenged by the new physics which views the universe as a fluid and dynamic amalgamation of inter-relationships. Biologists such as Rupert Sheldrake are returning to the 'whole' after finding that the traditional scientific methodology of examining the 'part' not only failed to substantiate orthodox theories but refused to acknowledge many of the phenomena so obvious to the naturalist. There are those who are clinging to mechanistic analogies such as Richard Dawkins in

The Selfish Gene, but these scientists are beginning to appear reactionary in a time of scientific revolution, rigid in a time of flexibility and fluidity. Physics is again paralleling philosophy.

Architecture sits between the macro and the micro but is influenced by both. As a cultural activity it cannot stand apart from the concerns and aspirations of the societies that produce it. The purpose of the Green Audit research project is to map where, when and hopefully how the mass of social, technical, economic and formal activities being carried out under the 'green' banner are influencing architectural design and built form. The Audit has a policy of inclusion rather than exclusion and will also track projects and ideas which although not claiming an environmental agenda might be evaluted as being relevant to the focus of design and nature.

From the initial investigations certain strands are emerging. The strongest is undoubtedly still the technical response. In his Reith Lectures of 1995, Richard Rogers exemplified the view that current and future advanced technologies could redress the problems created by the cruder processes and products of industrialization. This view is dominant at the global and governmental scale and exemplified in much that came out of the Earth Summit at Rio in 1992. In architectural terms this is the greening of hi-tech. The legacy of Buckminster Fuller, the Metabolists and Archigram is clearly alive in projects such as Rogers' unsuccessful proposals for twin 150 metre towers in Vienna in 1994. The emphasis is on meeting 'the needs of the present without compromising the ability of future generations to meet their own needs'. *The Brundtland Report* is the basis of this position.

The notion of sustainable development is an alluring one, especially to growth-imperative economists who also tend to refer to sustainable growth. At the micro scale it is the world of the ethical consumer, taking the best of current technology and attempting to select future developments through either the action of the 'free market' or governmental intervention of the carrot and stick variety. At the level of the individual house, that by Bambek and Bambek, built in the base of a disused stone quarry outside Stuttgart, is an interesting example. Set over a newly formed lake, a Biotop(e) which has been filled with fish and frogs, a slender platform is suspended over the water to form an external eating space. Clad in highly reflective profiled metal cladding on a steel frame, the angular building shimmers amidst the ever growing vegetation. Adjoining caves contain the sauna, a box set under water with glazing to the world beneath the surface.

In terms of green building, most projects published in the architectural press are of a more prosaic type. The house by Brenda and Robert Vale in Nottingham freely utilizes current technologies such as photovoltaic cells on the pergola and highly processed krypton filled double glazing. The emphasis is on energy efficiency and the reduction of overall energy consumption. The designers described their building as:

A building that tries to minimise environmental impact without waiting for any further developments of technology and without asking society to bend its existing rules with regard to building standards.

The form of the Vale house can at best be described as neutral. Whilst the materials, superinsulated brick and block cavity walling, clay pantiles and a timber-framed conservatory, have been selected on quantitative assessments of embodied energy value and sustainable

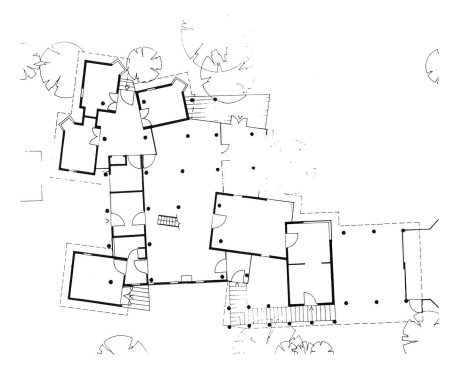

Figure 20.1
Jon Broome's house

sources, the final building form is mute. The most radical gestures are to invert the living and sleeping accommodation and use a composting lavatory for human waste. Its justification in journals has been on a numerical assessment of its physical performance rather than on any expressive statement of organic empathy. The lean-to conservatory is perhaps the most telling element of the house. The living spaces are only connected to the conservatory by relatively small triple-glazed, openable windows and two separate doors from the ground floor bedroom and hallway. Whilst there is an indication that the conservatory might be used as an additional living area, or as a winter garden, the house fails to use the possibilities of a conservatory as envisaged in the much earlier Autarkic House of the 1970s. The contribution of the Vale house is still considerable in technical terms, as it has been designed and built in accordance with current building norms and procurement procedures, even though it seeks to limit itself to certain technical issues and works within the parameters of existing legislation and lifestyles.

Other houses which have extended the agenda include the self-build houses, such as that built by Jon Broome, for his own use, in south London. Broome had worked for some time with the Walter Segal self-build housing venture which had enabled many who would otherwise have been excluded from our home-owning society to build their own homes, utilizing a timber system developed to allow unskilled labour to build with a minimum of industrial plant. He has continued his work with Architype, an architectural practice which has expanded the self-build possibilities of the Segal designs to achieve high levels of thermal performance and use of sustainable materials. One of the interesting issues is that this type of building connects back to the ideals of the Arts and Crafts movement without copying the forms. The reintegration of the designer and builder is part of the social development of green

Figure 20.2
Short, Ford and Associates, De Montfort University, engineering building. Courtesy of Short, Ford and Associates. Copyright Peter Cook.

building and parallels other integrative elements of the new sciences. Broome uses similar parameters to those of the Vales in choosing the materials for the house. Low embodied energy and sustainable sources are important but are also interpreted through the imperative of their being relatively easy and safe to work by hand. As design is integrated into construction, opportunities have been seized throughout the building phase.

It was intended that Broome and his partner, as the occupants, would complete their home around them, analogous to the making and maintaining of a nest or burrow. We replicate this process through DIY or the decorating and furnishing of our homes. Yet despite being seriously addressed by the Arts and Crafts and then later in the 1960s and early '70s, this process rarely figures in contemporary architectural design and theory which remains defined as a professional activity.

In form, the house addresses itself to more than function and performance. Broome states that he wishes the house to make connections between what he does and what he stands for. This philosophical connection is evident in the building in both plan and detail. The overall footprint of the house is defined by the presence of existing trees on the site. A regular grid of columns is set out across the site and the ground floor accommodation angles and splays between and around the grid to maximize view, capture sun or enclose and protect external space. The columns themselves are of Douglas fir with the minimum of working. The bark is stripped from the trunks but these vertical posts are still clearly trees similar in diameter to the trunks of the surrounding trees. These main posts pierce the first floor to carry the roof, giving the interior spaces, with floors and fitted furniture of timber boarding, the qualities of a tree house. The flooring of the ground floor is oak from the vats in a redundant vinegar factory, and the staircase makes visual reference to the ladder and tressle of the orchard. Small windows open into internal spaces as well as to the outside. The technical term for the wall construction is a 'breathing wall', a term that is especially appropriate for this house. The roof is covered with soil and planted with grass and wild flowers providing both poetic and practical shelter, the roof eaves extending to shade and protect as required. The Broome house is a humane and gentle proposition for the future dwelling, but it follows within the traditions of the villa and suburb rather than the density of urban existence. Its simple forms are reminiscent of the favella and squatter settlement, and its reliance upon manual labour over industrial production, combined with the use of local and second-hand material, points to the possibilities for habitation in a time of enforced leisure, the current euphemism for unemployment.

There is little in the area of high density and large scale housing which could be considered green, other than refurbishment projects from the Netherlands, France and Spain or the projects which retain an orthodoxy in planning terms and upgrade the external envelope to limit the energy requirements for environmental control. However projects such as the Engineering Building at De Montfort University by Short, Ford and Associates is an example of a large and complex building which has not only developed environmental control to minimize energy usage and maximize passive environmental control, but which has eschewed the overt use of technology as imagery for the building. It has been described as being clothed 'in historicist apparel', making reference to Ruskin and Viollet-le-Duc in its choice and use of materials (Dean Hawkes, *Architects Journal*, 9 March 1994). The vibrant red brick and tile hung facades, with their Gothic windows, are read against the forest of brick chimneys which form the flues for the passive ventilation system. Each of these is topped by a large louvered aluminium hood reminiscent of the helmeted chimneys of Gaudi's Casa Mila or the stacks atop Le Cobusier's Unité apartments.

For those architects who have maintained a spiritual focus in their designs, such as Christopher Day, the interest in ecologically sound design has brought their work to a wider public. The Rudolf Steiner design methods are producing consistently interesting buildings across Europe, America and Australasia. In *Places of the Soul* (1990), Day makes an impassioned plea for the recognition that architecture matters too much to be left to the stylistic preoccupations of architects: 'In terms of spiritual nourishment deeper than the glossy cosmetic, much of our daily surroundings approach bankruptcy.' Whilst not operating under an exclusively green banner, the works of Day and others who are using Steiner methods make for a wider spectrum of building types and all have a resonance unique to their belief in the holistic nature of human existence. The anthroposophical basis to the Steiner way of designing recognizes the earth as a living being:

Every new building deprives a plot of earth of the healing forces of the sun, wind, rain and animal life. The building must redeem this by its own qualities.
Kenneth Bayes, *Living Architecture* (1994)

The opening up of the eastern bloc has also revealed designers who have, through the vagaries of the systems within which they operated, been able to maintain the true organic craft traditions lost to western Europe with industrialization. Imre Makowecz from Hungary is one such designer. His magnificent churches and community centres are like the buildings of organic dreams. They are realized through the hands of local craftsmen who build, use and enjoy them; they are the closest

Figure 20.3
Bill Dunster's house at East Molesey, Surrey: a recent example of green design.

realization to the halls in William Morris's *News from Nowhere* completed to date. Although Makowecz has received many offers of work outside his native area, he has found as yet, that the skill resource necessary to create his designs is inadequate. He readily acknowledges nature as his inspiration and uses metaphors of bird or animal to generate the extraordinary forms of his buildings. Wherever possible, branching tree trunks are used as vertical supports; his community centre in Bak planned on the form of an eagle is as strong as Herb Greene's house despite its completion some twenty-five years later. It may be that these forms are so specific to the Hungarian experience that they would not transfer to other locations. But their potency connects to far deeper roots than the last 200 years of industrialization. There is no need for any justification in terms of ecologically sound design as they are part of the nature that surrounds them. They reek of nature and of man's ability to reach new heights of creation through working with nature rather than trying to dominate it.

The images and forms of technology are often illusory. Although 'intelligent buildings' have been anticipated for some twenty years, the prohibitive costs of many of the technologies involved has limited their realization. Intelligent glass that responds to external light and heat levels has been in production for many years. High performance glass that can withstand fire for considerable periods of time is also available. The possibilities of nano-technology could transform buildings into a myriad of tiny automatic, self-regulating systems which could produce a subtly changing and modifying environment at apparently little energy cost. What is however clear is that truly green design is more than a technological add-on. The social, political and economic structures which underlie the making of buildings will have to be reformed to enable designers to use their skills to provide ecologically sound environments in the broadest sense.

The practical, ecologically aware experiments made by building single or small groups of housing, usually in suburb or country, are important both for their role as prototypes and in sorting out problems and for their demonstration of the possibility of greener living. Care will be needed to ensure they do not experience the same problems as Biosphere II, the experimental re-creation of a microcosm of the earth's ecosystem, which apparently foundered at the human, social level rather than the technical level.

The ad hoc use of energy-efficient materials and construction are still useful, but all these green trials are patchy and as yet not fully backed by systematic investigation. Assumptions made now about what is the most environmentally favourable material or constructional method may not be deemed correct in a few years time, as our perceptions of the damage we are doing to ourselves become more clear. Nonetheless we must begin the task of testing all our current and future assumptions against complex criteria.

Software programs may be useful to evaluate the relative importance of the many factors involved, such as durability, maintenance needs and embodied energy costs (including that needed to transport materials or components to site and put them together). Studies can be done as to the effects of resource extraction and depletion on the natural habitat and which materials degrade biologically. Qualitative assessment can be made of the energy required for further processing, if materials can be recycled.

A centrepiece of the Green Audit will be a critical cross comparison of the factors – the material, economic, contextual and aesthetic – that go to make the Gestalt of a building and landscape.

Only man can decide what are to be the social, ethical and cultural green values. It may be that some materials and methods assumed to be green would fail such searching evaluation and other less obvious possibilities succeed. It is probable that no absolute or universal solutions are possible. It may be a question of steering in the right direction.

*

This book has been for the most part about people being constructive and positive. I have tried to show the continuity of awareness about the natural world and our relationship to it as displayed in the architecture of the last two centuries. The growing awareness of environmental issues and their centrality continues. Buildings in odd corners are found to excite and perhaps lead. The larger questions of changing priorities towards renewal, recycling, clearing up pollution are still being worked on but are nowhere near the necessary working order. The larger political questions of how urbanization can be equated with greener ways of living, have not really begun. Architecture follows, it cannot, except in tiny ways, lead political and social issues. It can express like any other language the issues and it can make tentative prototypes and perhaps dream of solutions. It may be that the green crisis will best be confronted by dour practical application in architecture and elsewhere, patching and mending what we have and how we do things. It may be that the dreams of the other ways of human settlement from the past, and in the future, will play their part. The renewable energy of the sun may then revive the desert city projects of Soleri; or the use of sun power combined with land scarcity, as the waters rise, make Taut's crystal alpine communities possible; or those to come may at best have to live in the equivalent of Badger's house, in the cellars of great houses left by humans who have long gone.

Time will tell.

Glossary

Beaux-Arts A rigorous and highly ornamental classical style originating in the Ecole des Beaux Arts in France.

Begijnhof The best known example of a hof – almshouses set round an open court – in central Amsterdam. The place has the feel of a village with houses of different dates and a clapboard chapel on the grass court.

Biotope A limited ecological region or area in which the environment is suitable for specific forms of life.

Brutalism A British architectural movement developed by young architects in the 1950s as a reaction to the formalism of the International Style (q.v.); characterized by the use of 'béton brut' (raw concrete) and other formulae of its own.

Cartesian Based on the philosophy of René Descartes, French philosopher (1596–1650), one of the fathers of Rationalism. In architectural terms a Cartesian approach is based on exploring the simple, single element before attempting to understand the complex.

Chaos Theory A theory developed during the 1980s that questioned the adequacy of scientific laws as a basis for predicting the behaviour of systems.

CIAM Congrès Internationaux d'Architecture Moderne, an international association of architects founded in 1928.

Deconstructive Architecture, Deconstruction, Deconstructivism A loosely constituted Neo-modern architectural movement deriving from Post-Structuralist French cultural theory (Derrida, Foucault). It is characterized by fragmentation, discontinuity and decentring. The term Neo-Constructivism is also used by some architects.

Dentil The lowest part of a classical cornice, incised to appear as a row of square blocks, named after their similarity to teeth.

Enclosures A process whereby English landowners fenced and hedged common land in the name of agricultural efficiency, authorized by privately sponsored Acts of Parliament.

Fordism System of assembly-line factory production originated by the American industrialist Henry Ford (1863–1947).

Garden City Urban form invented by Ebenezer Howard around 1900, characterized by low-density housing interspersed by green spaces with integrated industrial areas and cultural amenities (examples: Letchworth, Welwyn, Hampstead Garden Suburb).

Heisenberg's Principle of Uncertainty   A principle of physics which embodies the idea that an observer of any phenomenon interacts with that phenomenon, thereby rendering objective certainty impossible.

Hi-tech Architecture   Type of architecture originating in Britain in the 1970s in the work of Richard Rogers and Norman Foster which celebrates the use of precision crafted industrial components.

International Style   Term coined in 1932 to characterize uniform functionalist, 'white' modern architecture.

Maginot Line   French system of defences built in the 1930s along the Franco–German frontier, originated by André Maginot, minister of war 1929–31.

Nano technology   The technology of extremely small, miniaturized machines, tools or components on a microscopic or submicroscopic scale. K. Eric Drexler in the USA is one of the major visionaries in this area of science.

Neue Sachlichkeit   The new realism of German art and architecture in the 1920s following the earlier Expressionist phase.

Pattern Book   Illustrated book of 'correct' architectural features, plans etc. for use by provincial builders in the eighteenth century.

Pop Art   British and American art movement concerned with celebrating ephemeral consumer culture of the late 1950s to early 1970s.

Postmodern Architecture   An eclectic, pluralist movement defined by the historian Charles Jencks as a reaction against Modernism, and characterized by the American architect Robert Venturi in his book *Complexity and Contradiction in Architecture* (1966) in terms of the richness and ambiguity of modern experience. Central to it is the concern to express meaning, by signs, metaphors and stylistic allusions.

Pre-Raphaelites   An English artistic movement founded in 1848 by Dante Gabriel Rossetti and John Millais.

Purism   Movement in Modern architecture and painting of the 1920s developed by Le Corbusier and Amedée Ozenfant; its central tenet was that designed objects tend towards a purity of form as a natural result of the process of modern mass production.

Rosenhugel Pioneers   An Austrian social housing movement deriving their inspiration from rural and vernacular traditions.

Taylorism   System of scientific management originated by American inventor and engineer Frederick Winslow Taylor (1856–1915).

Triglyph   Blocks separating the metopes in a Doric frieze, each having two vertical grooves or glyphs and two half-glyphs at each end.

Bibliography

Works cited in the text

(In general these are given under the title by which they will be known to English-language readers, although the dates and places of publication refer to the original publication).

Part One: Introduction
Banham, R. (1960) *Theory and Design in the First Machine Age*, London
Giedion, S. (1941) *Space, Time and Architecture*, Cambridge, Mass., and London
Jencks, C. (1977) *The Language of Post-Modern Architecture*, London
Kaufmann, E. (1933) *From Ledoux to Le Corbusier*, Vienna and Leipzig
Pevsner, N. (1936) *Pioneers of the Modern Movement*, London
Pevsner, N. (1960) *Pioneers of Modern Design*, London
Venturi, R. (1966) *Complexity and Contradiction in Architecture*, New York
Venturi, R. (1972) *Learning from Las Vegas*, Cambridge, Mass.
Watkin, D. (1986) *A History of Western Architecture*, London

Part Two: The first return of the primitive hut
Adam, R. (1764) *Ruins of the Palace of the Emperor Diocletian at Spoleto*, London
Boullée, E. L. (1953) *Architecture, Essay on Art*, London
Coleridge, S. T. (1798) 'Frost at Midnight' in *Lyrical Ballads*, London
Gandy, J. M. (1805) *Designs for Cottages*, London
Gandy, J. M. (1805) *The Rural Architect*, London
Goldsmith, O. (1770) *The Deserted Village*, Dublin
Grigson, G. (1948) *An English Farmhouse and its Neighbourhood*, London
Harries, K. (1983) *The Bavarian Rococo Church: Between Faith and Aestheticism*, New Haven and London
Hawkes, J. (1951) *A Land*, London
Ledoux, C. N. (1847) *Architecture*, Paris
Loudon, J. (1833) *Encyclopedia of Cottage, Farm and Villa Architecture*, London
Lyall, S. (1988) *Dream Cottages*, London
Malton, J. (1798) *An Essay on British Cottage Architecture*, London
Papworth, J. B. (1818) *Rural Residences*, London
Payne Knight, R. (1805) *An Analytical Inquiry into the Principles of Taste*, London
Pevsner, N. (1958) *The Buildings of England. North Somerset and Bristol*, London

Plaw, J. (1802) *Rural Architecture*, London
Price, Uvedale (1794) *Essay on the Picturesque*, London
Repton, H. (1795–6) *Red Book for Blaise Castle*, City of Bristol Museum and
    Art Gallery
Rousseau, J.J. (1761) *La Nouvelle Heloise*, Lausanne
Rudofsky, B. (1965) *Architecture without Architects*, New York
Ruskin, J. (1835) *The Poetry of Architecture*, London
Sadleir, M. (1944) *Things Past*, London
Sedlmayr, H. (1957) *Art in Crisis: the Lost Centre*, London
Stuart, J. and Revett, N. (1762) *Antiquities of Athens*, London
Summerson, J. (1949) *Heavenly Mansions*, London
Thomson, J. (1748) *The Castle of Indolence*, London
Vitruvius (trans. M. Hicky Morgan, 1914) *The Ten Books on Architecture*,
    Cambridge, Mass.
Wood, R. (1753) *The Ruins of Palmyra*, London

Part Three: Natural selection and industrialization
Baillie Scott, H. M. (1906) *Houses and Gardens*, London
Banham, R. (1960) *Theory and Design in the First Machine Age*, London
Berger, J. (1974) *About Looking*, London
Blake, W. (1789) *Songs of Innocence*, London
Blake, W. (1794) *Songs of Experience*, London
Brehm, A. E. (1876) *Brehms Thierleben*, Leipzig
Brontë, C. (1847) *Jane Eyre*, London
CIAM (1933) *Athens Charter* (ed. Le Corbusier, Paris, 1943)
Darwin, C. (1859) *The Origin of Species*, London
Dickens, C. (1841) *The Old Curiosity Shop*, London
Dickens, C. (1854) *Hard Times*, London
Dickens, C. (1857) *Little Dorrit*, London
Dresser, C. (1859) *Unity in Variety*, London
Grahame, K. (1908) *The Wind in the Willows*, London
Howard, E. (1902) *Garden Cities of Tomorrow*, London
Laugier, M. A. (1752) *Essai sur L'Architecture*, Paris
Lyell, C. (1830) *Priciples of Geology*, London
Milne, A. A. (1926) *Winnie-the-Pooh*, London
Morris, W. (1878) *The Decorative Arts*, republished in *The Lesser Arts*
    (1882), and (1880) *The Beauty of Life*, in *Collected Works*, Vol. 22
    (1910–15), London
Muthesius, H. (1979) *The English House*, New York
Pater, W. (1878) 'The Child in the House', *Macmillan's Magazine*
Potter, B. (1910) *The Tale of Mrs Tittlemouse*, London
Rhind, W. (1840) *The Vegetable Kingdom*, Glasgow, Edinburgh and London
Rousseau, J.-J. (1762) *Emile, ou de l'Education*, Amsterdam
Ruskin, J. (1849) *The Seven Lamps of Architecture*, London
Ruskin, J. (1853), *The Stones of Venice*, London
Ruskin, J. (1854) *Lectures on Architecture and Painting*, London
Ruskin, J. (1859) *The Two Paths*, London
Ruskin, J. (1860) *Unto This Last*, London
Ruskin, J. and Acland, H. W. O. (1859) *The Oxford Museum*, London
Street, G. E. (1855) *Brick and Marble in the Middle Ages: Notes of Tours in
    the North of Italy*, London
Thomson, J. (1880) *City of Dreadful Night*, London
Unwin, R. (1909) *Town Planning in Practice*, London
Unwin, R. (1902) *Cottage Plans and Common Sense*, Fabian Tract No. 109,
    London

Voysey, C. F. A. (1915) *Individuality*, London
Wells, H. G. (1910) *The History of Mr Polly*, London
Wolf, J. (1861) *Zoological Sketches*, London
Wood, J. G. (1868) *Homes without Hands*, London
Wood, J. G. (1876) *Nature's Teaching*, London

Part Four: Modernism
Buffon, G. L. (1769) *Histoire Naturelle*, Paris
Coleridge, S. T. (1836-39) Lectures 1818, in *The Literary Remains of Samuel Taylor Coleridge*, London
Collins, P. (1965) *Changing Ideals in Modern Architecture*, London
Le Corbusier (1923) *Vers Une Architecture*, Paris; English translation (1927) *Towards a New Architecture*, London
Le Corbusier (1924) *Urbanisme*, Paris; English translation (1929) *The City of Tomorrow*, London
D'Arcy Thompson (1917) *On Growth and Form*, Cambridge
Goff, B. (1970) *Forty-four Realizations*, in David G. De Long (1988) *Bruce Goff: Towards Absolute Architecture*, MIT
Hitchcock, H.-R. and Johnson, P. (1932) *The International Style*, New York and London
Jackson, A. (1970) *The Politics of Architecture: A History of Modern Architecture in Britain*, London
Pevsner, N. (1943) *Outline of European Architecture*, London
Scheerbart, P. (1919) *Glass Architecture*, (ed. D. Sharp, 1972), New York
Scully, V. (1961) *Modern Architecture*, London
Taut, B. (1914) *Alpine Architecture*, (ed. D. Sharp, 1972), New York
Wright, F. L. (1932) *An Autobiography*, New York and London
Wright, F. L. (1939) *An Organic Architecture: The Architecture of Democracy*, New York and London
Wright, F. L. (1954) *The Natural House*, New York and London
Wright, F. L. (1958) *The Living City*, New York and London
Zevi, B. (1950) *Towards an Organic Architecture*, London

Part Five: The second return of the primitive hut
Alexander, C. and Jacobsen, M. (1974) 'Specification for an Organic and Human Building System', *The Responsive House*, MIT
Architectural Design (July 1967) XXXVII
Architectural Review (June 1947) 'The New Empiricism', CI, 606, pp 199–204
Architectural Review (December 1949) articles on 'Townscape', CVI, 636, pp 354–374
Architectural Review (January 1950) special number on 'The Functional Tradition', CVII, 637
Banham, R. (1966) *The New Brutalism*, London
Brett-Smith, R. (1966) *Berlin 45 – The Grey City*
Carson, R. (1951) *The Sea Around Us*, Oxford
Carson, R. (1962) *The Silent Spring*, Boston and New York
Carson, R. (1971) *The Dome Book*, Pacific Domes, California
Greene, H. (1976) *Mind and Image*, Lexington, Kentucky
Jameson, S. (1947) *The Black Laurel*, London
Newman, O. (ed.) (1961) *CIAM 59 in Otterloo*, London and Stuttgart
Pacific Domes (1971) *The Dome Book*, California
Schumacher, F. (1974) *Small is Beautiful*, London
The Whole Earth Catalogue, (1971) London

Part Six: Where we are now
Bayes, K. (1994) *Living Architecture*, Trowbridge
Day, C. (1990) *Places of the Soul*, Wellingborough
International Academy of Architecture (1989) *World Architecture*, London
Vale, B. and Vale, R. (1991) *Towards a Green Architecture*, London

John Farmer's bibliography of additional source material

Part One: Introduction
Banham, R. (1969) *The Architecture of the Well-Tempered Environment*, London
Giedion, S. (1948) *Mechanisation Takes Command*, Oxford

Part Two: The first return of the primitive hut
Addy, S. O. (1933) *The Evolution of the English House*, London
Lethaby, W. (1892) *Architecture, Mysticism and Myth*, London
Fergusson, J. (1872) *Rude Stone Monuments*, London
Fraser, J. (1968) *Village Planning in the Primitive World*, London
Grigson, G. (1948) *The Harp of Aeolus*, London
Harbison, R. (1980) *Deliberate Regression*, London
Heller, E. (1952) *The Disinherited Mind*, London
Heller, E. (1966) *The Artists Journey into the Interior*, London
Innocent, C. F. (1916) *Development of English Building Construction*, Cambridge
Kaufmann, E. (1955) *Architecture in the Age of Reason*, Cambridge, Mass.
Mainwaring, E. W. (1925) *Italian Landscape in Eighteenth Century England*, London
Nicholson, M. H. (1959) *Mountain Gloom and Mountain Glory: the Aesthetics of the Sublime*, Ithaca, NY
Oliver, P. (1969) *Shelter and Society*, London
Rapoport, A. (1969) *House, Form and Culture*, London
Rudofsky, B. (1977) *Prodigious Builders*, London
Schenk, H. G. (1966) *The Mind of the European Romantics*, London
Thomas, K. (1983) *Man and the Natural World 1500–1800*, London
Todd, R. (1946) *Tracks in the Snow*, London
Turner, T. H. and Parker, J. H. (1851) *Some Account of Domestic Architecture in England from the Conquest to the Tudor Period*, (6 vols) Oxford
Varma, D. (1957) *Gothic Flame: a History of the Gothic Novel in England*, London
Viollet-le-Duc, E. (1860) *Military Architecture*, London
De Zurko, R. (1957) *Origins of Functionalist Theory*, New York

Part Three: Natural selection and industrialization
Barber, L. (1980) *The Heyday of Natural History*, London
Betjeman, J. (1952) *First and Last Loves*, London
Blossfeldt, K. (1929) *Art Forms in Nature (1900)*, London
Buckley, J. H. (1967) *The Triumph of Time. A Study of the Victorian Concepts of Time, History, Progress and Decadence*, London
Chandler, A. (1971) *A Dream of Order; the Mediaeval Ideal in 19th Century Literature*, London
Clark, K. (1929) *The Gothic Revival*, London
Collins, G. (1960) *Gaudi*, London

Conrad, P. (1973) *The Victorian Treasure House*, London
Darley, G. (1978) *Villages of Vision*, London
Haeckl, E. (1904) *Art Forms in Nature*, Leipzig
Hitchcock, H.-R. (1958) *Architecture of the 19th and 20th Centuries*, Harmondsworth
Hitchcock, H. R. (1954) *Early Victorian Architecture*, London
Hobhouse, C. (1937) *1851 and The Crystal Palace*, London
Hulme, F. E., Mackie, S., Glaisher, J. and Hunt, R. (1872) *Art Studies from Nature as Applied to Design*, London
Hulme, F. E. (1874) *Plants, their Natural Growth and Ornamental Treatment*, London
Irvine, W. (1956) *Apes, Angels and Victorians*, London
Jeffries, R. (1875) *After London*, London
Madsen, S. T. (1967) *Art Nouveau*, London
Morris, W. (1887) *A Dream of John Ball*, London
Morris, W. (1890) *News from Nowhere*, London
Naylor, G. (1971) *The Arts and Crafts Movement*, London
Richards, J. M. (1946) *Castles on the Ground*, London
Richards, J. M. (ed.) (1973) *The Anti-Rationalists*, London
Ritterbush, F. (1968) *The Art of Organic Forms*, Washington
Rosenberg, J. (1963) *The Darkening Glass: a Portrait of Ruskin's Genius*, London
Schwarzbach, F. S. (1979) *Dickens and the City*, London
Sussman, H. (1968) *Victorians and The Machine*, Cambridge, Mass.
Thoreau, H. D. (1849) *A Week on the Concord and Merrimack Rivers*, Boston
Thoreau, H. D. (1854) *Walden*, Boston
Wichmann, S. (1977) *Jugendstil, Art Nouveau: Floral and Functional Forms*, Munich

Part Four: Modernism

Eisner, L. (1969) *The Haunted Screen*, London
Jean, M. (1960) *The History of Surrealist Painting*, New York
Kiesler, F. (1966) *Inside the Endless House*, New York
Kracauer, S. (1947) *From Caligari to Hitler*, Princeton, NJ
Mendelsohn, E. (1926) *Amerika*, Berlin
Ozenfant, A. (1931) *The Foundations of Modern Art*, London
Paz, O (1970) *The Castle of Purity*, London
Sharp, D. (1966) *Modern Architecture and Expressionism*, London
Spilka, M. (1963) *Dickens and Kafka*, Bloomington
Tate Catalogue (1971) Leger and Purist Paris, London
Yorke, F. R. S. (1934) *The Modern House*, London
Yorke, F. R. S. (1937) *The Modern Flat*, London
Yorke, F. R. S. (1937) *The Modern House in England*, London

Part Five: The second return of the primitive hut

Alexander, C. (1979) *The Timeless Way of Building*, New York
Alldis, B. (1973) *Billion Year Spree: A History of Science Fiction*, New York
Arguelles, J. (1975) *The Transformative Vision*, London
Armytage, W. H. G. (1968) *Yesterdays Tomorrows: A Historical Survey of Future Societies*, London
Ayrton, M. (1962) *Drawings and Sculpture*, London
Ayrton, M. (1967) *The Maze Maker*, London
Ayrton, M. (1971) *The Rudiments of Paradise*, London
Baird, G. (1970) *Alvar Aalto*, London

Butti, K. and Perlin, J. (1980) *A Golden Thread: 2500 Years of Solar Architecture and Technology*, New York and London

Le Corbusier (1961) *My Work*, London

DeWolfe, I. (1963) *Italian Townscape*, London

Fiedler, L. (1968) *The Reurn of the Vanishing American*, New York

Festival of Britain Catalogues (1951) London

Fussell, P. (1977) *The Great War and the Modern Memory*, London

Gerber, R. (1955) *Utopian Fantasy: A study of English Utopian Fiction since the end of the 19th Century*, London

Gleik, J. (1987) *Chaos: Making a New Science*, New York

Hadfield, M. (1964) *Gardens of Delight*, London

Hadingham, E. (1987) *Lines to the Mountain Gods: Nazca and the Mysteries of Peru*, London

Hamilton Finlay, I. (1977) Exhibition Catalogue, London

Hawkes, J. (1962) *Man and The Sun*, London

Hepworth, B. (1970) *A Pictorial Autobiography*, Bath

Kidder Smith, S. (1950) *Sweden Builds*, Stockholm

Kienholz, E. (1970) Exhibition Catalogue, London

Landow, G. P. (1982) *Images of Crisis: Literary Iconology 1750 to the Present*, Boston and London

Laurie, P. (1970) *Beneath the City Streets*, London

Levi, P. (1984) *The Periodic Table*, New York

Levi, P. (1987) *The Wrench*, London

Levi, P. (1989) *Other People's Trades*, London

Lopez, B. (1986) *Arctic Dreams*, London

Mallory, K and Ottvar, A. (1973) *The Architecture of Agression*, London

Marx, L. (1964) *The Machine in the Garden*, London

Mumford, L. (1971) *The Pentagon of Power*, London

Nash, P. (1949) *Outline: An Autobiography*, London

Neumann, K. (1959) *The Archetypal World of Henry Moore*, London

Novak, B. (1980) *Nature and Culture: American Landscape and Painting 1825–1875*, London and New York

Olderman, R. (1972) *Beyond the Waste Land: the American Novel in the 1960s*, New Haven and London

Olgyay, V. (1963) *Design with Climate*, Princeton, NJ

Oliver, P. (1987) *Dwellings – The House across the World*, Austin, Texas

Pearson, D. (1989) *The Natural House Book*, London

Richards, J. M. (1958) *The Functional Tradition in Early Industrial Buildings*, London

Richards, J. M. (1965) *Modern Architecture in Finland*, London

Scully, V. (1962) *The Earth, the Temple and the Gods*, New Haven and London

Shepheard, P. (1953) *Modern Gardens*, London

Steiner, G. (1971) *In Bluebeard's Castle*, London

Tassi, R. (1979) *Sutherland: the Wartime Drawings*, Milan

Tunnard, C. (1938) *Gardens in the Modern Landscape*, London

Weightman, J. (1973) *The Concept of the Avant-Garde*, London

Wells, H. G. (1945) *Mind at the End of its Tether*, London

Wines, J. (1986) *Site: Projects*, Tokyo

Part Six: Where we are now

Sheldrake, R. (1990) *The Rebirth of Nature: the Greening of Science and God*, London

Editor's note on the text and illustrations

Chapters 1–3 and 14 were fully written up by John Farmer before his death, and set the tone for the rest of the book. Earlier versions found among his papers show very clearly that he had moved away from an earlier academic style to a more oral mode. His voice comes across very clearly in his final version and we have tried to ensure that this happens throughout the book.

The condensed version had no equivalent to the substantial coverage of Ruskin in Chapters 8 and 9. However, in an accompanying note to Sally Richardson, the sponsor at WWF, he wrote: 'I have other stuff I can't find room for – you might ... On Ruskin who despite all that has been written about him, is still not seen as the Green Giant [he] undoubtedly was'. Reading his Ruskin material it is clear that it was originally intended for this book, and was omitted mainly because of its scale (he did envisage another, larger book, of which it could have formed a chapter). The 'other stuff' also included an essay on the Herb Greene House (Chapter 18). To quote again from the note that accompanied the condensed version, 'The buildings are the Fruit and I am concerned with the Tree': the inclusion of two chapters that are exclusively concerned with individual buildings enables us to see what fruit this particular tree – the tree of green thought and sensibility – bore at crucial moments in our history.

There is another source that I have used, and that is John Farmer's RCA doctoral thesis. An (unsent) letter to the publisher indicates the intended close relation at certain points between the book and the thesis. This, together with a number of fragments found among his papers, has enabled me to complete Chapters 5, 6, 8, 11 and 12.

I have myself contributed linking passages, and more substantially to Chapters 4, 15 and 16. Additional material for the remaining chapters has been written by:

Judith Farren Bradley, Architect and Senior Lecturer, Kingston University School of Architecture (Chapters 10 and 19).

Stuart Durant, Reader in the School of Art and Design History at Kingston University; author of *Ornament* (1985), *C.F.A. Voysey* (1992) and *Palais des Machines* (1994) (Chapter 7).

Trevor Garnham, Architect and Senior Lecturer, Kingston University School of Architecture (Chapters 13 and 17).

Members of the Green Audit group of the Kingston University School of Architecture (Judith Farren Bradley, Bryan Gauld, Bill Holdsworth, Euan McPhee) (Chapter 20).

Original photographs for this book have been taken by:

John Farmer

Augustus J. Farmer

Members of the Green Audit group of the Kingston University School of Architecture (Bryan Gauld, Senior Lecturer and Sophie Cameron-Tillett, Research Assistant).

Material from the Kingston University slide collection has been kindly provided by Alan Kent, Faculty Librarian

Members of the Green Audit group

Judith Farren Bradley DipArch, RIBA
Sophie Cameron-Tillett BA (Hons)
Eur Ing Bryan Gauld BSc, MSc, MPhil, DIC, CEng, MICE, AIWSc
Anne Goldrick BA (Hons), DipArch
Eur Ing Bill Holdsworth MSc, MASHRAE
Sue-Ann Lee MA (Hons) MSc
Anthony J. Miller BSc, BLA, ALI
Euan McPhee BSc, MSc, PhD, CBiol, MIBiol, MIEEM

Kenneth Richardson

Since taking an MSc at the Bartlett in 1987–88, Ken Richardson has taught history of architecture at Kingston University, where he was Head of the School of Art and Design History until 1994. Earlier he taught literature to architecture students, often jointly with John Farmer, who was a close friend and colleague for over twenty years. His previous experience as a writer and editor began with *Twentieth Century Writing: A Reader's Guide to Contemporary Literature* (1969).

Index

7-15-26 Coutts 84-85 (31-46) 64428